Idiosyncratic
REBT

Windy Dryden

PCCS BOOKS
Ross-on-Wye

PCCS BOOKS LTD
Llangarron
Ross-on-Wye
Herefordshire
HR9 6PT
UK
Tel +44 (0)1989 77 07 07
e-mail enquiries@pccsbks.globalnet.co.uk
www.pccs-books.co.uk

Idiosyncratic REBT

British Library Cataloguing in Publication Data.
A catalogue record for this book is available from the British Library.

ISBN 1 898059 52 7

Cover design by Old Dog Graphics
Printed by Bookcraft, Midsomer Norton, Somerset, UK

contents

	Preface	i
1	Windy Dryden	1
2	Albert Ellis	15
3	Raymond DiGiuseppe	31
4	Paul A. Hauck	47
5	Sue Walen	61
6	Emmett Velten	75
7	Monica O'Kelly	89
8	Nando Pelusi	105
9	Michael Neenan	119
10	Kristene A. Doyle	131
11	Ann Vernon	143
	Contributors	159
	Index	163

preface

Once I tell somebody in the field that I am a Rational Emotive Behaviour therapist, they make certain assumptions about the way that I practise, usually based on their knowledge of REBT gained through the writings of the founder of REBT, Albert Ellis. They may even have seen the infamous Ellis–Gloria film, which was made over thirty years ago, and assume that this interview is a reliable guide to how I and other REBT therapists practise REBT.

The idea that all REBT therapists practise REBT in the same way is grossly inaccurate and while there is a good deal of similarity in our practice there is also a good deal of difference too. This book is designed to explore this difference. The idea for the book came when Dan David, editor of the *Romanian Journal of Cognitive and Behavioral Psychotherapies*, invited me to write an article for the inaugural issue of this new publication. I accepted and mused for a while about the topic of my paper. The idea suddenly came to me that I would write an article showing my idiosyncratic practice of REBT. I did, it was published and it appears here by kind permission of the Romanian journal. I then thought that REBT therapists and trainees might benefit from reading about how a number of leading REBT therapists practise REBT in their own idiosyncratic manner and this volume was born.

I asked each contributor to outline 12 points of practice that taken together demonstrates their idiosyncratic practice of REBT. Now, REBT therapists tend to be a bunch of rugged individualists and the fact that all but one complied with my request exceeded my expectations. The exception was Albert Ellis and I think that he has deserved being given the license to write his chapter his way.

I hope that you find the book useful and I thank Pete Sanders, my old 'bumping' partner from Aston days, for being willing to take the risk of publishing such an idiosyncratic project.

Windy Dryden
London and East Sussex

1

Windy Dryden

In this chapter, I concentrate on my idiosyncratic practice of Rational Emotive Behaviour Therapy (REBT) and outline the reasons why I practise it in the way that I do. In particular, I discuss the importance of:

i.   developing relationships with clients based on the principle of 'informed allies';

ii.   developing a 'case conceptualisation' with complex 'cases';

iii. developing an REBT-influenced problems and goals list with clients;

iv.   working with specific examples of target problems at the beginning of therapy;

v.   identifying the critical 'A' in the assessment process;

vi.   focusing on thinking 'Cs' as well as emotional and behavioural 'Cs';

vii. helping clients to develop and rehearse the full version of rational beliefs;

viii. encouraging clients to voice their doubts, reservations and objections to REBT concepts and to the REBT therapeutic process;

ix.   deliberately instructing clients in the skills of REBT;

x.   encouraging clients to take responsibility for their change process;

xi.   using vivid methods to promote change;

xii. using humour to develop rapport and promote change.

While this list of modes of practice is not designed to be an exhaustive account of my REBT practice, it is meant to indicate what I particularly emphasise with clients from an REBT perspective.

Introduction
To those outside the cognitive-behavioural therapeutic tradition, all CBT approaches appear the same. This, of course, is far from the truth and while CBT approaches share some important similarities, they also differ from one another in other important ways (cf. Dobson, 2001). For example, while REBT is similar to Beck's cognitive therapy in some respects, it differs from it in others (Dryden, 1984; Haaga & Davison, 1991).

When we consider a specific CBT approach like REBT are we on safe ground in assuming that all REBT therapists practise REBT in the same way? The answer is: it depends. Thus, Robb, Backx & Thomas (1999) found in their survey sample of REBT therapists on the Albert Ellis Institute referral list that when faced with clients who articulated the insight problem (i.e. 'It makes sense, but I don't really believe it yet'), therapists generally responded with cognitive interventions. Warren & McLellarn (1987), in their earlier survey of the same listed therapists, found that 'most RE[B]T therapists follow the philosophies and practices of RE[B]T as espoused and advocated by Ellis' (p.71). However, they also found that a 'significant number of therapists disagree with Ellis in some of his philosophical views and appeared to adapt the practice of RE[B]T to their own preferred style' (p.71). On the latter point, Warren & McLellarn found that 36% of their sample reported using irrational belief inventories as an assessment procedure; 56% reported using rational role reversal with 38% of clients; and 46% suggest that their clients (38%) listen to audiotapes of therapy sessions as a homework assignment.

Given that REBT therapists do seem to practise REBT in different ways, while at the same time concurring on some of its main theories and practices, we need to know more about individual differences among REBT practitioners. In this chapter, then, I will take the lead and outline my own practice of REBT, focusing particularly on what I emphasise in my practice and why I do so. Space considerations mean that I am unable to discuss any of these points in depth and I will rarely have an opportunity to detail *how* I make the interventions I discuss (see Dryden, 1999; Dryden, Neenan & Yankura, 1999 for a more detailed discussion on these points).

Developing relationships with clients based on the principle of 'informed allies'

Although REBT employs a variety of cognitive, emotive, imaginal and behavioural techniques (Ellis & Dryden, 1997), it needs to be stressed that these techniques are used within the context of a therapeutic relationship and as such the development, maintenance and ending of this relationship needs to be considered. It is my view that the REBT literature has tended to underplay the importance of this relationship, a trend that I have tried to counterbalance in some of my own writings (Dryden, 1999; Dryden, 2001). In these writings and in my own practice of REBT, I emphasise a concept that I have called the principle of 'informed allies'. This concept comprises the principle of 'informed consent' and the tripartite idea of the working alliance first introduced by Bordin (1979), which I first introduced into the REBT literature in the late 1980s (Dryden, 1987). Bordin's conceptualisation of the working alliance highlights the therapeutic bond that develops between therapist and client, the *goals* of the enterprise and the therapeutic tasks that therapist and client undertake during the life of the therapeutic relationship to facilitate goal attainment.

I operationalise the 'informed allies' concept in my practice of REBT in the following ways:

i.   Early on in therapy, I outline the REBT model of psychological disturbance and psychological change to my client in bite-sized chunks to facilitate client understanding, using when appropriate the client's presenting problems. I also give them an idea of how I practise REBT and what this means for their participation in this process. I then ask them if they give their *informed consent* to proceed. Three outcomes are possible:

(a) the client wishes to proceed, so we do;

(b) the client is unsure. Here I usually offer a short-term contract so that the client can experience REBT in action and thus make a more informed decision to proceed or not; and

(c) the client does not wish to proceed. Here I attempt to discover what therapeutic approach may 'fit' the client better and effect a suitable referral.

ii.   In practising REBT I attempt to develop a suitable *bond* with my client. There are a number of issues that I keep in mind in doing so:

(a) *Informal vs. formal*. Clients differ with respect to their wishes for an informal or formal relationship with their therapists. As long as these wishes are healthy and do not unwittingly perpetuate the clients' problems, I am happy to meet their preferences on this point.

(b) *Directiveness*. While REBT is an active-directive, persuasive approach to therapy, I tend to be less directive and less overtly persuasive with clients who are reactant in personality organisation and who react adversely to attempts to influence them. With these clients I am explicit about REBT concepts and emphasise their choice concerning whether or not they implement these concepts in their life.

(c) *Humour*. Clients differ widely concerning their response to humorous interventions in REBT. While I prefer to practise REBT with a sense of humour (see below), I am quite happy to practise REBT in a more serious vein when this is required. I often have an intuitive 'feel' concerning a client's 'humour quotient', but when I am unsure about whether or not a client will respond well to my brand of humour, I offer 'trial' jokes (in the same way that an analyst makes trial interpretations) and gauge his or her response to these. I also ask for feedback on my humour and adjust my therapeutic style according to the feedback I receive.

iii.   In my experience as a supervisor of trainee REBT therapists, I often find that trainees lose sight of their clients' *goals* as they work with their clients over time (Neenan & Dryden, 2001). I am mindful in my own practice to keep my focus and that of my clients on their goals for change. In doing so, I consider that I am being a good role model since one of the ways in which clients maintain their psychological problems is lack of mindfulness about their healthy goals. I will discuss goals further later in this chapter.

iv.   I mentioned earlier that the technical aspects of REBT are often highlighted in the literature. From a working alliance perspective, I am particularly concerned about the following issues concerning therapeutic *tasks:*

(a) that clients understand (i) what their tasks are; (ii) what my tasks are as an REBT therapist and (iii) the relationship between both sets of tasks;

(b) that clients understand the relationship between their therapeutic tasks and their therapeutic goals;

(c) that clients are deemed capable of executing their tasks before they are asked to carry them out;

> (d) that clients are trained to carry out their therapeutic tasks as appropriate;
> (e) that I carry out my therapeutic tasks with skill, care and enthusiasm; and
> (f) that I suggest the use of therapeutic tasks that are potent enough to help clients to achieve their goals.

Developing a 'case formulation' with complex 'cases'

Beginning with the pioneering work of Persons (1989), cognitive therapists have espoused the value of carrying out case formulations to aid therapeutic intervention. REBT therapists have not embraced this concept as readily and indeed, my work on the subject is the only publication that centrally addresses this issue from an REBT perspective (Dryden, 1999). Indeed, when I showed a pre-publication copy of this work to Albert Ellis, he questioned the efficiency of making case formulations prior to therapeutic intervention in REBT. His point was that therapists can waste valuable therapeutic time making such formulations and that they could better use such time helping clients to address and overcome their psychological problems. This would be true if therapists carried out lengthy pre-treatment case formulations with all of their clients, but I am not suggesting this, nor is it my practice. My view about conducting a case formulation is this. I will do one when:

i.   *The referral is a complex one.* Once the client has given their informed consent to proceed with REBT and if it transpires that the client has complex problems, I will carry out a full case formulation before making any substantive change-based interventions since doing so will help me to understand the complexity of the client's 'case' and help me to save time in the longer run. This meets Ellis's inefficiency argument.

ii.   *The client isn't making progress as anticipated and/or I am stuck with the client.* When I predict that I can help a client, but the client doesn't make the anticipated progress or I get stuck and don't know why, I will then tend to do a full case formulation with that person. This often helps me to understand why the client isn't making the anticipated progress and/or why I am stuck and suggests avenues for intervention that had not previously occurred to me.

Let me now briefly describe the factors that I consider when I do a formal case formulation. I call this doing a 'UPCP', which stands for 'Understanding the Person in the Context of his/her Problems', because I do not like referring to a person as a 'case' (Dryden, 1999). This involves:

i.   obtaining basic information and utilising initial impressions;

ii.   developing a problem list;

iii.   identifying goals for therapy;

iv.   developing a list of problem emotions ('Cs');

v. developing a list of problem critical 'As';

vi. identifying core irrational beliefs;

vii. identifying dysfunctional behavioural 'Cs';

viii. identifying the purposive nature of dysfunctional behaviour;

ix. identifying ways in which the client prevents or cuts short the experience of problems;

x. identifying ways in which the client compensates for problems;

xi. identifying metapsychological problems;

xii. identifying the cognitive consequences of core irrational beliefs;

xiii. identifying the manner of problem expression and the interpersonal responses to these expressions;

xiv. identifying the client's health and medication status;

xv. developing an understanding of relevant predisposing factors;

xvi. predicting the client's likely responses to therapy;

xvii. negotiating a narrative account of the UPCP for consideration with the client.

For more detailed information on how to conduct a UPCP together with a case example see chapter 5 in Dryden (1999).

The final point that I wish to make on 'case formulations' is one that Ellis has made informally in many of his professional workshops. This is that competent REBT practitioners build up a working picture of their clients as they proceed in therapy and share this with their clients as a way of fine tuning these more informal case formulations. Albert Ellis is very good at this, as those who have witnessed him conducting therapy or been supervised by him will testify, but he has not written on this subject to any significant degree and this aspect of REBT has tended to be neglected.

Developing an REBT-influenced 'problems and goals' list with clients
As I listed above, conducting a problem and goals list with clients is an important component of a 'UPCP' or REBT 'case' formulation. It is my practice to develop such a list with virtually all of my clients (and not just when I am conducting a 'UPCP') since this helps both of us to keep on track throughout the therapeutic process. This is probably common practice among REBT therapists. What may be different is the way in which I do this.

Rather than ask my clients to develop a problems and goals list in their own way, I encourage them to use an REBT-inspired formula in doing so (Dryden,

2001). Usually, I help them to use this formula in a session and then once they have understood it, I suggest that they complete it as a homework assignment. I will now provide this formula and illustrate its use with a client example.

Formula for specifying a problem
Problem = Type of situation + inferential theme + unhealthy negative emotion + unconstructive behaviour/subsequent unrealistic thinking.

Example of specified problem
Whenever my boss asks to see me (type of situation), I think he is going to criticise me (inferential theme) and I feel anxious about this (unhealthy negative emotion). I deal with this anxiety by overworking so that he has nothing to criticise me for (unconstructive behaviour).

In helping clients to set goals, I encourage them in the first instance to keep the type of situation and the inferential theme the same and change the remaining factors. In doing so, I am being consistent with the traditional REBT approach which states that it is important at the outset *not* to change 'A' until clients have achieved a fair measure of change at 'B'. Following the tradition set by Wessler & Wessler (1980), 'A' here incorporates the situation and the inference about the situation.

Formula for specifying a goal
Goal = Type of situation + inferential theme + healthy negative emotion (*rather than* the unhealthy negative emotion) + constructive behaviour/subsequent realistic thinking (*rather than* the unconstructive behaviour/subsequent unrealistic thinking).

Example of specified goal
Whenever my boss asks to see me (type of situation) and I think he is going to criticise me (inferential theme), I want to feel concerned about this (healthy negative emotion) *rather than* anxious. I want to deal with this situation by doing the same level of work as if things were going well (constructive behaviour) *rather than* overworking.

Note that in the goal formula and example I encourage clients to specify their healthy emotional, behavioural and/or thinking goals as well as what they are going to strive not to feel, act and/or think; hence the emphasis on the phrase '*rather than*' in both formula and example.

I also help clients to distinguish between overcoming psychological problem (OPP) goals and personal development (PD) goals and to set both if relevant. Since this issue is outside the scope of this chapter, I refer interested readers to Dryden (2001).

Focusing on specific examples of target problems at the beginning of therapy and working them through
In my view, one of the most common errors that trainee REBT therapists make at the beginning of the REBT therapeutic process is to work with clients at an abstract, non-specific level rather than at a specific level (Neenan & Dryden, 2001). Of course, I endeavour to avoid making this error whenever I can. I do

so by encouraging clients to identify a problem from their problem list that they would like to work on. The selected problem is known as the 'target problem'. Then I encourage clients to identify a specific example of this target problem that we can work on and I explain why it is important for us to remain with this example and work it through. I explain that people make themselves disturbed in specific situations or when imagining specific situations and that given this, working with a specific example of their target problem will help us both to identify key elements of the ABC framework.

Thus, working with a specific example helps clients to identify with greater clarity than would be the case when working with abstract examples:

i.   the aspect of the situation (actual or inferred) they particularly disturbed themselves about (known as the 'critical A' — see below);

ii. their primary unhealthy negative emotion (emotional 'C');

iii. their unconstructive behaviours or behavioural impulses (behavioural 'C'); and

iv. their subsequent distorted thinking (cognitive 'C').

I then encourage my clients to stay with this specific example until I have helped them to identify, challenge and change the specific irrational beliefs that they held in this situation, and encourage them to imagine themselves responding to the critical 'A' while holding their specific rational beliefs and while acting constructively and thinking realistically. Finally, I encourage them to practise their rational beliefs and associated constructive behaviour and realistic thinking while facing the situation at 'A' which contains the inferential theme under consideration. When clients have done this, I help them to capitalise on their progress by encouraging them to generalise their learning to other relevant specific situations. Finally, I contend that working with specific examples of target problems helps guard against REBT becoming an overly intellectualised enterprise which it can easily become if the therapist works with the client at a general, abstract level.

Identifying the critical 'A' in the assessment process
In REBT theory, the concept of 'A' (or activating event) is deceptively simple. As its name implies, it is an event that activates something. Now, of course, it does not activate the person's emotional, behavioural and thinking responses at 'C' because that would be antithetical to REBT's ABC model of psychological disturbance and health. Rather, 'A' activates the person's belief and it is this 'A' x 'B' interaction that accounts for the person's psychological responses at 'C'. However, what actually constitutes an 'A'? This is where the distinction between an actual event and an inference about that event becomes salient. One point is important here: Ellis could have used 'A' to refer to an actual event, but he didn't. He clearly uses the term 'activating' when referring to 'A'.

To complicate matters a little further, some of us now use the term 'critical 'A'' (Dryden, 1995) to denote the core component of a situation that actually triggers the person's beliefs at 'B'. In using this term we recognise that there are many possible 'As' in a situation, but only one triggers a belief which accounts for a particular emotional-behavioural-cognitive response at 'C'. To make life even more complex for the REBT therapist, a client can experience several emotions in what Wessler & Wessler (1980) have called an emotional episode — an episode in which the client experiences emotions (and, I would add, behaviours and thinking responses as well) — and that each of these emotions are triggered by its own set of beliefs about a different critical 'A'.

When 'As' are inferential they have recurring themes when paired with different emotions. This was noted over 25 years ago by Beck (1976), whose thinking on this point has had a decided effect on my own with respect to the nature and role that 'As' play in the ABC model. For instance, when a client reports anxiety, look for the inferential theme of threat or danger in their report; when depression is reported look for loss or failure, etc. (see Dryden, 1995 for an extended discussion of this issue).

In my view and experience, critical 'As' are often inferential in nature. Given this, in identifying the critical 'A' in a specific ABC I often merge the actual with the specified inferential theme in the client's account (e.g. 'I was most anxious about my girlfriend looking over my shoulder' (actual situation) 'in case she found someone else more attractive than me' (inferential theme).

I have devised a number of different ways of identifying critical 'As' (see Dryden, 1995) and now see the importance of distinguishing between inferences at 'A' and inferences at 'C' (see below). Thus, my practice of REBT features an emphasis on helping the client and myself to identify and work with the critical 'A' in any highlighted emotional episode. This can often be a complex procedure and one which novice REBT therapists struggle to do well and succinctly.

Focusing on thinking 'Cs' as well as emotional and behavioural 'Cs'
I mentioned above that inferences can occur both at 'A' and at 'C' in the ABC framework. When inferences occur at 'C' in this framework they denote the fact that beliefs can not only have emotional and behavioural consequences, but thinking consequences as well. There are a variety of ways of dealing with thinking consequences in REBT. Thus, one can:

i.   deal with them as 'As' rather than as 'Cs' (e.g. as activating events for a subsequent ABC: let's suppose that everybody in the room does laugh at you, now how would you feel about that? Or as inferences as part of an inference chain: and if everybody in the room does laugh at you, what, for you, would be anxiety-provoking about that?);

ii. challenge their distorted nature (e.g. 'What is the likelihood that everybody in the room will laugh at you?); or

iii. educate clients about how they create them and to use them to identify the ABC in which they occur as a 'C'.

I find that while I do, at times, use the first two strategies listed above, I increasingly use the third strategy. Thus, if a client says that she is scared of speaking in public because she fears that everybody in the room will laugh at her, I show the client how they create this distorted inferential 'C'. I ask her questions such as 'what would have to happen for you not to fear that everyone in the room will laugh at you?' If she says: 'For me to have a sense of confidence about what I am talking about', I will show her that the opposite of this is likely to be her critical 'A' and teach her how she creates the aforementioned thinking 'C' by using the ABC framework. Thus:

'A' = Not being confident about what I will be talking about to a group
'B' = I must be confident about what I am talking about and it is terrible if
I'm not
'C' emotional = anxiety
behavioural = urge to cancel the talk
thinking = 'If I give the talk everybody will laugh at me'

Helping this client to dispute the irrational belief in the above example means that it is far less likely that she will create the thinking 'C' than if the irrational belief remains unchallenged. If the thinking 'C' persists then it can be dealt with by using the other two strategies listed above.

Finally, I want to note that it is a feature of my practice of REBT that I train my clients to identify the cognitive distortions in their inferential thinking so that they can treat these distorted inferences as thinking 'Cs' rather than to challenge them as distorted inferences as cognitive therapists are more likely to do. In this way, my practice of REBT differs from the practice of cognitive therapy.

Helping clients to develop and rehearse the full version of rational beliefs
As is well known, according to the REBT theory of psychological disturbance and health, irrational beliefs are at the core of the former and rational beliefs are at the core of the latter. Consequently, it is a major task of REBT therapists to help their clients to identify, challenge and change their irrational beliefs and to replace them with rational beliefs which need to be rehearsed and acted on sufficiently often if they are to make a significant difference in the clients' emotional lives. So far, what I have said would feature in the practice of virtually all REBT therapists. What characterises my practice that might not be sufficiently present in the therapeutic work of my colleagues is the emphasis that I place on what I call full versions of rational beliefs.

As I have noted elsewhere (Neenan & Dryden, 1999), a rational belief normally has two components: one that asserts the presence of the partial rational belief and the other that negates the presence of the irrational belief. Thus, if my client holds the following demand: 'I must do well in my examination', I help him, in this case, to develop and rehearse the following alternative full preference: 'I want to do well in my examination (asserted partial preference), but I do not have to do so (negated demand)'. I strive to do this consistently with all forms of rational beliefs (full preferences, full anti-awfulising beliefs, full HFT beliefs and full acceptance beliefs). I have found that when I do so my client is less likely to transmute her rational beliefs back into irrational beliefs than when I work with the partial versions of rational beliefs (e.g. I want to do well in my examination) (Dryden, 2001).

Encouraging clients to voice their doubts, reservations and objections to REBT concepts and to the REBT therapeutic process
One of the major features of REBT is that it has an explicit model of how people disturb themselves and what they need to do to undisturb themselves. Another major feature of this therapeutic approach is that it endeavours to teach this model to clients whenever possible and whenever appropriate. It is a feature of my practice to encourage clients to voice doubts, reservations and objections they have to any of the REBT concepts that I am teaching them or to any aspect of the REBT therapeutic process. My clinical experience has been that clients frequently harbour such doubts etc. and if these are not brought to light and examined with clients then they will have a decided negative influence on the therapeutic process. I have found it to be especially important to communicate to clients that I am very open to having REBT criticised in this way and to respond to these criticisms in a non-defensive manner. I also compliment clients for speaking their mind, which is, I have found, a good strategy for unearthing further doubts etc. later in the therapeutic process. Common doubts are too numerous to list here (see Dryden, 1995, 2001), but a few examples will suffice:

- acceptance means resignation
- accepting others means condoning their behaviour
- musts are motivating
- because preferences allow failure, they make it more likely that failure will occur. Musts, on the other hand, because they don't permit failure make failure less likely to occur
- REBT is simplistic
- REBT is brainwashing.

From this illustrative list, the deleterious effect of such doubts on the practice of REBT can be clearly seen and reinforces the importance of encouraging clients to reveal their doubts etc. and the importance of dealing with them in a sensitive but authoritative manner.

Deliberately instructing clients in the skills of REBT
I have always remembered a comment that Maxie C. Maultsby Jr. made at the very first workshop on REBT that I attended in 1977. He said that in essence effective therapy is self-therapy. In other words, clients will benefit from psychotherapy to the extent that they apply the principles of the therapeutic approach in their own lives. This fits very well with an educationally oriented approach such as REBT and over the years I have elaborated this concept to the point that I have recently published a book entitled *Reason to Change: A Rational Emotive Behaviour Therapy (REBT) Workbook* (Dryden, 2001). While this is a self-help workbook, I use the material with my clients since it gives step-by-step guidance with examples on how to use some of the major REBT techniques. My practice is to devote a portion of each therapy session to the work that clients have done between sessions on the workbook and the rest of the session on clients' target problems. In this way, I can monitor the progress that my clients are making on their problems and on their REBT skill development.

Of course, not all clients take to the skills development emphasis of the *Reason to Change* workbook and thus flexibility is the watchword here (as elsewhere). With such clients, I suggest that they do not use the workbook at all and I take a non-workbook approach with them. However, I deliberately instruct most of my clients in the use of core REBT skills and therefore this is an identifiable and key aspect of my practice of REBT.

Encouraging clients to take responsibility for change

Deliberately instructing clients in the skills in REBT is part of a wider emphasis that I place on encouraging clients to take responsibility for change. Thus, at the outset I outline my tasks as an REBT therapist and their tasks as REBT clients (Dryden, 1995). These are basically as follows:

*   specify problems
*   be open to the therapist's REBT framework
*   apply the specific principle of emotional responsibility (i.e. acknowledge and act on the idea that I largely make myself disturbed by the holding a set of irrational beliefs
*   apply the principle of therapeutic responsibility (i.e. acknowledge and act on the idea that in order to undisturb myself I need to dispute my irrational beliefs, rehearse and deepen my conviction in my rational beliefs and act and think in ways that are consistent with these developing rational beliefs and that I commit myself to doing this regularly)
*   disclose doubts, difficulties and obstacles to change.

In addition, I ask my clients, also at the outset of the therapeutic process, how much time they are willing to devote to helping themselves *per day*. I point out to them that the best predictor of progress in the cognitive therapies is the regular completion of homework assignments.

Throughout therapy, I remind clients that I don't expect them to do my job and I am not able to do theirs. Once again, I want to stress that this emphasis on client responsibility for change is modified according to the client's present capability for taking such responsibility.

Using vivid methods to promote change

In the early 1980s, I published a series of papers (collated in Dryden, 1986) on what I called vivid RE[B]T. Vivid interventions are those that bring the therapeutic process to life and I argued then as I still do now that such interventions instigate change more effectively than non-vivid interventions. A good example of this is vivid representations of 'As' where such 'As' are presented in clear and emotionally impactful ways, enabling clients' beliefs and feelings to be evoked and worked with in therapy sessions.

Thus, my work is still characterised by the use of such methods and I apply the same caveats as I described in the 1986 compilation [e.g. don't overuse vivid interventions in therapy sessions, don't use them with clients with a tendency towards a histrionic response and when you use them with clients use intellectualisation as a defence, introduce such methods gradually and at an initial 'low dose' of vividness, increasing this 'dose' if such clients respond well to the initial 'dose' (see Dryden, 1986 for a fuller discussion of vivid REBT).]

Using humour to develop rapport and promote change

The final distinguishing feature of my REBT practice that I want to discuss is my use of humour to develop rapport and to promote change. Although I mentioned the use of humour in the first mode of practice that I discussed in this chapter, I wanted to include it separately since it is such a defining characteristic of my work.

I find it difficult to describe my use of humour in REBT. It is something that one has to observe to understand. However, it is a combination of puns, witticisms, bringing together disparate aspects of a client's experience in humorous fusion, self-mocking and jokes. I don't, on the other hand, make much use of rational humorous songs (Ellis, 1987). Now, I don't want you to get the idea that my sessions are full of humour since this is not the case: I am serious when I need to be and often. However, I have found that my humorous interventions do lighten the therapeutic atmosphere to good effect, particularly in REBT group therapy. My experience is that humour is a therapeutic factor in that it helps clients to take themselves seriously, but not too seriously. It also serves to remind clients of a therapeutic point between sessions. My clients are wont to say that one of my humorous remarks came into their mind at an appropriate time and reminded them of a salient REBT concept that they were then able to translate into practice. In this sense, humour can also be seen as a vivid intervention.

I hope that I have conveyed in this chapter my idiosyncratic practice of REBT and that this encourages other REBT therapists to discuss their own particular way of practising REBT.

References

Beck, A. T. (1976). *Cognitive Therapy and the Emotional Disorders*. New York: International Universities Press.

Bordin, E. S. (1979). The generalizability of the concept of the working alliance. *Psychotherapy: Theory, Research and Practice, 16*, 252–60.

Dobson, K. S. (ed.) (2001). *Handbook of Cognitive-Behavioral Therapies*, (2nd edn.). New York: Guilford.

Dryden, W. (1984). Rational-emotive therapy and cognitive therapy: A critical comparison. In M. A. Reda & M. J. Mahoney (eds.), *Cognitive Psychotherapies: Recent Developments in Theory, Research and Practice* (pp. 81–99). Cambridge, MA: Ballinger.

Dryden, W. (1986). Vivid methods in rational-emotive therapy. In A. Ellis & R. Grieger (eds.), *Handbook of Rational-Emotive Therapy, Volume 2* (pp. 221–45). New York: Springer.

Dryden, W. (1987). The therapeutic alliance in rational-emotive individual therapy. In W. Dryden, *Current Issues in Rational-Emotive Therapy* (pp. 59–71). London: Croom Helm.

Dryden, W. (1995). *Preparing for Client Change in Rational Emotive Behaviour Therapy*. London: Whurr.

Dryden, W. (1999). *Rational Emotive Behaviour Therapy: A Personal Approach*. Bicester, Oxon: Winslow Press.

Dryden, W. (2001). *Reason to Change: A Rational Emotive Behaviour Therapy (REBT) Workbook*. London: Brunner/Routledge.

Dryden, W., Neenan, M. & Yankura, J. (1999). *Counselling Individuals: A Rational Emotive*

Behavioural Handbook, (3rd edn.). London: Whurr.

Ellis, A. (1987). The use of rational humorous songs in psychotherapy. In W. F. Fry & W. A. Salameh (eds.), *Handbook of Humor in Psychotherapy: Advances in the Clinical Use of Humor.* Sarasota FL: Professional Resource Exchange Inc.

Ellis, A. & Dryden, W. (1997). *The Practice of Rational Emotive Behavior Therapy,* (2nd edn.). New York: Springer.

Haaga, D. A. F. & Davison, G. C. (1991). Disappearing differences do not always reflect healthy integration: An analysis of cognitive therapy and rational-emotive therapy. *Journal of Psychotherapy Integration, 1*(4), 287–303.

Neenan, M. & Dryden, W. (1999). *Rational Emotive Behaviour Therapy: Advances in Theory and Practice.* London: Whurr.

Neenan, M. & Dryden, W. (2001). *Learning from Errors in Rational Emotive Behaviour Therapy.* London: Whurr.

Persons, J. (1989). *Cognitive Therapy in Practice: A Case Formulation Approach.* New York: Norton.

Robb, H., Backx, W. & Thomas, J. (1999). The use of cognitive, emotive and behavioral interventions in rational emotive behavior therapy when clients lack 'emotional' insight. *Journal of Rational-Emotive & Cognitive-Behavior Therapy, 17*(3), 201–9.

Warren, R. & McLellarn, R. W. (1987). What do RET therapists think they are doing? *Journal of Rational-Emotive Therapy, 5*(2), 71–91.

Wessler, R. A. & Wessler, R. L. (1980). *The Principles and Practice of Rational-Emotive Therapy.* San Francisco: Jossey-Bass.

2

Albert Ellis

I have done REBT so many times in public, with both professional and lay people, that I am sure that most REBT practitioners have largely or partly copied my style. Good! In this article, however, I should try to describe some aspects of my presentations that, for better or worse, are somewhat unique to me.

First, let me present *my* goals and values with new clients. I, of course, want to help them — preferably fast *and* thoroughly. I'd very much like to see them become significantly less disturbed and more self-actualizing from the first session onward; *but* I want to see them *get* better rather than merely *feel* better. Often, my two goals conflict, but *I* do my best to abet *both*.

I, of course, want my clients to like me — who the hell doesn't? But I want them, even more, to like themselves (yes, above me) and especially to like REBT — because they make it so helpful to them. Oh, yes — and to teach it to others to help themselves with. Because I, prejudicially, think REBT is so good, I want my clients to widely spread it around their community and the world — which, I fear, can greatly use it! So, I really push to help my clients help themselves — and help others.

I also distinctly want my clients to think, feel, and act for themselves — and only very partially to please me. I sort of like their dependence on me — but not too much! I want them to *use* me, but not too *need* me. I like their personal approval, but can also very *easily* live without it. Again, let them love REBT more then me!

I also want my clients to be individuals in their own right and to get what *they* really want, for their *own* good, and not just for what they think they should want. Yes, they *probably* should desire to help others — in addition to their strong desire to help themselves.

Which brings me to another of my goals. I, naturally, want to understand my clients. But, for their sake and mine, I want to understand their disturbances — how long they have had them, how intense they are, how likely they are to hold on to them — despite their and my great efforts to improve them. So I very quickly, in most cases, make a *tentative* diagnosis. Are they light neurotics, serious neurotics, severe personality disorders, or afflicted with psychosis? I don't have to know, and will find out much more precisely a little later. So at the start, I gather some important diagnostic material showing how long and intensely they have been disturbed, how dysfunctional their close relatives are, what therapy they have previously had, how it has worked, what medication they have been taking, and so on.

As I have said, my diagnosis is *tentative* — and is not merely for insurance purposes. I want to see, according to what I briefly find, how I preferably should proceed with REBT, what unusual resistances I may meet, how I shall prepare my client for rough possibilities, how far I can probably go with this particular client, etc. Whatever I find and conclude, I fairly rapidly go on. As I have often noted (Ellis & Dryden, 1997) in using REBT, therapy can be an important part of assessment. How the client reacts and acts to this kind of therapy can often provide an accurate kind of diagnosis and prognosis for her or him. So, with my revisable diagnosis in mind, I usually quickly proceed with the therapy and introduce the theory of REBT.

I discover the clients' referral sources, partly to see how much they know about REBT. If, for example, they have read some of my books or listened to some of the Institute's cassettes, I assume they know something about REBT and make my introduction brief. If, as usual, they know little about REBT, I outline its main theory. I usually, at the start, say, ' I am going to give you a model of what REBT is and how you can use it. What I am going to tell you in the next several minutes may well be the most important information you have ever learned in your entire life. If you use it! Listen carefully and see!'

I thereby encourage attentive listening and hint at the hard work to come. Then I usually give my clients my famous model of human disturbance and what they can do about it. I show them, in this model, that if they don't know how much money they have in their pocket or purse, and merely *wish* that it will be a minimum of ten dollars, when they look to find out, and see that they only have nine dollars, they will most likely feel the *healthy* emotions of disappointment, regret, and frustration. But if they insist, before looking, that they *absolutely must* at all times have a minimum of ten dollars, they will most probably experience the *unhealthy* negative feelings of anxiety, depression and anger. They almost all see this very quickly and in doing so, learn, first, that negative feelings — including strong feelings — can be definitely *healthy* or *unhealthy*; second, that *preferences* almost always lead to healthy negative feelings when they are thwarted; but absolutistic musts, shoulds, and demands, usually lead to unhealthy — disturbed — negative feelings. Third, my clients learn that they have a *choice* of whether or not they *make themselves* healthfully sorrowful or unhealthfully upset when unfortunate thoughts happen to them.

I emphasize that REBT is a *constructivist* or *choice* theory and that they can construct, deconstruct, and reconstruct their useful and dysfunctional thoughts, feelings, and behaviors. I usually do this, once I have known my clients for only a few minutes. Why do I not go out of my way to go more slowly before I theorize about REBT? Well, sometimes I do, if my initial assessment indicates that this is desirable. But I often find that my quickly showing clients what REBT is so that they can effectively now use it is one of the best ways to gain rapport or alliance with them. It tends to show them that I *care* to help them; that I am *confident* that I can; that they can soon *help themselves* if they follow me; that I have *expertise* in doing therapy and doing it quickly; that I am giving them a *choice* of thoughts, feelings and behaviors that *they* can select; that I will *strive* to do my best to help them; that I have confidence in them and their ability to change; and that I and REBT are fully on their side.

If I find that I am going too fast for particular clients, I slow down, spend more time bonding with them, and look for other ways to ally with them or reach them. Doing so, I'd better keep their goals and values more in mind than my own!

I follow up in the next few minutes with more of the general principles and practices of REBT, not necessarily putting them in the same order each time. For one thing, I show my clients, seriously and humorously, that they have many rational beliefs (RBs) and many irrational beliefs (IBs) but that practically all the latter include one, two, or three *musts*: (1) 'I *absolutely must* perform well and be loved by significant others — or else I am a turd for behaving turdily as I must not do!' (2) 'Other people *absolutely must* treat me kindly and fairly — or else I know what hell they should roast in eternally!' (3) Conditions must *always* be the way I want them to be and never deprive me — or else I *can't stand it*, can't be happy *at all,* and had better kill myself!' My clients' reactions to my seriously and humorously pointing out their musturbating again show me how to keep proceeding — or to change my foolish therapeutic ways.

I also, near the end of the first session, show my clients the 'ABCs' of REBT: activating events or adversities ('A') that happen to them; rational and irrational *beliefs* ('Bs') about their 'As'; functional or dysfunctional consequence ('Cs') that follow from 'A' and 'B'. Then I usually pick a consequence that they intensely have and specifically want to relieve; and I show them how to find and dispute ('D') the IBs that go with consequence. I briefly show them the realistic or empirical ways to dispute, the logical ways to dispute, and the pragmatic or heuristic ways to dispute their IBs.

I thus help my clients to proceed to their effective new philosophy (E) and to construct some rational coping statements that they can strongly repeat to themselves several times, until they feel and act on them (Ellis, 1994, 2000, 2001a, 2001b, 2002).

I especially emphasize the philosophic aspects of REBT during my first few sessions. I show how I originally derived it from many ancient and modern philosophies; and I especially show my clients how Alfred Korzybski in 1933, in his book *Science and Sanity*, pioneered in showing his readers that practically all humans are 'unsane' because of their strong tendencies to overgeneralize. Their worst overgeneralizations, I show them, are people's absolutistic *shoulds*, *oughts*, and *musts*.

Special ways of using emotional aspects of REBT
Usually during the first or first few sessions, I emphasize that REBT, since my first paper on it in 1956 at the American Psychological Association in Chicago (Ellis, 1958), holds that thinking, feeling, and behaving are not separate processes, but are *holistically integrated* and circularly affect each other. Therefore, REBT uses *many* cognitive, emotional, and behavioral methods; and, of course, unlike some of the other cognitive behavioral therapies (CBTs), it emphasizes emotional-experiential-evocative methods — especially unconditional other-acceptance, unconditional self-acceptance, and unconditional life-acceptance.

Moreover, I preferably use the thinking and behavioral methods of REBT in a strong, emphatic, and emotional manner, and I urge my clients to strongly do the same. Thus, they are encouraged to *forcefully* dispute their IBs, to *powerfully* do effective cost benefit ratios, and to *strongly* focus on and repeat their rational coping statements (Ellis, 1999, 2001a, 2001b).

Using Windy Dryden's (1999) cognitive-emotional method, my clients are taught to recognize that they often hold their RBs *lightly* and *unvigorously* and shown how to forcefully argue with them — as well as their IBs — until they get themselves to hold their RBs much more convincingly. Thus, they are not merely shown how to dispute their IBs, but also to argue with and dispute their lightly held, unconvincing RBs, such as 'I don't *have to* perform well at important tasks but can fully accept myself if I act ineffectually.' They can use realistic disputing to challenge this rational belief, by asking themselves, '*Why* can I accept myself when I perform poorly? Why am I *always* an *acceptable* person even when my performance is unacceptable?' They can also use logical disputing of this RB: 'Does it follow that because I greatly desire to perform well, that I *must* do so? Does it follow that I and everyone who performs poorly is *never* an inadequate person?' They can heuristically dispute this light RB: 'I will usually create anxiety and depression if I think that I absolutely must act well! So, I'd better not create self-defeating musts!' They can argue with this RB by asking themselves, 'Why are *musts* self-defeating? Aren't they often really helpful?' My clients, I teach, can vigorously and emotionally argue against *both* their IBs and their lightly held RBs.

Special ways of using behavioral aspects of REBT
REBT, of course, stresses *active-directive* therapy and I may well be one of the worst 'abusers' in this respect. I actively *push* my clients into productive action, somewhat modeling myself after Alfred Adler's (1926) *encouragement*. But I also emphasize their using cognitive methods *actively*. Thus, I induce them to fill out many REBT self-help forms, hand them to me to go over with them, and keep revising and improving them. I urge them, as did George Kelly (1955), to *act* on their disinhibiting thoughts and resolutions. I push them to think about modeling after people who have conquered adversity and to *act* on that thinking. I encourage them to read REBT books and pamphlets and to *discuss* and *debate* their ideas with other people. I emphasize their visualizing self-efficacious and anti-phobic behaviors — and encourage them to force themselves to carry out some of the visualized endeavors.

Once again, REBT revised thinking is accompanied by validating *action*. Although clients have the will or choice of changing themselves, will power includes deciding to change (cognition), determining to change (emotion), and *action* to change.

Else, will has no *power*. Moreover, I continually show my clients that even the decision to change and a *determination* to do so has definite *action* tendencies. My use of REBT steadily urges clients to 'push your ass' (PYA) to think differently, to feel differently, and of course to behave differently. So, I keep pushing my ass to get them to keep pushing their asses. At my urging, they are pushed to practice, practice, practice healthy thoughts, feelings and behaviors. Practice doesn't make perfect — but it helps protect my clients' emotional health!

So, expectably, I check my clients' homework. Not merely their behavioral homework — where at least they clearly can see that they often don't do. But also their cognitive homework — which they easily and unconsciously forget to do, do very lightly or think they do well when they really don't. So I check their new healthy cognitions, to reassign many of the neglected ones, give reinforcements for doing them adequately, recommend penalties for steady avoidances, and link them up with several behavioral procedures.

My clients' working to change their dysfunctional feelings can often be tricky. They easily use rational emotive imagery, can get in touch with their anxiety, depression and rage, and fully feel them, especially when I give it to them during a session. But they only lightly work at changing their unhealthy negative feeling to a healthy negative feeling; they only do so a few times, though we agree on their doing it doing it for 30 days in a row; they incorrectly change it by changing the adversity they are imagining and upsetting themselves about; they incorrectly change their unhealthy negative feeling to a positive feeling; and they goof in other ways of doing REI. So again, I monitor them and help them behaviorally correct this emotional exercise.

My style of therapy

My style of doing REBT with my regular clients starts off by being very active and direct. If clients know little about REBT — which is usual — I try to teach them its fundamentals during the first few sessions. As I noted in the first pages of this chapter, I commonly start with my analogy of supposing that they don't know how much money they have in their pocket or purse and, just before they look to find out how much, they tell themselves, at first, 'I would like, really prefer to find a minimum of ten dollars, since I may eat, take a cab, or go to the movies.' Then they find that they only have nine dollars — one less. How, I ask, would you feel under these conditions. About 90% of them say, 'Disappointed or regretful' or 'Not too bad.' I say, 'Good! That's a healthy negative emotion. If you said *anxious*, *depressed*, or *angry* then you would be having an *unhealthy* negative emotion — quite different. Not getting what you *want* leads you to have healthy feelings.'

Secondly, I get my clients to suppose that before looking to discover how much money they have in their pocket or purse they strongly tell themselves and believe, 'When I look in my pocket or purse, I *must*, really *must*, *at all times* find a minimum guarantee of ten dollars. I've got to! I absolutely must!' I ask, 'If you believed this before looking and then only found nine dollars again and couldn't possibly get any more, how would you then feel?'

About 80% of my clients reply: 'Anxious,' 'depressed,' or 'angry:' 'Yes,' I say, 'because of your *must*, your demand. But it's the same nine! The only thing you changed was your *must*. REBT shows you that you practically never disturb yourself without a *must*. The loss of a *preference* will make you healthily sorry, disappointed, or regretful. But a *must* will disturb you. When you *want* something and don't get it — too bad. When you think you absolutely *need* it and still don't get it, it's *awful* and *terrible* — and you disturb yourself.'

The great majority of my clients quickly see this. If not, we further discuss the crucial importance of their *demanding,* instead of *preferring*, to get what they want.

Finally, if this point sinks in, I say, 'The third time before you look to see how much money you have in your pocket or purse, you say to yourself the same demand as the second time, 'I absolutely *must* at all times find a minimum guarantee of ten dollars. I *have to*. I must!' You then look in your pocket or purse and find *fifteen* dollars. How would you feel?' Practically all my clients reply, 'Great!' 'Fine!' 'Happy!' 'Wonderful!'

'Fine!' I say. But a few minutes later when you *still* have the fifteen dollars — you haven't lost it and you haven't changed your demand to, 'I now need twenty more dollars,' — a thought would occur to you to make you feel anxious or panicked. What would that panicking thought be?

About 60% of my clients give the right answer: 'Since I absolutely *need* a minimum of ten at *all times*, I would think, I *now* have 15. But suppose I spend six or lose six. How awful!' Those who don't come up with this correct answer, I tell it to them, and almost all of them immediately see the important point I am making. 'When you *prefer* something and don't get it, you feel that that's unfortunate and too bad. But when you demand any *guarantee* that you get it, you're cooked. The universe doesn't have guarantees in it — just, at most, high degrees of probability.'

With this analogy, I usually give my clients, in the first session, some of the basic principles of REBT. By seeing how well they react to these principles I often can assess how disturbed they are, how likely they are to benefit from REBT, how long their therapy may take, how they will take to my active-directive teaching methods, and how I had better change my most common style with them. So, their *reactions* to my analogies and to my brief lectures about REBT give me very useful information about my clients.

With a few of my clients, especially those who are passive and don't work hard themselves to change, and with those who like to chatter on about their 'horrible' lives, I am sometimes much more passive. I may finally conclude that they may somehow benefit from therapy even when they don't work at it. So, I listen endlessly to them, try to sneak in as much REBT as I can, and occasionally spend months inactively. I rarely get rid of them as clients, though a number of them, after refusing my attempts to help them actively use REBT, see that therapy 'isn't working' and eventually drop out.

How I use humor in REBT

As I have noted in several papers and cassettes on therapy (Ellis, 1977a, 1977b, 1987) people often are overly serious about their disturbances and lose their sense of humor. Therefore, at the psychological clinic of the Albert Ellis Institute in New York we give all our clients a sheet of eighteen rational, humorous songs. They are to use these lyrics, which are set to well-known American and international tunes, to interrupt their disturbed feelings and to dispute the irrational beliefs behind them cognitively, emotively, and behaviorally. At my workshops and lectures at the Institute and in other cities, I also include the singing of some of these rational, humorous songs to help the participants see some of the main points of REBT and actually use them on themselves. A few of my humorous songs follow:

LOVE ME, LOVE ME, ONLY ME!
  (Tune: *Yankee Doodle Dandy*)
Love me, love me, just dear, only me
Or I will die without you!
O, make your love a guarantee
So I can never doubt you!
Love me, love me totally — really, really
    try dear;
But if you demand love, too
I'll hate you till I die, dear!

 Love me, love me all the time
Thoroughly and wholly!
My life all turns to slushy slime
Unless you love me solely!
Love me with great tenderness
With no ifs or buts, dear.
If you love me somewhat less,
I'll hate your goddamned guts, dear!

YOU FOR ME AND ME FOR ME
(Tune: *Tea for Two*,
by Vincent Youmans)
Picture you upon my knee
Just you for me, and me for me!
And then you'll see
How happy I will be!
Though you beseech me
You never will reach me —
For I am autistic
As any real mystic!
And only relate to
Myself with a great to-do, dear!
If you dare to try to care
You'll see my caring soon will wear,
For I can't pair and make our sharing fair!
If you want a family,
We'll both agree you'll baby me —
Then you'll see how happy I will be!

I'M JUST WILD ABOUT WORRY
(Tune: *I'm Just Wild About Harry,*
by Eubie Blake)
Oh, I'm just wild about worry
And worry's wild about me!
We're quite a twosome to make life
gruesome
And filled with anxiety!
Oh, worry's anguish I curry
And look for it's guarantee!
Oh, I'm just wild about worry
And worry's wild about
Never mild about,
Most beguiled about me!

FAIL, FAIL AT THERAPY!
(Tune: *Hail, Hail the Gang's All Here*,
by Arthur Sullivan)
Fail, fail at therapy!
What the hell do we care!
We want effort-free care!
Why should we seek good aid
When we've got neurosis made?
Fail, fail at therapy!
Why should we be workers
When we make great shirkers?
Fail, fail at therapy —
And reinforce our lunacy!

GLORY, GLORY HALLELUJAH
(Tune: *Battle Hymn of the Republic*)
Mine eyes have seen the glory of
    relationships that glow
And then falter by the wayside as
    love passions come — and go!
I've heard of great romances where
    there is no slightest lull —
But I am skeptical!

Glory, glory hallelujah!
People love ya till they screw ya!
If you'd lessen how they do ya
Then don't expect they won't!
Glory, glory hallelujah!
People cheer ya — then pooh-pooh ya!
If you'd soften how they screw ya!
Then don't expect they won't!

I WISH I WERE NOT CRAZY!
(Tune: *Dixie*, by Dan Emmett)
Oh, I wish I were really put together —
Smooth and fine as patent leather!
Oh, how great to be rated innately sedate!
But I'm afraid that I was fated
To be rather aberrated —
Oh, how sad to be mad as my Mom and my Dad!

Oh, I wish I were not crazy! Hooray! Hooray!
I wish my mind were less inclined
To be the kind that's hazy!
I could, you see, agree to be less crazy —
But I, alas, am just too goddamned lazy!

LOVE ME GOOD, AS YOU SHOULD
(Tune: Brahms' *Lullaby*)
Love me good, as you should
And I'll be a good client!
Yes I'll be, you'll agree,
So compliant and so good!
If your therapy's tough,
I'll behave like a ruffian!
And I'll balk and I'll stew,
Though I screw myself, too!

(Lyrics by Albert Ellis. Copyright by Albert Ellis Institute.)

In my individual group therapy sessions I frequently use irony, skepticism, joking, witticism, absurdity, and other forms of humor to lighten up my clients, to let them see how silly are their irrational beliefs, to interrupt their grim moods, and to counteract their narcissism and overcome their taking life *too* seriously. Their feedback often shows that my humorous sallies are an important part of my therapy.

How I dispute my clients' irrational beliefs
I continually dispute my clients' irrational beliefs in the usual ways that I have described in my books, *How to Stubbornly Refuse to Make Yourself Miserable About Anything — Yes Anything* (Ellis, 1988*); A Guide to Rational Living* (Ellis & Harper, 1997); *How to Control Your Anxiety Before it Controls You* (Ellis, 2000); *How to Make Yourself Happy and Remarkably Less Disturbable* (Ellis, 1999); *Feeling Better, Getting Better, Staying Better* (Ellis, 2001a); *Overcoming Destructive Beliefs, Feelings, and Behaviors* (Ellis, 2001b); and *Rational Emotive Behavior Therapy* (Ellis & MacLaren, 1998).

I also regularly employ the realistic, logical, and pragmatic REBT methods of disputing that are described in Bernard & Wolfe (2000) and in Walen, DiGiuseppe & Dryden (1992). But, again, I do these methods of disputing in a highly forceful and emotive-evocative manner, because my form of cognitive restructuring, as I showed in my first presentations of REBT, stresses emotional and action-oriented elements (Ellis, 1958). I have recently emphasized how the cognitive aspects of REBT are integrated with its emotional and behavioral aspects (Ellis, 2001a, 2001b, 2002).

I have also shown how I do the disputing of irrational beliefs of clients in several related cognitive-emotive methods. Thus, I work out with my individual and group therapy clients rational coping statements, cost-benefit analysis of their goals and actions, psycho-educational reasons for changing their destructive philosophies, the recording and listening to their therapy sessions to see how irrational they respond to my disputing, modeling methods of changing their dysfunctional ideas and behaviors, and other ways of interrupting and restructuring their IBs.

My approach to treatment planning
I probably give less attention to treatment planning then do most other REBT practitioners. One reason for this is that a great deal of my treatment with individual therapy clients is not only brief but very brief. Yes, I see a large number of persons with severe personality disorder, and some of them I see for three or more years. Still, I may have contact with them (in person or by telephone) only a few times a year for much of this time.

Most of my regular clients I see for five to ten sessions; I see a great many for a total of three sessions; and almost 50 per cent of the people, I see only for a single session. Why do I see so many one-session clients? For a number of reasons. Some come from out of town and are only in New York a few days. Some have a specific emotional problem — such as being guilty about not loving their mother — and, using REBT, I can quickly show how to be sorry about their behavior but not guilty and self-damning about it.

Other single-session clients have a practical problem, such as how to have more frequent sex with their partner — which I can show them how to achieve immediately by refusing to define partnership sex as intercourse and allowing themselves to have alternative methods of satisfying themselves and their partners.

Still other clients come for a single session, to see if their present therapy is useful. Or as a screening session which our clinic requires for them to arrange to join one of my therapy groups. Or they decide that REBT requires too much work which they may be allergic to doing. Or because they find therapy too expensive. Or because they came with the idea of having only one or a few sessions. Et cetera.

Anyway, knowing from experience that I will often have a few (or less) sessions with a client, I rarely initially plan what course I will take with a new one. If I did so, I might largely lose time and energy in such planning. Before I hardly know it, he or she is no longer a client!

Moreover, since I at first don't know which of my REBT methods will work best with a particular client, and since I want to remain experimentally open to find out, I first have several sessions with a client to see how it goes — and by that time we are (successfully or unsuccessfully) finished. I always realize too, that a long-range plan with starting clients may limit us too much in our experimenting — and I am loath to set these kinds of restrictive limits.

How I change my approach as clients begin to improve
Many of my clients seem to significantly improve after a few sessions — but, of course, I don't exactly trust this. I see 'real' improvement as clients understand the main principles of REBT; implement them, particularly by doing cognitive, emotive, and behavioral homework in between sessions; maintain their improvement for several more sessions; and continue their maintenance, including overcoming some possible setbacks, for a few months more.

When clients seem to begin improving, I usually change my approach as follows:

1. I talk less and listen to them more as they report the details of their improving.
2. I get them to agree to take 'harder' and 'riskier' homework assignments — such as more 'dangerous' shame-attacking exercises.
3. I encourage them to bring up other forms of anxiety, depression, and rage than they first wanted to deal with. Thus, if they come to therapy mainly for their social anxiety and seem to be conquering that, I ask them about their possible public speaking, test taking, and other forms of anxiety, that they may not have yet discussed in detail.
4. I encourage them to have fewer sessions and to do more homework in between sessions.
5. I encourage them to keep listening to recordings of their sessions if they have made such recordings.
6. I encourage them to use REBT to try to help their friends and relatives with their problems.
7. I encourage them to think more about future life goals and about methods of actualizing themselves now that they are becoming less emotionally and behaviorally disturbed.
8. I encourage them to continue with their REBT reading and listening to cassettes and to attend some of the lectures and workshops that we keep

presenting at the Albert Ellis Institute. I particularly recommend my regular Friday Night Workshop, where for a mere $5.00 they can see me demonstrate REBT with public volunteers, can actively participate in helping the volunteers, and can meet other devotees of REBT.

9. If they are individual therapy clients, I sometimes recommend that they join one of the regular therapy groups that the Institute conducts; and if they are group therapy clients, I may recommend that they stop group sessions and make occasional individual therapy sessions.
10. I stress that psychotherapy is largely a continual self-help process, and that now that they are doing well with it they had better continue working and practicing it indefinitely.
11. I encourage them to have occasional check-up sessions with me to see how they are maintaining and progressing and to discover other areas that they can work on with REBT.

How I take a hard-hitting approach with some clients

I take a hard-hitting, quite active-directive approach with most of my clients, especially for the first few sessions. My goal, again, is to help them improve quickly *and* intensively and I assume that some of them will do so if I work hard at convincing them to follow my energetic modeling.

Some clients — particularly the many I see with severe personality disorders — make good progress and then stop working to maintain or continue it. Other clients make little or no healthy changes. If so, what do I do?

Somewhat perversely, and against my own inclinations, I sometimes slow down. I assume — perhaps wrongly — that these clients are willful and/or innately inclined slow movers and that we are in for a long haul. So, I persist, steadily but more slowly, with what I think are the best REBT methods for these clients, and stubbornly refuse to upset myself about their resistance. I especially give them unconditional other-acceptance (UOA) in spite of their frustrating resisting. Often, this works and they eventually learn and use REBT at their own pace.

When my clients are unusual 'resistors,' and I think they can benefit from a more hard-hitting approach, I try and test out several possibilities:

*   I discuss their resistance with them, to see if it is motivated by their irrational beliefs about therapy, such as 'I am unable to change myself, so why try?' 'Changing takes *too much* time and energy, so I'll get along with the problems that I have.' If I suspect that clients have these IBs, I probe for them and help them to dispute and act against them.
*   I try to get the clients to agree to do more homework, especially activity homework that counterattacks their resistance. Thus, if they have social anxiety and won't dispute their irrational beliefs that being rejected socially makes them totally unlovable, I try to encourage them to actually get rejected and thereby *see* that rejection is not terrible and that it can lead to other acceptance.
*   I consistently, in a number of ways, keep striving to help my resisting clients achieve three of the main goals of REBT: (1) unconditional self-acceptance (USA), *whether or not* they perform well or win the approval of significant others; (2) unconditional other-acceptance (UOA), *whether or not* other people treat them considerately and fairly; (3) unconditional life-acceptance (ULA),

or high frustration tolerance (HFT), *whether or not* the world in which they live presents them with grim situations (Ellis, 2002). Does the achievement by resisting (and nonresisting) clients of USA, UOA, and ULA make them completely undisturbed and happy? No. But it may considerably help!

Some of my unusual ways of doing REBT

Almost all possible ways of doing REBT have been invented — by myself and by other REBT practitioners. Let me describe a few that I often use and sometimes make routine procedures.

Phone sessions

I, at first, was sold on the idea that seeing clients face-to-face was quite necessary for good therapy, since the therapist watched their eyes, facial expression, and tone of voice and received valuable feedback from them. Then shortly after I began practicing therapy in 1943, I was forced to have several therapy sessions by phone with one of my female clients who was physically ill and couldn't attend regular sessions. In spite of her severe panic — including panic about being ill — we did very well together. I saw that phone sessions can be just as effective as those I have face-to-face.

Thereafter, I have had literally thousands of phone sessions for various reasons: (1) my clients couldn't get together to see me because of very rough weather; (2) I hesitated to see them personally because I had a cold or other contagious disease; (3) they lived quite a distance from my office and could only visit occasionally; (4) they were phobic and couldn't leave their home; (5) they were afraid to face me, but found phone sessions safer.

For these and other reasons, I welcomed phone sessions and have had thousands of them, and my clients have felt that they were just as good — and sometimes better — than regular sessions. I like them since I am less distracted by attractive clients; can concentrate very well over a phone; usually hear better when I use my earphones attached to my phone; find that clients are more prone to keep appointments and take advantage of expensive phone rates to have quick and more concentrated phone sessions; find that clients save themselves much travel, time and parking fees; and can service more clients than I can see face to face. So I keep getting enthusiastic comments from many phone session clients. Viva Alexander Bell!

Recorded sessions

I do not favor sessions in which clients record their problems and I tell them my impressions and I make suggested homework assignments on another tape recording. They take too long. I cannot ask questions while listening to clients' recordings and they cannot ask me questions until they listen to my tape. But, for one reason or another, clients insist on taped sessions, and I oblige them. We do fairly well by exchanging tapes, but I think not *as* well, as by live voice exchange.

Written sessions

People often write me, email me and ask me to send them back brief answers to their problems. I refuse to do so and refer them, instead, for regular or phone sessions with me, one of the Fellows or Associate Fellows of our Institute.

Occasionally, they want to pay for written sessions. I have tried this medium a few times but find them too time-consuming. So I rarely do them.

Internet sessions
I have done a few sessions on the Internet, with clients typing out their problems and my typing back my therapeutic suggestions. This, too, I find time-consuming unless we can actually talk to each other via Internet and phone combination. When I have done so, that is quite efficient.

Conclusion
As I show in this chapter, I often do REBT in somewhat unusual, idiosyncratic ways and styles. I find that when I use a style that is close to my preference, I do better than when I use conventional styles. This, however, is a subjective opinion and may be inaccurate. Considerable research could be done to check my impression, and that of many other REBT practitioners I have talked with, that an idiosyncratic style is preferable to a 'regular' one. Most of us seem to think so; but of course we could be fooling ourselves!

References
Adler, A. (1926). *What Life Should Mean to You*. New York: Greenberg.

Bernard, M. E. & Wolfe, J. L. (2000) *The REBT Resource Book for Practitioners*. New York: Albert Ellis Institute.

Dryden, W. (1999). *Rational Emotive Behavior Therapy: A Training Manual*. New York: Springer.

Ellis, A. (1958). Rational psychotherapy. *Journal of General Psychology, 59*, 35–49.

Ellis, A. (1977a). Fun as psychotherapy. *Rational Living, 12*(1), 2–6. Also: cassette recording. New York: Albert Ellis Institute.

Ellis, A. (1977b). *A Garland of Rational Humorous Songs*. New York: Albert Ellis Institute.

Ellis, A. (1987). The use of rational humorous songs in psychotherapy. In W. F. Fry & W. D. Salameh (eds.). *Handbook of humor and psychotherapy* (pp.265–88). Sarasota, FL: Professional Resources Exchange Inc.

Ellis, A. (1988). *How to Stubbornly Refuse to Make Yourself Miserable About Anything — Yes, Anything!* New York: Kensington Publishers.

Ellis, A. (1994). *Reason and Emotion in Psychotherapy*. (Revised edn.). New York: Kensington Publishers.

Ellis, A. (1999). *How to Make Yourself Happy and Remarkably Less Disturbable*. Atascadero, CA: Impact Publishers.

Ellis, A. (2000). *How to Control Your Anxiety Before it Controls You*. New York: Citadel.

Ellis, A. (2001a). *Feeling Better, Getting Better, Staying Better*. Atascadero, CA: Impact Publishers.

Ellis, A. (2001b). *Overcoming Destructive Beliefs, Feelings, and Behaviors*. Amherst, New York: Prometheus.

Ellis, A. (2002). *Overcoming Resistance: A Rational Emotive Behavior Therapy Integrated Approach*. New York: Springer.

Ellis, A. & Dryden, W. (1997). *The Practice of Rational Emotive Behavior Therapy*. New York: Springer.

Ellis, A. & Harper, R. A. (1997). *A Guide to Rational Living*. Revised edn. North Hollywood, CA: Melvin Powers.

Ellis, A. & MacLaren, C. (1998). *Rational Emotive Behavior Therapy: A Therapist's Guide*. Atascadero, CA: Impact Publishers.

Kelly, G. (1955). *The Psychology of Personal Constructs*. New York: Norton.

Korzybski, A. (1933). *Science and Sanity*. Corcord, CA: International Society of General Semantics.

Walen, S., DiGiuseppe, R. & Dryden, W. (1992). *A Practitioner's Guide to Rational-Emotive Therapy*. New York: Oxford University Press.

3

Raymond DiGiuseppe

In this chapter I identify 12 ways that reflect my variations of the practice of rational emotive behavior therapy (REBT) as follows:

i. to work at developing the therapeutic alliance through clarifying the therapeutic goals, attaining agreement on the tasks to use, and attending to the therapeutic bond;

ii. the addition of strategies to enhance motivation for change;

iii. clients come to therapy re-moralized (and providing hope is more important than any other task);

iv. I attempt to avoid REBT jargon, and all discussions use the clients' words for REBT concepts;

v. although REBT focuses on the present, clients can learn to surrender their irrational beliefs by exploring how they learned them;

vi. I help the client develop explanatory schema to understand early traumatic events that are consistent with rational beliefs;

vii. I incorporate family system concepts as a complementary paradigm to REBT;

viii. I explain why gradual disputing of irrational beliefs is preferred over immersion in rational philosophies;

ix. developing new rational beliefs may be more important than challenging old irrational beliefs;

x. rehearsal may be a more important process of therapeutic change than insight;

xi. therapy may be more effective when dramatic strategies are used, such as metaphors and humor;

xii. challenging awfulizing may be the least effective and most offensive intervention in REBT.

The history of psychotherapy has always included great theories of interventions. A new professional joining our ranks must decide to be a psychoanalyst, systems therapist, gestalt therapist, cognitive therapist, or a rational emotive therapist. How can one assess the validity of these different theories? Each may have a kernel of truth or be the treatment of choice for certain people or for certain problems. However, they all have failed to provide guidance and effective interventions for all clients that psychotherapists encounter. For that reason, adhering to a single theoretical orientation has rarely been attractive to psychotherapists, and for the last fifty years most therapists have chosen to identify themselves as eclectic.

Some believe the alternative to theoretical orientations is science. As our profession moves toward the identification of empirically supported treatments (ESTs) for specific disorders, more psychotherapy treatment manuals have proliferated. Therapists could learn to follow the manuals for each EST and, therefore, have the flexibility to use different therapies with different clients and not commit to a grand theory. However, this proposition implies, for example, that if we have five empirically supported treatments (a low number) for each of 20 different diagnostic disorders (many more exist), a therapist would have to learn to use 100 different treatment manuals. This is an insurance company's dream. From Los Angeles to Moscow, every client with the same diagnosis would receive the same treatment. Yet psychotherapists, for now, are human, and the likelihood that they could master that much material and subsequently implement the techniques with integrity is poor. Do therapists need to learn a new manual for each disorder or are there general principles that apply across disorders? Modern psychotherapists face the dilemma of opting to follow a grand theory or using specific interventions for different disorders.

Most therapists choose to follow a theory. However, our clients want us to treat them as individuals and understand them as unique people. Clinical tradition has always supported the ideographic nature of psychotherapy and the development of treatments for the individual. Although most therapists follow a theory, we diverge from the theory at times when we find it lacking or it fails to address specific problems.

Windy Dryden has asked the contributors of this book to express how they implement REBT in their own idiosyncratic or unique way. The very nature of this task unmasks a fiction that has survived in the psychotherapy world: we do not all do the same therapy the same way. Psychotherapists often see themselves as creative, intelligent people who are too smart to follow manuals or theories slavishly. Our clients are too complex and diverse for us to treat them all the same. As a result, we all diverge from the master plan and great variance exists in how we practice psychotherapy. As well, part of the variance in practice results from who we are as people, not therapists. Some of us tell jokes and stories better than others. Some can act more empathically than others. However, much of what we do as individual therapists rests on our choices.

Dryden's task challenged me to justify the criteria I use for diverging from accepted practice. If I am an REBT therapist who is committed to that theory of psychotherapy and behavior change, on what basis do I decide how I will vary from its strategies and techniques and include differences into my practice of therapy? As a teacher, Dryden's task presents me with another problem. If therapists can never learn all of the treatment manuals, and no theory is 100% accurate and effective, how do I teach my students to diverge from their adopted theory when necessary? My solution is to add ideas from the science of psychology and behavior change to my framework of REBT where they are appropriate.

I have remained identified as a REBT therapist because the theory provides a bare bones framework for explaining psychopathology and treatment but allows a great deal of divergent interventions. The more specific and detailed the theory, the more stifling it is. I have augmented my practice of REBT with the following principles. This is not an exhaustive or static list and will change in the future — I hope.

Therapeutic alliance

Many researchers and clinicians (Horvath & Luborsky, 1993, for a review) have shown that a good therapeutic alliance facilitates psychotherapy and that this concept applies across therapeutic orientations. Many critics have identified REBT as not attending sufficiently to the therapeutic relationship. This may have been a valid criticism. Carl Rogers (1957) proposed that unconditional acceptance by the therapist was necessary and sufficient for change. Albert Ellis (1962) had a contentious debate with Rogers, arguing that the therapists' unconditional acceptance was neither necessary nor sufficient for change. Ellis's early argument was that people change for many reasons. Thus, we should recognize that many things facilitate change and, therefore, we should not overly focus on one strategy. Ellis never said that a therapeutic relationship was unimportant or that we should ignore it. He has said that therapists should unconditionally accept their clients. However, he does not believe that such an attitude or acts following from it are necessary nor sufficient. Clients can change without a therapist's acceptance, and even if therapeutic acceptance is present, it may not be enough.

Perhaps too much time in the REBT literature has focused on this old debate between Ellis and Rogers. Moreover, Dryden has since brought the tripartite concept of the therapeutic alliance to the REBT literature. Dryden's model focuses on agreement of the therapeutic goals, agreement on the tasks of therapy, and the development of the client–therapist bond. As Dryden discusses this topic, I will refer the reader to his chapter.

Motivation for change

Because my practice has focused on aggressive adolescents, adults with anger problems, and substance abusers, I am greatly aware of the poor motivation for change across these populations. Many of such clients are reluctant and/or coerced referrals. Trying to change a person's irrational beliefs when they do not wish to change their behavioral or emotional 'A' (activating event), usually results in a conflict. Clients will only agree to the process of challenging beliefs and replacing them if they want to change. Note that this topic could also fall under therapeutic alliance because it includes agreement on the goals of therapy. However, people who are unmotivated to change require different kinds of interventions compared to people who want to change but have not yet worked out with their therapist what they will target.

Prochaska and DiClemente (1988) have proposed that people differ in their attitudes toward change and some, called precontemplators, do not even want to talk about change. When people reach the action stage of change, they want to do things to reach their goals. Prochaska and DiClemente have proposed that psychotherapists match their intervention to a clients' stage of change. They also note that action stage interventions aimed at those in the precontemplative or contemplative stage will result in a negative response to therapy. Elsewhere (DiGiuseppe, 1995), I have written about the cognitive and behavioral interventions I have used to help people who do not want to change develop the motivation to change — before trying any standard REBT interventions. These strategies usually include extensive training in consequential thinking to help the person become aware of and think about the negative consequences of their emotional or behavioral 'C' (consequences). Next, I provide the client with education concerning what alternative emotion scripts are available to them. This usually involves first, choosing models that the client respects and second, observing their adoptive emotional reactions. For many of my clients I focus on motivational interventions before I proceed to the standard REBT techniques.

Providing hope

The problem of why so many clients leave therapy early and what makes them stay has intrigued me. Over the years I have searched the literature on the number of sessions clients typically remain in psychotherapy. I have also examined the actual session length for clients at the Albert Ellis Institute. Most consumers of mental health services stay for approximately four sessions. Perhaps 25 per cent stay beyond twelve sessions and only a very small percentage (2 or 3%) are interminables — in for long-term treatment. At the Ellis Institute, our mean session length is 17 sessions, our median is 11 sessions, and only 25 per cent stay for more than 22 sessions. Although Seligman's (1995) commentary on the *Consumer Reports* study suggests that more is better and up to one year is ideal, much research suggests that, at least in cognitive-behavioral therapy, most change occurs by the eighth to tenth session (Tang & DeRubeis, 1999). Thus, great controversy exists about the optimum duration of psychotherapy. Frank's (1973) seminal study of psychotherapy may provide a clue to this problem. He found clients come to therapy demoralized. However, making the appointment and some initial interventions by the therapist can serve to remoralize clients. Thus, through immediate intervention, therapists may provide hope to their clients early in therapy.

Consequently, because many clients leave therapy quickly and come to therapy demoralized, I question the professions' focus on first making a valid diagnosis, doing a thorough assessment, or making a case conceptualization. Rather, restoring hope needs to be the first task of therapy. Although I will be empathetic, listen with the third ear, and assess the problem, I want to immediately address some of the client's problems and intervene. By helping first, I convey that we can and will do specific things to help. I will give clients some task to complete between sessions to get them involved in the solutions. This remoralization or restoration of hope is my first chore. It requires that I intervene somewhere in the last half of the first session before I have completed my assessment and before I have completed my case conceptualization. I often choose an REBT homework sheet for this task so the client can learn how we will identify and challenge beliefs. I also usually assign clients an assessment task to log target behaviors, emotions, and corresponding thoughts. Hence, my first rule is that clients leave with hope. Immediately addressing their problems, teaching them the tasks of therapy, and assigning data collection assignments helps provide that hope.

Avoiding jargon

Socializing with a group of REBT afficionados usually includes jokes using the words 'awful' or 'must.' We almost define our sub-field by its jargon. The overuse of jargon has become a caricature of REBT and bad public relations. The words awful, terrible, must, should, worthless, and, of course, the phrase 'I can't stand it' represent the concepts of exaggerated appraisal of harm, demandingness, self downing, and frustration intolerance, respectively. I attempt to avoid such jargon when doing therapy and even when teaching about REBT. I have treated clients with REBT without using any of this jargon or even the terms 'A', 'B', or 'C'. Why? The use of jargon forces the client to learn our or Ellis's words for the concepts they represent, rather than the words the client uses to represent these concepts. If a client has described thinking an irrational belief, I will be more successful in having them challenge and replace that belief if I use the lexicon for that belief that the client has used. If I interject the REBT word for the client's concept, my challenges to the irrational belief are aimed at the REBT jargon word. As a consequence, the client may fail to transfer the challenges from the REBT word to his or her own word for the concept.

As illustrated in the following example, I learned the benefits of avoiding jargon early in my career while treating a depressed, 16-year-old, socially isolated boy. 'Sam' had no friends and few social skills. He referred to himself as a jerk. I quickly recognized his irrational belief as self-downing. For three sessions, I challenged his self- downing and tried to convince him that he was not a worthless person. We rehearsed replacing the idea that he was worthless with the rational belief that he was a worthwhile person. Eventually, Sam agreed to the homework assignment of talking to a peer. Upon doing so, the boy ignored him. Sam recited the mantra, 'I am not a worthless person.' At the next session, I asked Sam how he felt about being rejected. Sam said depressed. 'Why', I asked, 'were you not thinking that you are a worthwhile person?' 'Yes, I may be a worthwhile person', Sam replied, 'but I am still a jerk.' No transfer of learning had occurred from worthless person to jerk. Similar experiences across many cases occurred that year. As a result, I have since stopped teaching clients to use our words for their irrational beliefs and, alternatively, encourage the use of their words.

Furthermore, the use of jargon in REBT sessions sometimes results in clients perceiving the therapy as canned or non-spontaneous. Some therapists I have trained have said that they feel awkward or insincere when doing REBT. When further questioned, they reveal that they are trying to use REBT jargon or look for the must. Look for the must, yes, but better to look for the demandingness concept in the client's language — whatever the word(s) the client uses to communicate it. Again, I recommend always using the words that clients use for the concepts REBT posits to moderate psychopathology. This saves the step of clients learning a new vocabulary before learning to challenge and replace their irrational beliefs.

Exploring the past

Many clients believe that psychotherapy is about their past and learning how they became the way they are. However, REBT has always been a therapy based in the present. Our theory proposes that it is the client's rehearsal of their irrational beliefs that they have learned in the past that explains why they are disturbed now. REBT focuses on challenging the present beliefs as a mechanism of change. However, understanding the context in which one learned an irrational belief that led to a false conclusion may help the person abandon a given irrational belief. Thus, placing an irrational belief in its historical context is one of the many challenging strategies that I use to help clients stop rehearsing old, irrational beliefs.

Achieving insight into the origin of one's irrational beliefs is not difficult and does not require long-term psychic archeology. Asking clients how they may have learned to think in a disturbed way or when they can first remember thinking in a disturbed way usually brings forth a flood of memories. A discussion of these memories, from the perspective the client had as a child, can help the client understand how they may have constructed a given irrational belief. Clients are then asked to assume the perspective of themselves as an adult watching the same event or discussing the same memories. This perspective switch results in the original conclusion(s) no longer making sense: the irrational conclusion(s) the client made as a child are not the ones they would draw as an adult. I may also assign a homework task of rehearsing the remembered event with the client observing it as an adult.

Irregardless, such historical exploration appears neither necessary nor sufficient for change in my view. However, it can be another strategy used to challenge irrational beliefs and to construct new rational beliefs. Moreover, for clients who believe that exploration of the past is important, an historically based challenge to their irrational beliefs may be more credible and, therefore, more effective.

Developing explanatory schema
Kelly (1955) inspired many of the originators of cognitive-behavioral psychotherapy. His classic two volumes of work, *The Psychology of Personal Construct,* is referenced by most books in the field but read by few. Kelly's major premise was that humans think like scientists. They create theories or explanations for events. He posits that the reason the brain evolved to its current capacity is to understand and predict negative events. Mahoney (1991) called this process evolutionary epistemology. Such explanatory creations are part of who we are and may have helped us survive. Not having an explanation for crucial events in our lives is upsetting for humans. Once we think we understand an event, we believe (sometimes falsely) that we can predict and control the event. The generation of explanations for trauma or major life events may account for how clients develop the dysfunctional or irrational beliefs that cause their current disturbance. Challenging a client's irrational beliefs may help them to learn that what they believe is false, illogical, dysfunctional, and/ or anti-empirical.

As well, learning a new rational belief may help clients understand the irrationality of their old beliefs. However, new rational beliefs often do not explain why major life events occurred. I believe that humans create and maintain irrational beliefs because the irrational beliefs are consistent with or derived from explanations of important life events. Thus, clients may not give up their irrational belief(s) until they have an alternative explanation for the past event that their mind has attempted to understand. Our task in REBT is to create a new rational belief that may either include an explanation of a traumatic event or that is consistent with a new explanation of such events. Below is clinical example.

Bill came to our anger control group believing that he must not let anyone criticize him. He believed that he must respond to all criticism (or negative feedback) with attacks. This prevented people from dominating and controlling him. The group and I attempted to challenge his irrational belief and replace it with the idea that he does not have to control others and that he can stand it if others criticize him. Bill resisted giving up his irrational belief. Whenever anyone in the group reported an incident of receiving negative feedback, Bill questioned how they could tolerate that. During a discussion about a group member's experience of childhood abuse, Bill revealed that he too experienced abuse as a child from his father. A group member asked Bill if that experience had anything to do with his anger and why he would not tolerate any criticism. 'Yes,' he said. 'People will abuse you if you give them the opportunity. If I let my guard down with anyone, they will get me.' A discussion of this comment followed. Bill had a global attribution for his abuse: his father abused him because all people are potential abusers. It is no wonder that he resisted the challenges to his irrational beliefs. He must defend against all criticism because it is the start of abuse and can come from anyone. The group then focused on the truth of this explanation. Over the following weeks, Bill was surprised to learn that some people did not have abusive parents or spouses, and that other people were kind. The group continued to challenge his idea that his father abused him because all people are abusive. One night Bill came to the group and announced that he had had a great insight. Perhaps his father abused him because he was a poor father, and not because all people behaved this way. Hence, Bill switched to a specific attribution. With this new explanation for his past abusive experiences, he was less resistant to challenging his irrational belief that others must not criticize him. Bill quickly believed that he could tolerate criticism and learned to respond without anger.

Bill's explanation about his abuse may have created his irrational belief. His irrational belief was consistent with his explanation of the world. Attempts to challenge and replace his irrational belief failed because the causal attribution was operating. Once he developed a new causal attribution for the abuse, working on the irrational belief was easier.

A family systems perspective

Family systems theory has long presented itself as an alternative, competing theory in the psychotherapy field. This is unfortunate because all people live in families or work as part of a system. I prefer to see systems theory as a complementary rather than a competing paradigm with REBT (DiGiuseppe, 1988, 1989). Two main ideas from family systems theory apply to most cases on which I have worked. Therefore, I regularly attempt to incorporate these aspects of family systems theory into my therapy practice.

The first idea concerns the rippling effects of behavior change. A change in one person's behavior will influence or affect the behavior of others who may not like the change. Others affected by the client's change may attempt to undermine that behavior change. Our client's family members, coworkers, or friends may not like the change we have helped clients make and may try to subvert it in some way. As therapists, I think it is important to help clients to anticipate potential resistances and to develop plans for how to effectively deal with them. An example follows.

Len, a client in our anger management group, has been involved in a vicious court battle with his ex-wife over visitations. Presently, Len has supervised visitations with his two young children because of his verbal assaults on their mother. The first phase of treatment taught Len how to control his anger whenever he spoke to his ex-wife. This he accomplished in about four weeks of therapy. Len commented in a Pollyanna-ish manner that now that he had controlled his anger for three weeks, his ex-wife would behave civilly toward him. However, from a strategic view, this seemed unlikely. I needed to predict who would want Len to stay angry. Because Len lost his temper publicly, his ex-wife was winning in court. Len's anger outbursts made it easy for his wife to exclude him from their children's lives and to win financial concessions. I asked Len to consider that his wife may become more provocative toward him as he improved. I recommended that he prepare to deal with escalating activating events from her. Len thought that I was cynical but he conceded, and we practiced rational emotive imagery where he acted mannerly in response to his ex-wife's anticipated verbal assaults. He rehearsed the rational statements and stayed calm. Later, Len called his wife to arrange the next supervised visitation with his children. His ex-wife asked for a doubling of the child support payments and reported that he could not see his children until he could support them like a real man. Len started to feel rage and wanted to scream and curse at her. However, that reaction would have been unwise because his wife has taped their phone calls in the past and would forward them to the court. Len invoked the rational coping statements, stopped himself from escalating, and just ended the conversation. Thus, by using a systems perspective, the group and I had helped Len anticipate escalating activating events and gain control of his anger.

A second principle of family systems theory I like to incorporate is the forward feedback loop. The classic example of this occurs in abusive couples. Men who become abusive often avoid talking about issues with their wives: the less he talks the more she pursues him. The more she pursues him, the more upset he becomes and the less he talks. The less he talks, the more she pursues him. Hence, a vicious cycle unfolds. I instruct clients on this cycle to become aware of how others will receive their behaviors. Most men I see for relationship problems believe that if they control their anger and remain calm, their marital arguments will cease. However, calmness for them means not reacting. When they work hard at being rational and calm, they avoid yelling and also talking. However, given the forward feedback system, this attempt to remain calm results in an escalation of the behavior that they do not like. Thus, they are not rewarded for the work and improvements that they have made. The missing piece is perspective taking. If they can remain calm, problem-solve, and imagine what their partner wants rather than what they want, they may think of a response to end the conflict. This insight usually results in therapy progressing to some form of assertiveness training. The men practice responding in a way they think their wives would like. Thus, the forward feedback loop principle of family systems theory is a useful complement to REBT.

Gradual disputing

When I first became committed to REBT, I enjoyed fervently convincing people of new rational beliefs. We do not need other people's approval. The universe does not have to behave as we think it must, and nothing is awful. These rational beliefs are difficult for people to accept at first. To this day, I meet many REBT practitioners who attempt to convince clients first of the most abstract, extreme, rational positions. Such strong adherents of REBT often alienate clients by their extreme positions.

As a young therapist I noticed that I was not always convincing. It occurred to me that my treatment strategy clashed with a major theory of attitude change I had learned and completed research on as an undergraduate. Social psychologists Sherif and Sherif (1967), proposed the social judgement theory of attitude change. They assumed that people perceive social attitudes similarly to physical stimuli. Based on the original research of Fechner (e.g., 1860), they thought people would react to communications aimed at challenging one's attitudes. Sherif and Sherif believed that people had a continuum of positions around an attitude they held. That is, people could linearly rate a set of attitudes as close to or away from their own. Hence, some communications promote attitudes considered similar to one's own and, therefore, are judged as not different. Alternatively, other communications promote attitudes considered dissimilar to one's own and, therefore, are judged as different (the just noticeable different concept (JND) from Fechner). The JND concept falls within what Sherif and Sherif call the latitude of non-commitment. Just noticeably different attitudes are not considered inconsistent with or contrary to one's own position. However, farther away from one's own attitude lies a group of attitudes perceived as antagonistic or inconsistent with one's own position. Sherif and Sherif call this the latitude of rejection. In turn, Sherif and Sherif caution that expressing an attitude too distant from the position a person holds (latitude of rejection) fails to induce attitude change. Alternatively, communications aimed in the latitude of non-commitment can shift a person's attitude. Specifically, each communication progressively shifts the latitude of non-commitment. Targeting successive communications within the shifting latitude of non-commitment produces the greatest amount of attitude change.

As a consequence, for many years I have not attempted to convince clients (or therapists new to REBT) that nothing is awful or that they can stand anything. I believe people perceive such statements as cold and insensitive because they are in their latitude of rejection. Instead, I attempt to convince someone, in stages, that they can tolerate a little more frustration — and a little more and a little more. Although I adhere to this attitudinal gradualism, I do not necessarily believe that all change is gradual — just most cognitive change. As well, I would not necessarily use only graduated exposure instead of flooding. However, with respect to attitude change, direct comparisons between graduated and extreme communications have produced unambiguous findings in support of the graduated method. This finding has been lost on most REBT therapists.

Challenging the old or developing the new

An old debate in psychology goes back to Descartes (1955/1649) and Spinoza (e.g., Gilbert, 1991, 1993). Do we have a coping or master model of change? Do we forget old responses or do we remember them but learn a longer string of responses with the last item in the string being an adaptive response? Descartes believed in the power of thinking and insight. He believed that when individuals learn a new response, a connection is made between the stimulus and the new response. The connection between the same stimulus and the old response is forgotten, bypassed, or disconnected. Alternatively, Spinoza argued against forgetting. Spinoza believed that we retain all past connections. More specifically, we learn new connections in addition to the old. This debate continues today in experimental psychology.

One's position on this issue has implications for therapeutic interventions in cognitive-behavioral therapy. If one sides with Descartes, one would be more likely to challenge irrational or dysfunctional cognitions. For once we establish insight, the connection between the A and the old irrational belief will be broken. Alternatively, if one sides with Spinoza, one would pay less attention to insight and challenging the old bonds and, instead, work to establish new ones. Consider the issue this way. After one successfully changes an attitude, does the 'A' elicit the new 'B' and then the new 'C', or does the 'A' elicit the old 'B', then the old 'C', and then we rehearse a new alternative 'B' in response to the old 'C'?

In my experience, people do not appear to forget old responses. Entrenched responses are always there and seem never to be forgotten. It appears that we learn new responses that are triggered by the old. Teaching people to recognize their old patterns and to use them as cues to generate rational coping statements appears crucial for successful therapy. If a therapist fails to do this, the client may learn to interpret the continued existence of irrational beliefs and negative emotions as failure. This will result in their not using the positive strategies they have learned. Some impressive research in the treatment of anxiety and anger, the AMT or anxiety/anger management training (Suinn, 1995), rests on the principle that one attends to the experience of affective arousal and uses these cues to rehearse the new statements that therapy has provided.

This takes me to a revolutionary idea in REBT. Possibly challenging irrational beliefs is less important: Teaching the client to generate new, rational, alternative beliefs may be more important. A recent dissertation by Leiber (2002) compared REBT treatments that included both disputing and teaching new rational beliefs versus treatment that did no disputing and only taught new rational beliefs. Disputing did not add to the effectiveness of teaching new rational beliefs. I have long anticipated this result and my version of REBT focuses more on teaching and rehearsing new rational beliefs than challenging old ones.

Cognitive change through rehearsal

Because REBT relies on changing what people think to change their emotions, one might consider REBT a truly cognitive theory. For example, once people examine the evidence against their irrational beliefs and the support for new rational beliefs, ideally, a rational brain decides to give up the old irrational beliefs and to adopt rational replacements. Unfortunately, change is not that simple. Many people report that although they understand that their irrational beliefs are incorrect and that rational beliefs are correct, they still have trouble changing. This disconnect between what people know to be true and how they react presents the greatest obstacle to cognitive theories of psychotherapy.

Obviously people do not change their emotional reactions entirely because of verbal arguments aimed at their thoughts. Possibly, the verbal arguments do not even change their thoughts. This state of affairs implies that psychotherapists must rely on other strategies besides verbal discourse. Remember a key insight of REBT theory: people continue to rehearse irrational beliefs. This same principle that contributes to or maintains psychopathology can, alternatively, be used as a strategy to foster adjustment — practice, practice, practice. Thus, I include many techniques to rehearse rational alternative beliefs that clients and I have generated. Imagery strategies, homework sheets, and rehearsal of rational self-statements are all procedures that I encourage clients to continually employ. Most important is the idea of practicing rational coping statements whenever they experience their disturbed emotion. When clients ask me when they should practice their rational emotive imagery, I respond, 'whenever you practice your irrational emotive imagery'. I also want to convey to clients that they often rehearse irrational beliefs while simply anticipating activating events. As a result, when clients catch themselves, they are more likely to reverse the process and imagine the same activating event with rational coping statements.

Thus, although we consider REBT a cognitive therapy, cognition does not change by insight alone. I think insight counts very little for the changes people make. Rehearsal may be the most important factor. Therefore, I want to include as many rehearsal exercises in session and in homework as I can.

Creative challenges

Many authors have written much about challenging and disputing irrational beliefs and convincing clients to adopt more rational ones. When we engage in this process, we are persuading our clients to believe new things and to act differently. I believe that good therapists have learned rhetoric and can be convincing. However, what in our education as therapists teaches us to be convincing? Persuasion involves more than logical disputing. To convince people to take steps to change we often need to build on some value that they endorse. I like to use an example from the American Civil War to illustrate how strategies focusing on including a value endorsed by the client can facilitate clients' behaving differently.

Major Joshua Lawrence Chamberlain (one of my personal heroes), who saved the union forces at little round top in the battle of Gettysburg in the American Civil War, took a sabbatical leave from Bowdoin College to enlist in that war. He was a professor of rhetoric, a job to which he returned after combat. After the battle of Appomattox, General Grant gave Chamberlain the task of disarming Robert E. Lee's Confederate army. Imagine asking soldiers to surrender their arms after the most costly and bitter war of the century. Chamberlain knew this would be a hard sell, so he created a situation that displayed the maximum respect for the vanquished to restore their pride during this difficult task. The major had the union army band play the confederate anthem as Lee's troops marched in parade to the place where they handed in their muskets. Similarly, therapists are more likely to be convincing if they can creatively find a way to challenge clients' irrational beliefs while simultaneously preserving the clients' pride and dignity. Such strategies as those of my hero, Major Chamberlain, are not deduced from any theory of psychotherapy. Hence, we need to incorporate principles beyond those offered in traditional theories of psychotherapy into our practice.

Two strategies that I consider essential to being convincing are metaphors and humor. According to the Merriam-Webster Dictionary, a metaphor is 'a figure of speech in which a word or phrase literally denoting one kind of object or idea is used in place of another to suggest a likeness or analogy between them' (1993).

Psychotherapists have misused metaphors in psychotherapy because of the false assumption that we can unconsciously communicate the meaning a therapist has for a metaphor to the client. Metaphors are symbols and we cannot assume that all people attribute the same meaning to a given symbol (see Muran & DiGiuseppe, 1990, for a review). To use metaphors successfully, several steps are necessary. First, the therapist must have clear the idea he or she wishes to communicate to the client or wants the client to remember. Next, the therapist must choose a content area in which to select the metaphor. This should be a content area about which the client knows a great deal and that the client values. For example, religious metaphors work well with religious clients but are likely to fail on those who have no religious training or interest.

After the content area is chosen, the therapist must pick a symbol or element within the content area that has analogous characteristics to the idea the therapist wants to communicate. Finally, the therapist introduces the metaphor to the conversation and checks to see if the intended meaning is understood by the client. By using an analogy to something familiar, clients attach a symbol and its respective meaning to a new content area. Because I believe that metaphors have mnemonic value, the new connection is also more likely to be remembered. An example of the use of metaphor follows.

Jeff, a narcissistic client, reported alternating between feeling angry at himself and depression when he failed at some minor professional tasks. Jeff set unrealistically high standards for himself. He expected no mistakes from himself and could be considered a perfectionist. I attempted to show Jeff how he condemned himself for failures that other people would not even notice. However, all my attempts failed. Jeff had attended Catholic schools from first grade through Law school. He was proud of his Jesuit education and his church affiliation. So, I chose theology as a content area, and searched for a metaphor in theology that could show the foolishness of his high standards and condemnation. I found one, Lucifer. I asked Jeff who was God's greatest creation. He looked perplexed. 'Well, it was the first and best angel, Lucifer. But Lucifer was not happy to be just the best angel and second to God. He (or she) wanted to be God. Does that sound like you? You are always striving to be error free, like a god.' He chuckled in agreement. 'Well,' I continued, 'what happened to Lucifer? He went from being right up there next to God, to being condemned to hell. Now, does that sound like you? If you cannot be perfect and God-like, you condemn and make a hell for yourself.' Jeff got it.

I went on to point out that the expectations he had for himself, he did not have for others. He would never condemn me or other group members for the types of sins we committed. We, mere mortals, would get absolution for such acts. Yet Jeff would not absolve himself. Not only was he condemning but he was arrogant. Jeff was expecting more from himself than of other humans. Jeff had all or nothing thinking — perfection or condemnation. All these points I had discussed with Jeff before but he had failed to see the point. He could not see the package of beliefs as dysfunctional. However, the Lucifer legacy summed it up with one word because he was familiar with the story. When Jeff came to future sessions, I would ask him whether he had deposed God yet. He would laugh and get right to the point of discussing how he had succeeded or failed at challenging his dichotomous thinking of perfection or condemnation.

Humor is another important rhetorical device that allows people to hear things they might not otherwise listen too. Humor also increases attention and enhances memory. I consider it an important part of therapy. However, after years of teaching psychotherapy, I admit being clueless about how to teach others to be funny.

Awfulizing

Although demandingness and musts represent the core of irrational thinking and human disturbance, other irrational beliefs have been identified as contributing to human disturbance. Of these, I think the most controversial is the notion of *awfulizing*. Ellis (1994) has defined *awfulizing* as believing that something is 100% or more bad. Nothing can be 100% or more bad. Therefore, nothing is *awful*. No-one other than Ellis has defined *awful* this way. Once you realize that nothing can be *awful*, things can vary from 1% to 99% bad. This is supposed to be helpful. However, the argument does not convince people. I have never successfully challenged a person's awfulizing beliefs. As a consequence, I have avoided challenging this irrational belief. Whether Ellis is philosophically correct or not appears irrelevant. Most people perceive awfulizing disputes as insensitive and caustic.

Moreover, this argument has caused REBT much loss of prestige in the therapeutic community. Rorer (1989), offering a less extreme interpretation, has suggested that *awfulizing* statements are arbitrary statements of the negative valence assigned to a stimulus. He posits that *awfulizing* statements are irrational because they are arbitrary and they prevent one from confronting the feared stimulus. Rorer's argument is reasonable. However, I am not sure that challenges to *awfulizing* statements based on his definition are any more effective.

In my practice, I choose to avoid this issue. Rather, I have replaced it with a less elegant approach. When clients say an event is *awful*, I ask them if they mean it is dangerous: What is in danger — your life, your ego, or your reputation? This we can discuss. We can decide whether the client really is in danger and/or whether they *can stand* the threat or survive the assault. This I can sell. Anti-awfulizing I cannot.

Conclusion

Some people have conceptualized REBT as outlined by Albert Ellis. As the founder and chief protagonist, his conceptualization may be true. However, each of us brings something different to REBT, and idiosyncratic definitions of REBT add to the melting pot through such discussions as this book provides. I hope the result will be an enriched theory. My version of REBT includes most of the techniques practiced by Ellis with the following additions and modifications: focusing on the therapeutic relationship, motivating clients to change, generating hope in the initial sessions, exploring the historical context of irrational beliefs, developing explanatory schema of traumatic events that are consistent with rational beliefs, using a systems perspective, using humor and metaphors to change clients' thinking, and avoidance of awfulizing disputes.

References

Descartes, R. (1955/1649). The passions of the soul. In E. S. Haldane & G. R. Ross (translators), *The Philosophical Works of Descartes* (Vols. 1–2). New York: Dover.

DiGiuseppe, R. (1988). A cognitive-behavior systemic approach to the treatment of conduct disorder children and adolescents. In N. Epstein, W. Dryden & W. Schelsinger (eds.), *Cognitive Behavioral Therapy with Families* (pp. 183–214). New York: Bruner/Mazel.

DiGiuseppe, R. (1989). Cognitive therapy with children. In A. Freeman, L. Buetler, H. Arkowitz & K. Simon (eds.), *Comprehensive Handbook of Cognitive Therapy*. New York: Guilford Press.

DiGiuseppe, R. (1995). Developing the therapeutic alliance with angry clients. In H. Kassinove (ed.), *Anger Disorders: Definition, Diagnosis, and Treatments* (pp. 131–49). Washington, DC: Taylor & Francis.

Ellis, A. (1962). *Reason and Emotion in Psychotherapy*. New York: Lyle Stuart.

Ellis, A. (1994). *Reason and Emotion in Psychotherapy* (Rev. edn.). New York: Birch Lane.

Fechner, G. T. (1860). *Elemente der Psychophysik*. Leipzig: Breitkopf und Häärtel.

Frank, J. (1973). *Persuasion and Healing* (2nd edn.). Baltimore, MD: John Hopkins University Press.

Gilbert, D. T. (1991). How mental systems believe. *American Psychologist, 46*, 107–19.

Gilbert, D. T. (1993). The assent of man: Mental representation and the control of belief. In D. M. Wegner & J. W. Pennebaker, (eds.), *The Handbook of Mental Control* (pp.57–87). Englewood Cliffs, NJ: Prentice Hall.

Horvath, A. & Luborsky, L. (1993). The role of the therapeutic alliance in psychotherapy. *Journal of Consulting and Clinical Psychology, 61*(4), 561–73.

Kelly, G. (1955). *The Psychology of Personal Construct*. New York: Norton.

Leiber, D. (2002). The effect of disputing strategies of irrational beliefs on depression. Unpublished doctoral dissertation, Hofstra University, Hempstead, NY.

Merriam-Webster's Collegiate Dictionary (10th edn.). (1993). Springfield, MA: Merriam-Webster.

Mahoney, M. (1991). *Human Change Processes: The Scientific Foundation of Psychotherapy*. New York: Basic Books.

Muran, C. & DiGiuseppe, R. (1990). Towards a cognitive formulation of metaphor use in Psychotherapy. *Clinical Psychology Review, 10* (1), 69–85.

Prochaska, J. & DiClemente, C. (1988). *The Transtheoretical Approach to Therapy*. Chicago: Dorsey.

Rogers, C. (1957). The necessary and sufficient conditions of therapeutic personality change. *Journal of Consulting Psychology, 21*, 95–103.

Rorer, L. C. (1989). Rational emotive theory II: Explication and evaluation. *Cognitive Therapy and Research, 13*, 531–48.

Seligman, M. (1995). The effectiveness of psychotherapy: The Consumer Reports study. *American Psychologist, 50*, 965–74.

Sherif, C. & Sherif, M. (1967). *Attitude, Ego-involvement, and Change*. New York: Wiley.

Suinn, R. (1995). Anxiety management training. In K. D. Craig & K. S. Dobson (eds.), *Anxiety and Depression in Adults and Children* (pp. 159–79). Thousand Oaks, CA: Sage.

Tang, T. Z. & DeRubeis, R. (1999). Sudden gains and critical sessions in cognitive-behavioral therapy for depression. *Journal of Consulting and Clinical Psychology. 67*(6), 894–904.

4

Paul A. Hauck

My idiosyncratic style of practicing REBT is condensed under the following twelve headings:

i.   two types of emotional problems: *intra*personal and *inter*personal;

ii.   intrapersonal problems: anger, depression, anxiety, low self-esteem, procrastination, etc., all emotions which largely do not involve others;

iii. *The Human Interaction Program (HIP)*, (1): interpersonal problems, how we create them, the *three principles of human interaction*;

iv.   *The Human Interaction Program (HIP)*, (2): interpersonal problems, how to control them, the *three rules of assertion*;

v.   the goals of human interaction;

vi.   the six conditions required to make the rules of assertion work;

vii. the four options always available at the moment a frustration appears;

viii. the importance of living in a condition of *Just Reasonable Contentment (JRC)*;

ix.   love and marriage; a definition of love and the implications derived from the definition;

x.   a compatibility test: a brief exercise to determine the suitability of a partner;

xi.   idiosyncratic teaching tools;

xii. genteel counseling.

In the following pages I will explain how I have fashioned my own style of counseling using REBT as the foundation. In doing so I have changed my life and the lives of many of my clients. However, in the past, being so sure of the salubrious effects of learning to think rationally, I would tend to wade into the fray and attempt immediately to disperse the demons my clients were suffering from. To my surprise, they would sometimes not show up for future appointments. A study of this matter showed me that I acted too hastily and did not allow my clients to empty themselves of the angers and hurts with which they came to me. Apparently I was doing the equivalent of amputating limbs before I searched for the source of the pain.

In time I learned to make haste slowly and to allow people to cry, to whine, and to scream at those who had tormented them for years. And it was not until some ventilation was released that they were ready to calm down enough to converse with me as their teacher while they assumed the role of the student (Hauck, 1972; Maultsby, 1975; Dryden, Neenan & Yankura, 1999). Not until then did I feel ready to enter into a program of self-recovery and rational rejuvenation. It is not always a simple matter to judge when that period of readiness has arrived. I still want to push forward at times before my clients are fully prepared for a life change, but these errors are far fewer today. When I feel the time for instruction is ready, I seek an answer to two questions: (1) Are these problems indirectly caused by the clients themselves? or (2) Do they heavily involve others? (Ellis & Harper, 1997).

Two types of personality problems: intrapersonal and interpersonal
Some types of problems, the intrapersonal ones, are clearly confined to the frustrations clients are having practically only with themselves. Some examples would be when a man is worried he will lose his job, a student is depressed over failing to enter the college of his choice, or an artist berates himself for not getting back to his easel to finish the portrait he promised his client.

At the same time these emotions are raised in therapy it is not uncommon if other problems are also brought forth, those that involve others. For instance, the artist who is angry at himself and feeling guilt over his lack of self-discipline may also complain angrily about the harsh treatment he is receiving at the hands of his irate wife who needs him to sell more of his work so they can pay their bills. Therapists will lose sight of their goals if they do not make a strategic choice at this point over what they intend to address first. The most frequent of the intrapersonal problems are anger, depression, fear, low self-esteem and procrastination.

The artist in question could be suffering from guilt over failure to live up his expectations and those of his wife. His anger at himself is the feeling of guilt (Hauck, 1973). There is no need to go into the dynamics of anger in depth since relieving his guilt feelings will also remove his anger. But what is causing his failure to use his talents more productively? It is his inability to make himself do what he knows he can do and had better do. In short, he has a problem with procrastination (Ellis, 1957).

Counseling would now focus on the five steps so common to REBT that help people over their laziness. I now hand the client my wallet-size card on self-discipline. As he reads it out loud I make comments and give explanations of key points that I feel are most relevant to his case. He is advised to study the card daily, or to read my book, *How to Do What You Want To Do: The Art of Self-Discipline* (Hauck, 1976). The major points of this technique are: (1) it is easier to face difficult tasks than it is to avoid them; (2) it is more important to do than to do well; (3) divide large tasks into small ones; (4) analyze what you did correctly and what you did incorrectly; and finally (5) reward yourself for what you did right and penalize yourself for what you did wrong.

Assuming that he could apply these principles and get back to work he might still want to understand why he is often depressed. I would then teach him the REBT theory of emotional disturbance (Ellis, 1961, 1962) and show him that his depression arises out of his talking to himself in one, two or three ways: (1) self-blame, (2) self-pity and (3) other-pity (Hauck, 1976). If his anger needs to be addressed so that he and his wife can communicate more effectively when frustrations arise, I explain the three psychological mistakes all angry people make when they make themselves angry (Hauck, 1974; London & Monjes, 1994). I give him my card that is a very brief outline of my book, *Overcoming Frustration and Anger* (Hauck, 1974). The three mistakes are: (1) if I want something I must have it, (2) if you refuse me I shall conclude that you are a bad person, and (3) being very severe with you will change you from a bad person into a good person.

If the problem is one of jealousy I give the client my card on *Overcoming Jealousy and Possessiveness* (Hauck, 1981). Again, three major errors must be challenged to control those feelings: (1) you are inferior to everyone your partner talks to, (2) being inferior will surely cause you to be rejected sooner or later, (3) rejection is unbearable and proves what you always knew, that you are unworthy.

The final common intrapersonal emotions I shall mention as one of those issues all REBT therapists are well advised to be familiar with are worry, fear and anxiety. Again, having written a book on that subject (Hauck, 1975), and having produced a card that carries the essential facts of understanding those feelings, I point out that worry and fear arise from three irrational ideas: (1) we interpret a frustration in its most severe terms by making mountains out of molehills, (2) we believe things outside of ourselves have the power to upset us, and (3) obsessing about 'horrible' consequences will reduce them.

Notice that in dealing with the usual emotional problems my approach has been a traditional one: to focus on rational and emotive techniques to train clients to remain calm. Although behavioral strategies were never totally neglected, even when we referred to our movement as RET, the focus of that modality was not formal and not conceptualized as an equivalent technique to deal with interpersonal problems (Robb, Backx & Thomas, 1999). I felt for years this was an area that needed attention and to this end I wrote several books which highlighted behavior as a target: *Marriage Is a Loving Business* (1977); *How To Stand Up For Yourself* (1979); *Overcoming The Rating Game: Beyond Self-love — Beyond Self-esteem* (1991); and *How To Cope With People Who Drive You Crazy* (1998).

Interpersonal problems: how we create them: the three rules of assertion
I have observed on many occasions that I make a very comfortable living from the fact that most of my clients have serious problems with other people. They are unaware of being controlled by the irrational idea that one should be upset and disturbed over other people's problems and disturbances. Therefore, they come to me wondering what they could do about the difficult people in their lives, or as I described them in my book about crazy makers (1998): (1) the brutes, (2) the brats, (3) the control freaks, (4) the losers, and (5) the neatniks who live with slobs. It was when I was repeatedly confronted with this group of abused clients that I learned to pay close attention to what they were doing wrong. It finally dawned upon me that they were all unwittingly teaching others to abuse them.

The three principles of human interaction
I have these principles included on my card about the psychology of love and marriage (Hauck, 1984): (1) you get the behavior you tolerate, (2) others will not change their behaviors until you change some of your behaviors first, and (3) stop being excessively tolerant.

These principles apply not only to individuals but also to groups of individuals, such as corporations and governments. I maintain that those who annoy us do so because *we taught them to do so*. The principles of reinforcement apply here as readily to human behavior as they do to the rat laboratory. I, therefore, spend time showing the clients how their permissiveness actually taught their frustrators to behave in annoying ways. When they balk at this interpretation I remind them that if they did not teach others to behave so rudely, then who did? Was it the man in the moon? Was it I? Of course not. It was the clients because they did nothing to prevent themselves being treated negatively. At this point they protest that they have often yelled at their children to quiet down and to come to the dinner table, but to no effect. I respond that this does not disprove my point. Either the penalty was not strong enough and might work if increased, or it was truly the wrong method to use and another should be attempted.

Some will be upset when it is pointed out that *they allowed the problem* to take root. Had they behaved differently they would not have had the problem at all. So the fault must be theirs, which generates feelings of guilt. This trend must be avoided immediately. When it occurs I point out to them that they *can* hold themselves *responsible* but *not guilty*. Just because we are permissive does not mean that those who are indulged have no choice but to accept the indulgence. They have the complete freedom to refuse to be spoiled and to turn down whatever offers are made in that direction.

Common errors we make occur when we allowed others to bully us, to borrow our money and not repay it on time, to play upon our sympathies or try to make us feel guilty. And unless we do something about it they will continue abusing us. Since it was we who taught our clients to abuse us, we now have to teach them to stop doing so. And, as is so often said among REBT practitioners, 'Whatever you learn you can unlearn,' or 'Anything you can talk yourself in to, you can talk yourself out of.'

The goals of human interaction: cooperation, respect and love
At this point I give my clients another card on assertion. What we want from others is simply (1) cooperation, (2) respect and (3) love. The following three rules of assertion show us how to obtain those three conditions. Granted, at first blush, these goals will seem impossible to achieve using the three rules of assertion. However, with patience and logic, it is usually not very difficult to show clients that the three rules of assertion usually work.

How do they differ from one another? By the degree of sacrifice each calls for.

Cooperation
Cooperation asks only that we show others minor courtesies such as holding a door ajar for someone with an arm full of packages. Offering someone change to make a phone call is a matter of civility. Minding your neighbor's child for a short while as the mother drives to the pharmacy for medicine is a kindness that fills an important need without great inconvenience.

Respect
This word has three definitions: (1) admiration, (2) appreciation, and (3) mild fear. We respect those we admire, such as great composers, artists and scientists. How else can we describe our feelings for the astronauts who landed on the moon other than by using a word like *admiration*?

The second way we show respect is through *appreciation*. We respect our parents for the huge sacrifices they made for us throughout their lives. Their selflessness is nothing short of awesome and deserving of our deepest gratitude.

Lastly, we respect those whom we *mildly fear,* such as our parents, teachers, the police and our employers. Since they can all frustrate us greatly, it behoves us to be on their good sides. It is that quiet threat of potential discomfort in our relations with authority figures that makes many relationships work harmoniously.

Love
This is the third goal we seek in interpersonal relationships. Our greatest sacrifices are for those we love, which can include our wealth and our lives. Seldom is this done for mankind in general. It is almost exclusively confined to family members. It is the most sought-after emotion and just about the least understood. And when it is pointed out to clients that love between adults is barely possible without the presence of mild fear, they become incredulous.

The three rules of assertion
There is no system I am aware of today that guarantees us more strongly that cooperation, respect and love can be achieved, than when applying the Human Interaction Program (Madsen & Madsen, 1980).

First, people do something good to you, do something good to them. $(+ = +)$.

This is Skinner's reinforcement principle, plain and simple. Each time a kindness is given to us (the left side of the equation) and it is responded to with an equally kind act (the right side of the equation), the effect is to strengthen the behavior on the left side.

Secondly, if people do something bad to you and they do not realize they are being rude or inconsiderate, turn the other cheek, go the extra mile and forgive 'seventy times seven' as stated in Scriptures. This is done by calmly explaining how they are behaving badly and what we wish them to do instead. Then, wait for some time to pass to see if your objections have been understood and your recommendations followed. If the rude behaviors occur a second time, decide to move on to Rule Three immediately or give them another chance $(- = + \times 2)$. You can wisely do so by considering the fact that old habits do not die easily, or that we often do not learn a new behavior merely by having it pointed out to us once. In this way we follow the biblical injunction to turn the other cheek. However, we must do this cautiously since turning the other cheek repeatedly is tantamount to rewarding negative behavior. It is for this reason that I strongly advise clients not to tolerate bad actions more than twice. The powerful biblical injunction that we forgive seventy times seven is to be taken literally (which actually means that we always forgive others for everything).

Thirdly, if rude behavior occurs a third time, and reasoning twice about this matter has apparently not helped, then do something equally annoying to them $(- = -)$. To make this work, however, several emotions must be avoided.

The six conditions
Anger
This is crucial toward increasing our chances of modifying behavior. If we are going to be aggressive and nasty, we can be sure that others will respond in

kind. *When we stand up for our rights with anger we are being aggressive. When we stand up for our rights without anger we are being assertive.* I always recommend assertion unless we are being attacked in a violent way. Then, out of self-defense, we have no rational choice but to strike back. Let us learn to respond appropriately to frustrations in the form of annoyance, irritation and disappointment rather than with fury, hatred and brutality. Such a goal is not fanciful by any means. Practitioners of REBT can all cite time spans during which they were not angry at all, even for weeks, months or years. To get cooperation, respect and love it is necessary that we get others to work with us in harmony, not against us as in war. Eliminating anger from our repertoire is the first step toward modifying the behavior of others.

Guilt

To be an assertive person it is essential that we do not feel guilty for making others uncomfortable over their negative actions. It weakens our resolve to be firm and to help others over their immature habits. I refer to guilt as one of the three coward-makers that must be guarded against if we are to be assertive beings. My attack against this feeling starts with explaining to clients that guilt is created in two steps: (1) they have done something immoral or bad, and (2) they think of themselves as awful human beings because of what they have done (Hauck, 1991). I instruct them never to feel guilty over anything since that is paramount to hating oneself. Instead, it is enough that they *admit their guilt* for behaving badly and then proceed to work on correcting that faulty habit.

Other-pity

The second coward-maker is the pity we feel for those whom we are making uncomfortable. This is clearly self-defeating. To pity the child when he cries over the penalty, and then to lessen or eliminate the penalty, teaches the youngster to use crying in the future to manipulate the parent unless, of course, it appears the new lesson has been learned, thus making the full penalty unnecessary. We are not being caring persons when we teach our children, friends or employees to whine and become self-pitying when we try to help them mature by letting them suffer the consequences of their mistakes or disturbances.

Fear of rejection

Insecure persons are particularly vulnerable to this coward-maker. They believe that being rejected by those close to them is the worst of all possible fates. This weakness is a clear sign of their low self-esteem. They are self-raters of the worst sort and never feel comfortable with themselves unless they are constantly receiving approval from significant others. Teaching them never to rate themselves, only their traits and behaviors, is crucial for all counselors to learn. It is a serious problem and, in a conversation with Ellis some years ago, we agreed that self-rating is the most frequent and widespread emotional problem in the whole world, even more common than anger (Hauck, 1991).

Those four emotions must be avoided if clients are to become assertive in an efficient manner. Rule Three ($- = -$) is almost impossible to implement unless this skill has been mastered. However, there are two further emotional conditions that must be fully understood also before Rule Three will work. In these two instances, however, yielding to them is often the wiser course of action.

Fear of physical harm
To be passive with persons who threaten your physical safety is not neurotic, it is life-preserving. To avoid being battered it is better to flee from being injured, or to satisfy the demands of the assailant.

Fear of financial harm
If you are not wealthy and your boss orders you to work over the holidays you had better comply rather than lose your job. Smile, bow, laugh and flatter your supervisor over his dumb jokes if you want to be smart and make your life comfortable. Life is not fair, and the sooner, the better, you realize that being practical is sometimes the logical and rational choice to make.

The four options
When our clients attempt to implement the HIP, especially Rule Three $(- = -)$, they are initially likely to run into complications that will make them think they are doing something wrong and that this system actually doesn't work. This is a mistake because they will have tried only *one* option and, not finding it satisfactory, believe they have hit a stone wall and must give up. On the contrary, if one option does not bring forth the desired results we are free to use three others. The four choices are:

Option one: toleration without resentment
Now that we have learned from our clients that there are crazy-makers in their lives (Hauck, 1998), and we have described to them why those difficulties were allowed to arise, we now ask them what they want to do about those problems. The most logical question would be to determine whether or not the problem could safely be ignored. Not every issue in our lives needs to be confronted. We want to pick our battles. By teaching clients to think of the rational idea which states that it is not horrible and awful if things happen to us which we disapprove of, we teach them to decatastrophize. This teaches them to tolerate frustrations and to lump them gracefully (Alberti & Emmons, 1995).

This is a prerequisite for healthy living. Day in and day out we normally overlook frustrations that are not worth getting aroused over. That quality itself defines the term maturity. Grown-ups simply do not make mountains out of molehills, children do.

Option two: protest, cold war, or strike
When reasoning does not work and we do not want to tolerate certain behaviors, we will not explain a third time why the behavior had better change. *We will now do something, not say something,* to make others so uncomfortable over what they have done that they will think twice about frustrating us again (Hauck, 1980). Keep the equation $(- = -)$ in mind and you will not be confused as to what you had better do. This is a time-honored method of handling disputes and has been used by negotiating bodies in governments and labor unions for decades.

A woman complains about the sloppy habits of her husband and two teenage children. She has reasoned with them forever to pick up their dirty clothes and put them in the laundry hamper. The wet towels should not be left for her to pick up after they shower. And the children could be neater and bring some order to their rooms. She seeks counseling and breaks out in tears as she recounts the frustrations at home.

In the first session it is quite apparent we are dealing with an *interpersonal* problem. Furthermore, it is also apparent that she has turned the other cheek and gone the extra mile, not once, unfortunately, but hundreds of times. That being the case, where does the REBT therapist begin? I would suggest that we do not deal with her anger and depression: that will come later. What she needs to know more than anything else is how her problems were created, and what she can do about them now. She is ready to learn about HIP.

The three principles of human interaction show her that she is indirectly teaching the family bad habits. She has used Rule Two $(- = + \text{ x } 2)$, not twice as is advised, but time after time. Her yelling at them to change, while not making them sufficiently uncomfortable to take her seriously, literally taught them that they could be sloppy and get away with it. Therefore, she was immediately advised not to complain about their sloppiness again but to go home and make them uncomfortable in other ways. She was then introduced to Option two, protest, cold war and strike.

To this end she now picked up her husband's wet towels and placed them on the driver's seat of his car. The assortment of clothes she picked up from the floors of the children's bedrooms were simply put in a garbage sack and stashed away in a corner of the garage. When the family quizzed her over what happened she simply reported that she wants the house to be tidy and if others don't want to do it for themselves, she'll do it in any way that suits her.

The lady was slow at putting this plan into action because she struggled with guilt and the fear of rejection from her husband. Two sessions of dealing with the dynamics of guilt and fear of rejection left her strong enough to get back to her plan of asserting herself.

The family did not take kindly to this, naturally. They rebelled and the husband, in particular, resisted. I suggested she make him more uncomfortable by not doing his laundry and if that did not work to refuse to cook or to be intimate and wait to see what his reactions would be. Usually that much pressure gets results in a fair amount of time. However, that did not happen. He became more sullen and complained that those duties were hers because she was the housewife. He did all sorts of things he didn't care about but had to if he wanted to keep his job. So what gave her the right to think she had to have everything perfect in her life?

My client reported to me that she was getting discouraged with counseling and that it wasn't working. I have learned to expect this reaction. People often feel a good plan should work quickly and if it doesn't they might as well throw in the towel. They seem to forget that the people they want to correct have plans of their own and often get angry when being coerced to change their lifestyle. Instead of letting up I informed her that she could do any one of three things: (1) get tougher and tougher until he gave in to a reasonable degree: (2) get a separation or a divorce or (3) tolerate his sloppiness *with* resentment (Beck, 1988; Borcherdt, 1996; Hauck, 1980).

She chose to increase the pressure and it eventually worked. Her calm demeanor, the absence of angry scenes, and her refusal to be goaded into a fight all helped toward the family seeing the reasonableness of her protests and realized that she meant business.

Many counselors shy away from urging their clients to get this tough. *To do so ignores the basic laws of learning, which state that we get the behavior we tolerate* (Dryden & Gordon, 1991). *Or, put more technically, we get the behaviors we reward.* Once that is clearly seen as a fact of psychological life and that the choice has to be left up to the client, it is worth trying to see what happens. If clients refuse or are frightened to proceed with getting tough, they can be urged to consider the next option.

Option three: separation or divorce

This is the big one. Separation is the atomic bomb. Divorce is the nuclear bomb. It is not available to those married partners who are totally dependent on the spouse. And those of religious persuasions that forbid divorce are also excluded from utilizing that solution. All others usually consider it when life becomes very strained and filled with more unhappiness than pleasure. We quit our unfair jobs, leave neighborhoods that have turned unsuitable, and break up with friends who seriously disappoint us. Separation makes a great deal of sense and can be a lifesaver.

Option four: toleration with resentment

When we get right down it, this is why many of us in the business of counseling make a nice living. Most disturbed people tolerate disturbing and frustrating behaviors and then suffer the emotional consequences of that decision. This choice always leads to more suffering while any of the first three offer relief. For example, to tolerate without resentment brings instant relief since the position is taken that the frustration is not worth bothering with. Using the second option, protest, also brings relief albeit after some struggle and strain. A separation or a divorce, the third option, is also stressful, but with time can lead to great improvement in one's life. Toleration with resentment, however, is always more painful and should be avoided at all costs. If people find that they cannot leave a bad situation, they had better learn to live with it as gracefully as possible, and thereby preserve their sanity (Beck, 1988; Borcherdt, 1996; Hauck, 1974, 1976, 1977, 1984; London, 1997), or review the first three options and forcefully make a choice.

JRC

Many people have a difficult time deciding if they have a right to protest and become assertive. At such times I point out the serious consequences of ignoring their needs and allowing themselves to live unfulfilled lives for months or years on end. The consequences of being thoughtless to oneself is explained by the concept I introduced some years ago (Hauck, 1979).

JRC stands for Just Reasonable Contentment. It is the perception that tells us whether we are comfortable in our lives or if we are under stress and feel we must take action to change things for the better. Hopefully all of us will go through life above the JRC or at least spend as little time as possible below it. Sadly, we have all had our share of joyless days without them causing us serious psychic damage. Many of our clients, however, cannot make the same claim. We have all counseled clients whose lives were shattered and who lived with minimal satisfactions for years. Yet, they somehow felt they did not deserve better or realized how important it is to them and those with whom they lived to achieve a life above the JRC. To live below the JRC interminably will lead to consequences that had better be guarded against.

The first symptom of this condition is that one feels *chronically unhappy*. Secondly, when unhappiness prevails long enough the result will surely be the *appearance of symptoms of disturbance*. Thirdly, in due course the suffering and unfulfilled person will *fall out of love* with those who do not provide the love and psychological nourishment sought after, be they spouses, parents or one's children. And fourthly, when that condition continues long enough, *the disillusioned person will want to end the relationship*. This is a natural process, it is logical, and it should not surprise anyone. When deep desires and needs are unfulfilled, love dies. Driving this point home to passive and overly tolerant persons will sometimes motivate them to exchange their passivity for assertion (Mills, 1993).

If people will still not change, decide to put up with the problem and tolerate it without resentment (Option 1), or leave the relationship (Option 3).

Teaching the psychology of love and marriage

Few relationships are as important and as misunderstood as are those involving love and marriage (Hauck, 1977; Wolfe, 1992). I define love as that powerful feeling you have for someone or something that has, is, or will satisfy your deepest desires and needs. Several unexpected conclusions derive from this definition that are crucial for our clients to understand if they are to achieve reasonable happiness in their relationships.

It appears that unconditional love is a serious mistake except in the case of infants, feeble adults and pets. All other relationships must meet certain criteria for love to be forthcoming. The definition minces no words when it cautions us that we love those persons who are good to us, and that we dislike those who are inconsiderate of us. Love must be earned. It should not be taken for granted. We are each in a relationship for that reasonable degree of contentment we think we need to be happy. Lacking that, the love suffers. Love, just as with a job, is highly conditional. If we would handle our marriages as sensibly as we do our occupations we'd have far fewer divorces (Hauck, 1984).

When counseling a couple with marital problems I usually get a list of their deep desire and needs during the first few sessions, either with both clients present or when I counsel them separately. I regard this as crucial because it will tell us what the major stumbling blocks are between the couple that will have to be addressed in the coming sessions.

I first inquire what the client wants from the partner that would make the marriage ideal. The responses are often quite revealing but are too few. Marital unhappiness is caused by a group of complaints, seldom by one or two irritations. I systematically inquire into the following areas of conduct which are likely to harbor resentments: (1) finances, (2) children, (3) sex, (4) religion, (5) relatives and in-laws, (6) work, (7) socializing, and (8) irritating and annoying habits. Then I ask the clients to pick out which among the collected complaints is the most serious and which is the next most serious. If I have done this in privacy with one of the partners, I later read the list to the other partner and ask them if they can guess what their spouse claimed was the single most serious criticism registered by their spouse or significant other. This gives us a good idea of how much awareness there is between these people and how fast we can proceed to explore a problem.

When I have a clearer picture of the dynamics operating between the two, I am prepared to teach them both the facts of life about assertion. They will both have to make sure they know what they want from each other. This will involve reasoning with each other no more than two times about any item of disagreement and then it will involve a series of confrontations meant to make each partner increasingly frustrated until a change is made or they decide to separate.

Love has three faces, not just one (which insists that we must give others everything they want). That is nothing more than indulgence. Love is shown by (1) rewarding good behavior (*appreciation;* + = +); (2) reasoning with them no more than *twice* (*patience and understanding;* − = + x 2); and (3) penalizing undesirable behavior (*firmness;* − = −). We all understand the need to be firm with our growing children lest they fail to acquire controls. We cannot ignore the need to be firm with adults for the same reasons (Meichenbaum, 1974; Rachman & Teasdale, 1969).

If you are unaccustomed to urging people to be confrontational, then start by teaching them to be assertive over small issues. Never send a client home with the urge to start a revolution. That is dangerous and is likely to backfire. Make haste slowly.

The compatibility test

The crucial question couples in marital distress need to know is whether they are in fact compatible and if so, in what ways that compatibility exists. To this end I often determine how fulfilled the persons in a relationship think they are. The test consists of three questions: (1) Does your partner *understand* your deepest desires and needs? (2) Is your partner *capable of fulfilling* your deep desires and needs? (3) Is your partner *willing* to fulfill your deepest desire and needs? A No answer to any of the questions weakens their compatibility.

Our teaching tools

Never forget that in practicing REBT you are being a teacher and are using debate as one of your techniques to convince your client he is wrong in his thinking and you are right in your thinking. If he can prove that you are wrong, you are willing to listen and be convinced. But if that does not happen, you expect the client to go along with you.

To ease and hasten the learning process, do not hesitate to use the time-honored tools of the teacher's trade: books, audiotapes, wallet-size cards, letters, VCR tapes, and telephone coaching. I use these techniques to great advantage and positively recommend them to all counselors. I believe that the more we all know about human behavior the healthier we are likely to be.

Let me say a few words about the summary cards. They make the point very strongly that our clients want information from us as well as empathy. A number of years ago, one of my clients asked me to write down a remark I had made for fear that he would forget it. He came back two weeks later and told me that he had stuck the paper on his refrigerator and one of the children had removed it. Could I give him another note? While doing so he mentioned that there were other thoughts he wished he could refresh himself on after our sessions and he then suggested I put them on a wallet-sized card which he could comfortably take with him. I took up his idea and put all the twelve irrational ideas on such a card but phrased them to express the rational and healthy versions rather than the irrational and unhealthy ones. The interest in such cards was striking. So I decided to put nine of my books in summary form on color-coded cards and they have gone down surprisingly well. The anger card is in red, the depression one in blue, the jealousy card in green, the worry and fear card in yellow, et cetera.

This technique is especially appropriate for those clients who normally do not enjoy reading. To suggest they read a book is a waste of time. To hand them a card, however, which they can whip out of their wallets or purses any time they feel anger or depression coming on, is another matter entirely. Some have reported avoiding disturbances any number of times by quickly resorting to the cards when they were about to act in a self-defeating manner. Some wear their cards out and call me for fresh cards.

Genteel counseling
Albert Ellis, through the strength of his personality and intellect, ran his show exactly as he liked it, profanity and all. He justified this style of counseling in the belief that a strong emotive element during counseling was often helpful in getting clients to pay attention. Reason, though powerful when once accepted, is often feeble to those who will not heed it. Thus Ellis justified bluntness, being highly directive, and using a salty vocabulary.

His followers often followed suit and became equally as profane as the master. In truth, some clients welcomed this down-to-earth encounter. They felt a kinship with a professional person who talked at a level they were accustomed to. When a touch of profanity puts clients at ease it can be considered a therapeutic device as long as it is used with discretion.

We who have grown up professionally in this movement are sensing a need to limit profanity in counseling. I, for one, am of that persuasion although I have been as guilty of rough language as most imitators of Ellis have been. The older I get, however, the more genteel I want to be. Being socially polished, sensitive, tactful, tasteful and genteel in my demeanor is much to be preferred and greatly to be recommended as an idiosyncratic counseling style. It is time that REBT counselors made it a routine style.

References

Alberti, R. & Emmons, R. (1995). *Your Perfect Right*. (7th edn.). San Luis Obispo, CA: Impact. (Original edn., 1970.)

Beck, A. T. (1988). *Love Is Not Enough*. New York: Harper & Row.

Borcherdt, B. (1996). *Head Over Heart in Love*. Sarasota: Professional Resource Press.

Dryden, W. & Gordon, J. (1991). *Think Your Way to Happiness*. London: Sheldon Press.

Dryden, W., Neenan, M. & Yankura, J. (1999). *Counseling: A Rational-Emotive-Behavioral Handbook*. (3rd edn.). London: Whurr.

Ellis, A. (1957). *How to Live with A Neurotic*. New York: Crown Publishers.

Ellis, A. (1962). *Reason and Emotion in Psychotherapy.* New York: Lyle Stuart.

Ellis, A. & Harper, R. A. (1997). *A New Guide to Rational Living.* North Hollywood, CA: Wilshire Book Company.

Hauck, P. (1972). *Reason In Pastoral Counseling.* Philadelphia, PA: Westminster Press.

Hauck, P. A. (1973). *Overcoming Depression.* Philadelphia, PA: Westminster Press.

Hauck, P.A. (1974). *Overcoming Frustration and Anger.* Philadelphia, PA: Westminster Press.

Hauck, P. (1975). *Overcoming Worry and Fear.* Philadelphia, PA: Westminster Press.

Hauck, P. (1976). *How to Do What you Want to Do.* Philadelphia, PA: Westminster Press.

Hauck, P. (1977). *Marriage Is A Loving Business.* Philadelphia, PA: Westminster Press.

Hauck, P. (1979). *How to Stand Up for Yourself.* Philadelphia, PA: Westminster Press.

Hauck, P. (1980). *Brief Counseling with RET.* Philadelphia, PA: Westminster Press.

Hauck, P. (1981) *Overcoming Jealously and Possessiveness.* Philadelphia, PA: Westminster Press.

Hauck, P. (1984). *The Three Faces of Love.* Philadelphia, PA: Westminster Press.

Hauck, P. (1991). *Overcoming the Rating Game: Beyond Self-love — Beyond Self-esteem.* Louisville, KY: Westminster/John Knox.

London, T. (1997). *REBT Questions: A Study Guide to Rational-Emotive-Behavior Therapy.* Evanston, IL: Garfield Press.

London, T. & Monjes, A. (1994) *Managing Anger in and out of the Classroom: A Rational Emotive Behavior Approach.* Evanston, IL: Garfield Press.

Madsen, C. H. & Madsen, C. K. (1980) *Teaching Discipline: A Positive Approach to Educational Development*, (3rd edn.). Allyn & Bacon.

Maultsby, Maxie C. Jr. (1975) *Help Yourself to Happiness Through Rational Self-counseling.* New York: Institute for Rational Living.

Meichenbaum, D. (1974). *Cognitive Behavior Modification.* Morristown, NJ: General Learning Press.

Mills, D. (1993) *Overcoming Self-esteem.* New York: Albert Ellis Institute.

Rachman, S. & Teasdale, J. (1969). *Aversive Therapy and Behavior Disorders: An Analysis.* Miami: University of Miami Press.

Robb, H., Backx, W. & Thomas, J. (1999). The use of cognitive, emotive and behavioral interventions in rational emotive behavior therapy when clients lack 'emotional' insight. *Journal of Rational-Emotive & Cognitive-Behavior Therapy, 17*(3), 201–9.

Wolfe, J. L. (1992). *What to Do When He Has a Headache.* New York: Hyperion.

5

Sue Walen

In this chapter, I outline several of the elements of my particular practice of psychotherapy, stressing what I have come to appreciate as the ones that are important to me in my work and in the enjoyment of my work. I include:

i.   the intimacy of sharing;

ii.   the importance of changing the 'As';

iii. the importance of affect;

iv.   acceptance of intense affect;

v.   deepening affect;

vi.   working fast;

vii. working at multiple levels;

viii. bringing in significant others;

ix.   use of adjunctive therapies;

x.   preference for certain techniques;

xi.   humor;

xii. getting older, getting wiser, slowing down.

First: some background
When I stumbled onto Albert Ellis's work in the 1970s, I was at an interesting juncture in my education. My graduate school work had been in experimental behavioral psychology, and although, in addition to the PhD, I acquired a severe allergy to rats and pigeons, I also acquired a sharp taste for empirical processes and a pretty good eye for discerning erroneous leaps of logic from data to conclusions. I emerged from school at a time when Behavior Modification was coalescing as a discipline of simple contingency programs to control small units of human behavior (as in the early work of Ayllon and Azrin, 1965, 1968), but it was considered very controversial.

I was out of the country for three years, returning in 1971 to find that Behavior Modification had begun to not only come out of the closet, as it were, but to branch into what would be called Behavior Therapy. Procedures of reinforcement, punishment, and extinction were being enriched by techniques such as desensitization, flooding, and relaxation. The early textbooks in Behavior Therapy were organized by chapter headings just like the list above (e.g. extinction techniques), but in my developing private practice, clients weren't coming in that way; they came with fears and sadness and troublesome behaviors and difficult relationships. To manage my own anxiety, I did what I always do: I set about studying. I had, for example, a referral of an adolescent boy who continued to wet his bed, much to his shame and the disgust of his parents. I prowled through my behavioral textbooks, went to the library journals, spoke to colleagues in the halls at the university to get ready to see this young man. Luckily, he didn't keep the appointment, and I continued to study, eventually organizing for myself an informal term paper on enuresis. I felt much more self-confident when the parents called, almost a year later, to ask if I would see the young man, who continued to wet his bed.[1]

During the years that this adolescent's problems were growing, I and two colleagues (Norma Hauserman and Paul Lavin) began to work together on these clinical topic 'term papers', trying to find teaching cases or well documented research papers on each of the 26 topics we chose, extracting tips and techniques and details of pitfalls and what we called 'nuggets' of good practice. The end result of three years of such labor was a book, long since remaindered and out of print, entitled *A Clinical Guide to Behavior Therapy,* published by Oxford University Press (Walen, Hauserman & Lavin, 1977). By the time of its completion and through this 'operation bootstrap' training, I felt like a reasonably competent behavior therapist, yet there were so many moments in sessions with patients when I knew I was flying by the seat of my pants. It was shortly after that when I heard my first lecture by Albert Ellis.

Dr Ellis gave me a framework. Instead of a pile of bones (different techniques), I felt I had been given a skeleton on which to hang them in such a way that they made sense and were interrelated. Moreover, the ineffable 'no-see-ums' of behaviorism — cognitions and emotions — were validated, clarified, and put in a place of central importance that made the whole far more understandable. My subsequent years of study at the Ellis Institute were rich with techniques, clinical nuggets, and even the rudiments of a philosophy of human behavior and behavior change. They were also enormous fun, and culminated in the first and second editions of *A Practitioner's Guide to Rational-Emotive Therapy* with Ray DiGiuseppe, Rick Wessler (Walen, DiGiuseppe & Wessler, 1980), and later, Windy Dryden (Walen, DiGiuseppe & Dryden, 1992).

In following years, I studied at the Beck Institute in Philadelphia, learning some of their technology, appreciating their respect for empirical clinical trials, and enjoying seminars with David Burns, who continued to ask the hard questions while being interested in internal personal experience. In the late 1980s, my consciousness of the importance of the biology of mental illness was raised, in part by caring for several difficult and suicidal patients, and in part by my own first diagnosed episode of major depression, which had dogged my heels for years without even having a name. I dove into the study of the brain and neurobiology, and continue to view it as an essential study for anyone working in REBT or any form of psychotherapy. Although quite handicapped by the lack of

---

[1] This case turned out to have a happy ending, although it wasn't related to my studiousness. Once again, he stood me up, but just the next month, a nice paper came out on working with the older enuretic patient, so I remained at high alert. Almost a year later, when he was 16, his parents called one more time for an appointment, and that night, emboldened by my observation that his son clearly wasn't 'growing out of the problem', the father loudly told his son, 'I mean it, kid . . . If you wet your bed one more time, you WILL go to that lady shrink!' He never wet his bed again.

a biology or chemistry background, I found good teachers, an occasional training workshop, the writings of Nancy Andreason (1985, 2001), *The American Journal of Psychiatry*, DRADA, and new websites to be good supports in keeping up with the emerging field of biopsychiatry. I see this study as important in making me a better diagnostician, an important link between the patient and psychiatrist as educator, explicator, and interlocutor, and most saliently, in giving patients the biology framework as an alternative to the 'badness' framework which so easily comes to their mind.

In the 1990s either I was getting more referrals of more difficult (axis II) patients or I was becoming more astute at recognizing them, but I began to see others in the broad discipline of cognitive therapy trying to grapple with them too. These patients were hard to relate to, mistrustful, often angry, had long histories of disrupted interpersonal relationships, and sadly, had life stories replete with horrific abuse or neglect, beginning in childhood and sometimes chosen in adulthood. I found the work of Jeffrey Young very exciting, and have been a student of his schema therapy approach as it has evolved over the past decade (Young & Klosko, 1993) . Once again, in addition to a theoretical framework, sets of techniques, and buckets of clinical nuggets, Young's work has illuminated for me the role of pathological early development and the complexity of recovery from that, all capable of assembly under a broad umbrella of cognitive and rational therapy.

Most recently, and more insistently since September 11th, 2001, I have been getting more training in trauma work and the anxiety disorders. I have found some excellent local instructors (such as Dr Sally Winston), and a rich lode of websites to help. One particularly useful resource over time has been the listserve for the Academy of Cognitive Therapy, a world-wide network of cognitive therapists whose questions and case discussions have provided a great deal of intellectual and clinical stimulation for me.

For me, therefore, one of the joys of being a clinician is that I not only learn *from* patients, but they provide the impetus to study. It's not the dry, rarified study of the academic world, but the moist, spreadable sharing of information as knowledge is applied to the patient's wounds (if you'll forgive the poetic license). I can't imagine a better job for an old academic.

The intimacy of sharing

I wish I had a better memory. I've never been one who could cite authors or references off the top of my head; I think I don't even put that kind of information into storage, frankly. Of the stored information, I've noticed over the decades, an intermittent sluggishness of retrieval. I sometimes compare my brain to the Magic 8-Ball in the toy store; you ask it a question and turn the magic ball over and one facet of a multi-sided object slowly bubbles up from the viscous liquid to rest against the clear plate at the bottom, saying, perhaps, 'ask again later.' There seems to be a particular disability with name retrieval, which is why I sit with the patient's folder, name exposed, in my lap during a session.

The one kind of information that is almost always available, however, are personal stories, and I include in these the stories of clients, friends, family, and of course, myself. Every year this resource grows deeper and wider, and is of enormous clinical utility. Teaching, reassurance, normalizing, not feeling alone, providing models, sharing tips — all of these come with knowing the intimate details of many human lives. The identity of the story's owner is not relevant, with one exception, perhaps; self-disclosure.

Relevance of self-disclosure, timeliness, amount, intensity, ability of the client to listen to it — these are the 'art' of personal sharing, an art which is shaped by good supervisors and by years of attentive interplay with patients. If you ask, they will usually tell you how your self-disclosure went, and what about it was helpful or not helpful. Generally, it is helpful to be discussing something which you, the therapist, have resolved, rather than something which actively troubles you at the moment. If the subject is something you have wrestled with long and hard, so much the better; your clarity and ability to empathically relate the story will likely be improved.

I think this kind of self (or other) disclosure is among the most powerful clinical strategies. It can enable the patient to feel safer, to believe she is in competent hands, to assess that the therapist accurately hears and understands, and it helps to close the wide gap of connection between the Helper and the Helpee roles.

The importance of changing the 'As'
New REBT therapists seem to believe that it is inappropriate if not downright subversive to make changing the A the primary therapeutic intervention. Over the years, I've found myself more and more frequently leaning in that direction, especially in situations of chronic unhappy marriage or demoralized students or employees.

Although it is now many years ago, I can recall my own confusion in my first marriage, having never spoken of my unhappiness to anyone, believing it was unseemly and perhaps unethical to discuss this personal relationship 'behind the other's back.' Attempts to discuss the relationship with my partner, even in a therapist's office, got us nowhere, except to deepen my own despair. I'd struggled for quite a few years to 'make peace' with the situation, to 'accept' my reality, to 'live around' the marriage and make happier moments when I could. Then, when I learned some REBT, I was really confused. I understood the model. My marriage was the 'A'; my unhappiness was the 'C', but what was I 'supposed' to do: change the 'A' or work on my 'Bs'? You can see from the form of the question itself, how simplistically I was locked into the problem.

Recently, I saw a young man who had been doing battle with a severe episode of depression, which had required hospitalization and trials of various medications to find a stabilizing tool. He had returned to his high school, a very fine academic institution noted for sending its graduates to very fine colleges and universities, but he was quite unhappy and unproductive. The high school, the parents, the referring psychiatrist, and the young man himself were looking for 'tools to help him cope' better, buckle down, and get back to work. No one was more surprised than the student when I asked him if he'd ever thought about transferring to another school to finish his high school career. He assured me that, although the wish had occurred to him, it was impossible because his parents wouldn't allow it, it probably couldn't be done, he'd been able to get As in the past, and if he didn't continue to get As in this school he wouldn't be able to get into Harvard, and if he failed at that, he wouldn't be able to have a successful career like his father, and all would be lost!

In both of these examples a happy ending was achieved, rather quickly and with almost immediate positive emotional feedback, by leaving the unhappy situation. Certainly there was a lot of cognitive work to be done in order to even consider the option seriously, to counter potential anxieties, shame, and guilt, and to effect the change. And one additional very helpful step was needed: to do what Ellis might call a hedonic calculation, or Young might review as a list of core unmet needs. In both instances, fundamental needs to feel connected, to 'belong', and to feel safe were long unmet, and the changes at least opened the possibilities of new options to get those needs met.

I often tell people a variant of the St Francis of Assisi prayer which I picked up at the Ellis Institute: namely, that there are only two sorts of problems in the world — those we can fix and those we can't. If the problem is solvable, the best choice is usually to calm down emotionally and work out a solution. If the problem is not solvable, to calm down and practice lumping it. The hardest part, in some cases, is deciding which kind of problem it is.

The importance of affect

I recently worked with an attractive but 'plain' young woman in her late thirties, who had intense anxiety problems, perhaps GAD. She was pleasant, but formal in her speech, and exuded an intense desire to please while remaining rather reticent in her manner. She described some interpersonal problems at work, and eventually revealed that she had never had a 'boyfriend.'

In trying to get a sense of her family of origin, her descriptions were particularly impoverished; it was a 'good' family, of 'nice' people, all of whom got along swimmingly, although all were alleged to be 'quiet people.'

> Me: What do you know of your father's life?
> She: He had a hard life . . . but I don't know any of the details.
> Me: Why is that? Have you ever considered asking him to
>   tell you some of the stories of his early life?
> She: Oh, no. It would make me sad.
> Me: Yes, and . . . ?
> She: (With astonishment) Why would I want to feel sad?

Why, indeed. To be able to relate to his life story with empathy, to share the intimacy of knowing and being known not just factually but emotionally, had never occurred to her. Alexythymia and affective avoidance were themes in the family dynamics, adopted perhaps in part to 'protect' each other from pain. At a practical level, all the children in the family were enrolled in vigorous individual sports, mostly competitive swimming through their high school years and beyond, and this emphasis on being constantly busy and competitively achieving provided a socially accepted way to practice avoidance of relationships, intimacy, and feelings. Yet, of course, the feelings were there, bubbling up as generalized anxiety, and occasionally, much to her dismay, bursts of anger.

REBT gave me my first clarity on emotions, and that when I asked what the patient was feeling, I'd better listen carefully to what came back, since the word 'feeling' has multiple meanings in our everyday speech. 'I feel cold' describes a physical sensation. 'I feel fat' is a self-perception. 'I feel the economy is stable' refers to an opinion. 'I feel that movie was terrible' is an evaluative statement. 'I feel happy', however, is what we're looking for: an emotional description. This discrimination immediately helped me to funnel patient comments into thoughts versus feelings, and I continue to be rather a stickler with both patients and students to limit the word 'feel' to mean 'affect.'

Patients often have complex layers of emotional problems. First, an experience may trigger multiple emotions simultaneously: e.g., sadness and anxiety and shame, which they can appreciate when the therapist repeatedly asks, 'what *else* might you have been feeling?' More difficult for the patient to see is the layering of emotional distress (in REBT, variously referred to as symptom stress or secondary symptoms). The primary affect(s), themselves, become a kind of secondary activating event, about which the patient cognates, which can result in another set of emotions. Frequently, we see guilt about C, shame about C, anxiety or depression about C. With a little help, sometimes drawing these connections on a blackboard, patients can quickly grasp the need to disentangle these emotional layers, working first with the secondary reactions.

It is at this juncture that I more recently began using mindful acceptance strategies. When the patient is struggling within himself about having his emotional pain, I might say something like, 'It's OK to feel your feelings. Let's take each of your judgements about your distress and gently put them on your hand and gently blow them off into the air (and I'll demonstrate). Let's do the same for your worries about the emotional turmoil you're in, one at a time, let's gently blow them away.' The metaphor might be different with different people, but the concept is: A feeling is a temporary state, neither bad nor good, and it need not be feared or avoided. It just is. We can calm down and observe how various internal and external experiences affect it.

I have found the writings of Steven Hayes (Hayes, Strosahl & Wilson, 1999), John Kabat-Zinn (1990, 1994), and Thich Nhat Hahn (1976) very interesting, inspirational, and helpful.

Acceptance of intense affect

Early on, I understood my therapeutic task to be the quieting of emotional distress. There is a distinction in REBT between emotional distress and emotional disturbance. Distress may be appropriate to an intense stimulus, while disturbance is considered unnecessary. For the new practitioner, it may be difficult not to misinterpret distress as disturbance, or to know how much distress to 'permit'. Now, in a sense, I encourage more distress. Over the years, however, I have come to appreciate the value of intense affect, and I worry more about the patients whose affect is damped or flattened or simply not what I would expect given the severity of the situation being described.

A simple example is the difficulty many of my women patients have with anger. In the private culture of many families, only adults, especially the males, are allowed to be angry; in others, no anger is allowed except that which seethes quietly, unspoken, but hovering like a toxic mist over the dining room table or in the car on family excursions. Many of my adult women patients do not even recognize that they *are* angry, although it leaks out of their pores behaviorally or in their tone of voice. These women often have a history of being punished for acting angry, or have seen negative consequences happen to their mothers when mothers got angry. As one woman said to me recently, 'what good does it do?' It was surprising to her to learn that anger plays an important role in our emotional life.

I asked her what life would be like if she had no pain . . . if the nerves in her body simply didn't let her feel any physical pain. At first she thought that was a good idea: a life free of pain. But when we continued to think about it, she easily recognized that the absence of pain would put her body in serious danger. She would be damaging her skin or her joints and never know that she needed to do something quickly, like remove her foot from a sharp object. Pain, in other words, had important informational qualities, even if it wasn't usually much fun to experience. The same could be said for other 'negative' emotions, such as anger; anger lets us know that someone has hurt us or is trying to do damage to someone or something we love. If we don't feel, we aren't recognizing the reality and are probably behaving in a maladaptive fashion.

Intense affect often occurs when core schemas are activated, even in the absence of clear early memories of the situations that may have laid down the early maladaptive schemata. Such is often the case in instances of chronic childhood abuse or neglect, even when it is not malevolent. Consider the case of the happily married woman who has panic when approached by her husband sexually. Suddenly, she feels profoundly unsafe and behaviorally she freezes. In her case, she was born with a bladder-urethral problem which required many childhood years of painful and humiliating treatment, which she quickly learned to endure by dissociating from the body experiences, and for which she was praised by the doctors, nurses, and family members who saw her through these ordeals. They formed a unanimous chorus, praising her for being such a 'good patient.' In taking her history, she almost forgot to mention this little fact, because it was long ago, medically necessary, and parentally endorsed. Her body and some core part of her brain remembered, however.

Even the intense affect of a major depression can have important informational value. A standard dictum in clinical practice is to instruct depressed patients that they are not to make *any* important life decisions until the illness is mitigated: they are not to quit their job, leave their marriage, or, most importantly, calculate whether their life is worth living or not! While that is usually good advice, it is also true that some patients will not take stock of the reality issues in their life situations until they are swept away in the dark waves of depressive illness. We must not overlook the potential, for example, for the stress of a bad marriage to exacerbate if not precipitate the onset of an episode of depression.

Deepening affect

Not only have I come to appreciate the value of intense affect, I sometimes find myself working to deepen affect, to intensify the patient's emotional experience. The easiest clinical example to consider is that of 'blocked grieving.' Recently, a mid-life woman was referred to me for REBT because she 'couldn't let go of her mother's death.' Her mother had died 5 months previously, rather suddenly, when the patient was visiting her parents in another state. She had flown into action to care for her distraught father, had coordinated the family arrangements for the funeral and cremation, the estate, the subsequent care of her father, comforting all the others in the family and neighborhood who were shocked at the death.

Obviously, the one person who didn't have access to her comfort was herself, and after not actively grieving for weeks on end, she felt 'strange' to suddenly begin. Our therapy was brief but highly emotive. She brought in photos and mementos of her mother, told stories of her mother's life and of their relationship, thought of many future activities she would never be able to share with her mother, wrote letters to her mother as if she were a child, an adolescent, a young mother, and her current age — all of which produced many tears and periods of great sadness after our sessions. She terminated with a plan for the spring to bring some of her mother's ashes to a special place she liked to hike by herself, and have a quiet private ceremony to honor her mother and mark the end of her season of grieving.

Working fast

I used to listen in wonder to tapes and workshop sessions of Dr Ellis; he so quickly could zoom in and identify core irrational beliefs and hammer away at them. I thought he was a wizard. Well, when I think about my own idiosyncratic practice of REBT, I realize that I work fast too now. I tend to get in quickly, and push for movement or change.

I think I mostly prefer first sessions. I like meeting the new person(s); I like the challenges of putting them at ease a bit, getting a quick sense of why they came in and why they came in *now*, what kind of family background they have, whether there are any medical or psychiatric complications, and what kind of help they think they would like. I like the guiding and shaping of the active therapist role as we help the patient tell what may feel like an elaborate and overwhelming tale to a stranger. I especially like it when I can teach something in the first session that feels helpful, either by reflecting back their data in a new array or in a new light, by normalizing, by decatastrophizing, or just by stimulating them to think in a new way. I often ask clients for feedback on an intervention or a session or a group of sessions, but my most favorite positive feedback occurs spontaneously, when patients open their eyes a little wider and say something like, 'I never thought of it like that!'

Working at multiple levels

It is my belief that skilled therapists are, *au fond*, good behaviorists. They keep a keen eye on what I originally learned as my 'ABCs': antecedents to behavior and consequences to behavior. After all, we humans, perverse as we can be, do seem to operate on that old Law of Effect: we tend to do and do again that which brings us pleasure or relief, and we tend to avoid that which hurts or brings negative consequences. At one level, I've got my ears tuned to what's going on behaviorally in the client's life, particularly in marital or family patterns.

Of course, I'm also looking at the 'ABCs' of REBT. Again, I think that among the greatest gifts I got in my training was the initial clarity of the distinction between a thought and a feeling (long since muddled by my more clever colleagues who find 'Bs' in 'As' and 'C-B' combinations and other theoretically interesting notions). I much prefer the simpler notion, which also seems much easier for my patients to understand. To realize that 'I feel like a loser!' is really a thought — and ONLY a thought — can be an eye-opening revelation to the patient, especially when they appreciate the 'B-C' connection: when I think that, I feel sad.

The various levels of cognition have always fascinated me. What surprises come up for the patient when we do a 'downward arrow' technique. Some seem particularly helped by understanding the various cognitive distortions their thinking contains; these are often the patients who will 'catch' others at these distortions in their daily contacts with family and friends. Some patients appreciate the dogmatic rules that Ellis has pointed out for us: the shoulds, musts, have-to's, and oughts (I sometimes punfully refer to this thinking as Oughtistic). Making contact with and recognizing very deeply embedded and affectively loaded beliefs learned in the crucible of the early family experiences is one of the most moving levels of work, for the patient and for me.

Keeping an eye on all of this and more, and monitoring the biologic state of the patient (e.g., med checks) as well as current events in their lives, maintaining awareness of the rapport with the patient, and keeping the focus on our therapy goals is what makes the hours fly by for me. Doing this work is mostly like being 'in flow.'

Bringing in significant others

Increasingly, over the years, I've become aware of the importance of bringing in significant others in the patient's life: to solicit information, to educate them, to help them learn ways to be more supportive in the patient's process, to enlist their help in sessions, and to have them demonstrate their caring simply by being present. In this capacity, I've invited in friends of adolescents, spouses, parents, children, even dogs.

It is also helpful for the 'other' to have seen and met me; I become something real that they share and can discuss. Obviously, I also have the opportunity to observe my client in these kinds of interactions, and get a much better chance of understanding how they act in the Real World, appreciating strengths as well as problems that might not show up in the structured therapy hour. Sometimes these visits allow me to form a bond with a significant other who also needs help, and to direct them to good resources.

Use of adjunctive therapies

I maintain an ongoing and evolving computer list of therapeutic resources in my community. I get items for this list from my patients, colleagues, local professional listserves on the web, newspaper and magazine articles, and so forth. Whenever I get negative feedback on any resource, I mark it by reducing the typeface and changing the color of the ink, so I won't have to make that referral again. My list has over thirty categories, and I think I've used all of them in the past several years. Here are some of my categories:

- Adoption Information
- Aging and Caring for the Elderly, including Alzheimer's resources
- Asperger's Syndrome
- ADD and ADHD Resources
- Career Counseling
- Children and Young Adolescents
- Chronic Medical Conditions and Chronic Pain Resources
- Specific Phobias, including fear of flying

- Gay and Lesbian Resources
- Group Therapists
- Legal Specialties
- Low Cost Therapy Options
- Neuropsych Testing and Referrals
- Physicians and Dental specialists
- Psychiatrists and their specialties
- Singles Resources
- Sleep Evaluation and Treatment
- Sports Psychology
- Substance Abuse, in and outpatient
- Therapists in other parts of the state
- Therapists who are fluent in other languages

This list has become a *large* notebook, which gets re-edited at least every 6 months. I also maintain readings lists in many of these topic areas. For example, I have lists of good books for parents who are contemplating divorce, parenting books, helpful readings in specific anxiety disorders and affective disorders, substance abuse, recovery from extra-marital affairs, sex books, and so on. I purchase many of the best of these books in paperback, and keep them in a 'lending library' area of my waiting room.

Preferences for certain techniques

I admit it: I prefer the behavioral and the cognitive strategies. As an old teacher, I still love that role, and think I have a bit of skill in taking complex ideas and making them more accessible and simple to grasp. I enjoy cognitive disputation, and finding ways to help the client to examine and think about their own thinking; this provides some of the creative moments for me. I enjoy role play and using humor and problem solving together, and the sense that it's the patient and me working as a team.

I'm much less likely to reach into my 'Bag O' Tricks' for a gestalt or experiential or metaphoric intervention. I continue to read and attend workshops on and enjoy experiencing such procedures, and I certainly can see that they can have an important if not essential role in the therapy practice, but I'm not as comfortable in these arenas. I think I gravitated to BT, REBT, and CBT because my brain seems to work best in a logical, linear processing style, and while I'm entranced and often delighted as I watch skillful experiential therapists work, I'm often a little befuddled about what actually happened and why. I've tried many new tools: I did the EMDR training, for example, and applied it to everybody who crossed my path in the following week, but it never stuck in my repertoire. You probably won't find me doing a two-chair technique, but I like the concept of dialoging from different 'parts of the self.'

I'm watching the cognitive-behavioral field now incorporating many Eastern, and Buddhist, and gestalt conceptions. They can be powerful eye-openers and change agents. I'll keep learning, and keep practicing, keep trying to 'get it' so that I can incorporate at least some of their 'nuggets' and perhaps thereby it'll become more comfortable.

Humor

Now here's another piece for which I am grateful to Dr Ellis; I don't remember learning anywhere else that humor is an important therapeutic tool, when used gracefully and wisely. I've enjoyed his lectures, replete with kibbitzing, word play, and even song-sheets with 'rational lyrics' no matter what size the audience. In the restroom of our office, we have framed copies of 'Musturbation is self-abuse' and 'I will not SHOULD on myself today', both testimonials to REBT wit and wisdom.

As a therapist, I note that I use paradox, whimsy, and model the ability to laugh at myself. While the patient is *never* the butt of a joke, by gently poking fun at the irrational beliefs or events which the patient views as catastrophes, we may help put the problems into more realistic perspective. As Ellis (1977, p. 269) has pointed out, 'A sense of humor, in itself, will not cure all emotional problems. But the refusal to take any of the grim facts of life *too* seriously largely will.'

Getting older, getting wiser, slowing down

As I enter my sixties as an 'orphan' and having lost several friends to death, I have found myself periodically reviewing how I am using the days of my life which I feel fortunate to have, and I am making changes and accommodations in a much more conscious and self-aware way. For example, I have left behind my university and psychiatry teaching jobs. While there was much that I enjoyed about that work, there was also a great deal of redundancy, of which I'm not fond. I tried experimenting with different course formats, different course materials, even teaching at different schools, and my experience kept informing me that I could stop without a sense of loss. I've more and more frequently turned down requests for lectures or workshop presentations, and writing requests as well (although the reader will no doubt note that I am writing this small chapter, which is perhaps a testament to Dr Dryden's persuasiveness). Having kept some years' worth of data on sources of referral to my practice, I long ago learned that these activities (lecturing and writing) were low probability for clinical referrals, but high probability for further requests to talk again or write again. While occasionally exhilarating, these activities are now mostly stressful for me — the writing because it is so isolating, and the speaking because, having left the daily desensitization of the classroom, my 'native' shyness and performance anxiety are at high enough levels to greatly diminish the pleasure of the task.

But I still love the clinical work. It has the elements I enjoy: variety, intimacy, independence, opportunity for creativity, and for further learning. I can't imagine ever retiring at this juncture (although I'm open to the possibility that I may change my mind on that), but I did experiment with reducing my 'service' days from 5 to 4 last year. That was such a pleasant experience, I opted to go to three days 'on' and four days 'off.' Currently, I'm on duty the first three days of the week, and these days fly by. Then I'm off duty, and those days fly too. I've let my body lead, and have found, as sleep lab data show, that I, like many of my age, do better if I allow myself a small nap in midday. My workday begins after that nap, and continues fairly late in the evening, when my brain seems to be in a very alert phase. Work days end with note-taking, reading/studying, and locking up till the next week. (Off duty days? Being with loved ones, gardening, fiddling, exercising, cooking, de-cluttering, organizing, and planning for and enjoying stimulating events. Nothing special, but mostly non-scheduled.) So, that's my version of getting older, feeling wiser and sharper as a clinician, working less and crafting a happy balance of work and play.

References

Andreason, N. C. (1985). *The Broken Brain: The Biological Revolution in Psychiatry.* New York: HarperCollins.

Andreason, N. C. (2001). *Brave New Brain: Conquering Mental Illness in the Era of the Genome.* New York: Oxford University Press.

Ayllon, T. & Azrin, N. H. (1965). The measurement and reinforcement of behavior of psychotics. *Journal of the Experimental Analysis of Behavior, 8,* 357–83.

Ayllon, T. & Azrin, N. H. (1968). *The Token Economy: A Motivational System for Therapy and Rehabilitation.* New York: Appleton-Century-Crofts.

DRADA: Depression and Related Affective Disorders Association. Website: http://www.hopkinsmedicine.org/drada.

Ellis, A. (1977). Fun as psychotherapy. In A. Ellis & R. Grieger (eds.), *Handbook of Rational-Emotive Therapy.* New York: Springer.

Hahn, Thich Nhat (1976). *The Miracle of Mindfulness: A Manual of Meditation.* Boston: Beacon Press.

Hayes, S. C., Strosahl, K. D. & Wilson, K. G. (1999). *Acceptance and Commitment Therapy.* New York: Guilford Press.

Kabat-Zinn, J. (1990). *Full Catastrophe Living.* New York: Delta Books.

Kabat-Zinn, J. (1994). *Wherever You Go There You Are.* New York: Hyperion.

Walen, S. R., DiGiuseppe, R. & Wessler, R. L. (1980). *A Practitioner's Guide to Rational-Emotive Therapy.* New York: Oxford University Press.

Walen, S. R., DiGiuseppe, R. & Dryden, W. (1992). *A Practitioner's Guide to Rational-Emotive Therapy* (2nd edn.). New York: Oxford University Press.

Walen, S. R., Hauserman, N. M. & Lavin, P. J. (1977). *Clinical Guide to Behavior Therapy.* Baltimore, MD: Williams & Wilkins.

Young, J. E. & Klosko, J. S. (1993). *Reinventing Your Life.* New York: Dutton.

6

Emmett Velten

In this chapter I will detail my idiosyncratic practice of REBT under the following headings:

i.   rapport;

ii. what kinds of problems do I *not* work with?

iii. socializing clients into REBT;

iv. socializing clients into REBT with me;

v.   rational optimism, hope, and faith;

vi. motivational re-direction;

vii. healthful versus unhealthful 'negative' emotions;

viii. do I understand the context and meaning of the client's problems?

ix. practical versus emotional problems;

x.   what do the 'A', the 'B', and the 'C' stand for?

xi. key questions for our beliefs;

xii. my own irrational beliefs.

This chapter is about some of my REBT-practice-related idiosyncrasies. These emotional, action, and cognitive consequences at 'C' are idiosyncratic because they combine several activating events at 'A' — REBT, the client, and the problems presented by the client—as perceived and constructed by 'me at B,' otherwise known as my Being, my Brain, my Body, my Belief System. Like many other human performances, the practice of any psychotherapy is a variable consequence. The therapist's idiosyncrasies are part of what makes therapy therapeutic. That is why comparative studies of therapies, which adhere to manuals and attempt to minimize idiosyncrasies, are dull, if not lifeless. Much cited and so beloved by those who thrill to claim that all therapies are created equal, such studies rightly control for the fact that what therapists earnestly think and say they do, may not be the whole story. Be that as it may, this chapter briefly relates, idiosyncratically of course, twelve points in my story, and it illustrates several ways in which my viewing and doing of REBT may differ from those of others.

Rapport

I think rapport is more important in REBT than in most other types of therapy, given that REBT practitioners are usually efficiently active-directive and (1) have the gumption, unlike conventional therapists, to take risks, and (2) in taking those risks, undoubtedly say the wrong thing much more often than do conventional therapists. The latter have a dire fear of rejection, which is exactly what would often happen to them if they shared their theories with their clients. The difference with REBT is that it has more than rapport to rely upon. However, just because REBT strives for efficiency and offers teachable, potentially effective methods does not mean that the client will take to it or remain in therapy. Without rapport, therapists and their theories still find wedded bliss, but they may do so in an absence of billable hours and benefited clients.

Having so said, idiosyncratic 'me at B' very likely does less than most REBTers in terms of consciously working to establish and maintain rapport. Why so?

Most of my clients have sought me out because they know I do REBT. Most typically, they find me through the internet, where I post a website, www.rebt-cbt.com, or through the Albert Ellis Institute in New York City. Like everybody else, I give talks and workshops, usually to professionals, and this generates referrals, but again, these referrals are people thought to be suited to REBT — or to me. The same thing is true of referrals by former clients.

Most would-be clients, therefore, contact me already knowing something about REBT and something about me as well, particularly if they have looked at my website, because it goes into some detail. These individuals, even if they are shopping for a therapist, have already put down some earnest money on the idea that one's beliefs are important in maintaining dysfunctional behavior, and they have gotten that far before they ever meet me.

When would-be clients call who have not read up much on REBT, I often refer them to my website as a fast way for them to get a good bit of information in much more compact and coherent form than I can provide by phone. Reading the material at leisure gives the caller more time to think and make an informed decision. In our phone conversation, I do outline key points about REBT and my practice of it, and I answer the caller's questions. Not surprisingly, my website highlights various sterling-sounding details of my years of practice, background, publications, honors, elected positions in organizations, and the like. It also features yours truly's mug-shot, smiling, informal, idiosyncratic.

Thus, clients usually reach me already having positive expectations. This is fortunate, because I am less a natural at establishing rapport, and less skillful at it, than the average therapist. One of my idiosyncrasies, you could say.

What kinds of problems do I *not* work with?

I practiced for decades in school, community, inpatient, and substance abuse treatment settings, so I can testify to the applicability of REBT to a vast array of types and intensities of problems. In recent years, however, I have had the luxury of a selective private practice, which gives more play for my idiosyncratic preferences. (And, yes, in case you are wondering, I do not have to depend on private practice for income.) I only accept private-pay clients, which means that my practice is hardly a representative sample of the client population.

Through website, telephone conversation, and talks and workshops, I outline the kinds of problems I most often work with. Usually, these are problems of everyday living, such as shyness and dating-mating issues; anxiety disorders, such as panic and phobias; dysthymia; procrastination, indecision, and other productivity problems; and life transition issues. This information may deter some people with other kinds or more severe problems from seeking my services, as indeed it is meant to do.

Though I don't particularly tout it on my website, I frequently work with people who show addictive problems, a group shunned by many, if not most, practitioners. My approach with other clients has been colored, I think, by my work with people with addictive problems (Ellis & Velten, 1992; Horvath & Velten, 2000; Velten, 1986, 1993, 1996, 2000a, 2000b; von Breton & Velten, 2000a, 2000b). Even in the case of heroin or crack addicts, however, my private-pay practice means such clients are hardly a random selection from the relevant population. They have managed to remain employed, usually at a legitimate job, and out of the hoosegow.

Probably more important — and more idiosyncratic — is the fact that my website mentions, and so do I, some of the problems I do *not* work with. Said website may imply that I do not work with these problems because I am a solo practitioner and often out of town, which while true, is not the whole truth. Also true are the facts that I don't like to work with some problems, don't have the expertise for others, and don't do well with still others. Among the nonstarters are partners who hate each other, custody issues, chronic pain, situations requiring psychological testing and/or court testimony, known crises in which the individual is suicidal or may need hospitalization, and mandated treatment.

When I talk with would-be clients by phone, I directly ask them what they want to work on. This information is usually rapidly elicited, and getting it helps me conceptualize the 'case' with an ABC thumbnail sketch. I do this not just in my own head, but aloud for callers who already know the 'ABCs' of REBT. For example, I may summarize: 'OK, let me see whether I've followed you so far. The situation at 'A', your activating event, is that your girlfriend left you and went back to her ex; and at 'C', consequences, your reactions you'd like to change, are that you feel extremely hurt and depressed about it. You're also obsessing about what you could have done differently to have kept her from leaving; and you've been calling her house to see if a man answers and driving by at night to see if his car is there. You've been telling yourself that you're never going to have a lasting relationship and this idea feels unbearable. Does that capture the gist of what you'd like to work on?' The caller then clarifies and amplifies on my sketch. If the person does not already know the 'ABCs' of REBT, I say essentially the same things, but without mentioning the letters 'A' and 'C' and the terms activating events and consequences.

I try to make it clear to prospective clients that I work in the here and now for the most part, and am not the one for someone who wants to delve in any detail into the past. Thus, those seeking 'inner child' or 'adult child' therapies, both of which I see as psychoanalytic in their suppositions and methods, can see that I am not the therapist for them (Velten, 1993). No client of mine has wanted age regression or reported past lives. No one's reported having been whisked into space and probed by alien abductors. Nor do multiple personalities darken my door. I think the absence of these phenomena in my practice stems from (1) informed referrals and (2) I do not pull for and manufacture such material iatrogenically.

In addition to information about the caller's problem, I listen for other information that suggests to me that the would-be client and I (and my solo practice) might not be a good fit. If the caller reports a therapist-ridden history, I assume that that chapter of the person's history is unlikely to have a happy ending through my ministrations. Florid or dangerous problems, suicide attempts, homicidal ideation, a history of mental hospitalizations, and having been on every medication in the book, are other major red flags.

I *never* try to talk a caller into making an appointment. If I sense any such dynamic looming in conversation with someone whose stated problems *do* sound like my cup of tea, I quickly drop my end of the rope (Miller & Rollnick, 1991). I may suggest that the caller interview a number of therapists.

Socializing clients into REBT

By website and/or by phone, I provide a snapshot of REBT as I see it, so that prospective clients can consider whether it's the therapy for them, and whether I am the therapist for them. From my perspective, the characteristics of REBT that epitomize it, and which I mention to prospective clients, are it (1) is a humanistic, practical, action-oriented therapy that says that how we think and what we believe — our attitudes — are crucial to how we feel and how we act; (2) largely focuses on the here and now and where we can go rather than where we have been; (3) views problem behavior as largely maintained in the here and now rather than remote-controlled from the past; (4) involves active work and practice, including homework experiments that target self-defeating habit patterns and help build new skills; and (5) advocates developing a philosophy that one can apply across many problems as they crop up in life.

As I make these points, which are integrated into a conversation in which I get an idea of what the caller wants to work on, and in which we may discuss making an appointment, I of course give people the time to react. I answer their questions, and they answer mine.

Socializing clients into REBT with me

Socializing clients into the mechanics of REBT with me has a number of somewhat idiosyncratic parts, because it is one of the consequences at 'C' that flow from 'me at B' in constructive interaction with the client and REBT. I will subsection some of the elements I see as important in socializing clients into REBT with me.

We work as a team

I see myself as hired by clients to help them with projects they *could* do alone. I emphasize that REBT is a collaborative form of therapy in which the two of us work together. As therapy progresses, I do all I can to teach clients to believe in themselves. Should they say they would still be poor slobs if not for me, I accept the compliment but firmly point out that they really did it themselves, though with some pointers and encouragement.

Scientific attitude

I tell clients that successful REBT requires open-mindedness and persistence on both our parts. Most REBT methods make good common sense, but it does take experimentation to find out what works for an individual. If some procedure seems not to be working or is not their cup of tea, I tell clients that we will figure out an alternative.

How frequent are sessions?
In answering that question, usually on the part of would-be clients, I emphasize that there is nothing sacred about any particular frequency of sessions. More important, I go on say, is what one does *between* sessions to tackle targeted problems and to learn how to become one's own therapist.

Why record my sessions?
An important idiosyncrasy of mine is that I like clients to cassette-record their sessions. Very few demur, and over the years I have noticed that non-recorders usually make much less progress in therapy than do recorders. I tell them that they will probably get more for their money's worth if they tape record their sessions and listen to them. Clients bring their own blank tapes to sessions. Listening to the recordings is the #1 homework agreed upon at each session. If the client chooses not to record sessions, I recommend that he or she make session notes and review them.

Many people are apprehensive about listening to their tapes. This is usually because they fear how their voices will sound, and they also would feel embarrassed at hearing themselves tell their problems, stutter, mumble, and the like, in the presence of 'the great white father.' Such reluctance is a C, so I may use it as a good opportunity to bring out and dispute irrational beliefs.

Why does therapy involve homework?
I explain to clients and prospective clients that progress requires actively targeting and tackling one's self-defeating habit patterns, not just insight. I indicate that we work together and will collaborate to develop homework experiments that target specific problems. At each session, we review what was experienced and learned from the homework, whether done or undone. In sessions, I use a one-page homework form on which I write whatever the specifics were that we agreed upon during the session. The client receives the original, and I keep the carbon copy. I usually am firm in stating that research findings suggest just what anyone would expect based on common sense, namely: homeworkers tend to make greater gains in therapy than do non-homeworkers (Persons, Burns & Perloff, 1989).

What about medication?
Would-be clients sometimes ask my opinion about medication. Perhaps they expect a definite pro-or-con opinion. I explain that I am neither for it nor against it as a policy. Whatever works for the individual is what I favor: different strokes for different folks. The strategy is to effectively intervene against problems, not to adhere to a particular ideology. I do ask clients to let me know about any changes in their medications.

Not infrequently, would-be clients volunteer that they do not want medication and are against the idea of it. While I respect the person's preferences, 'no medication ever' can be a way to avoid self-downing for 'weakness,' and sometimes it's an expression of heroic self-esteem. Psychologists in New Mexico can now prescribe psychiatric medication after they fulfill various provisos. I'm not particularly interested in that option for myself, once it becomes available in Arizona or California, the two states in which I am licensed.

Rational optimism, hope, and faith

I think of all motivation as divided into two beliefs: 'I want to change' and 'I believe I can change' (Horvath, 1999). The normal, beneficial human activity of encouragement gets short shrift in the REBT literature. I see it as quite important and stoutly encourage defeatist clients to keep trying and to have the same faith in themselves that I have. Not just depressed people, but many others are to some extent demoralized when they seek therapy. They may ignore, pooh-pooh, or not see their successes, or they may have trapped themselves in some pigeonhole.

It may emerge that the client has been persisting in unworkable efforts to solve problems and feel happier. From these failures, clients may have inferred and concluded there's solid evidence they 'can't.' I solidly come down on the side of 'can,' and often say that sometimes all we have to make is one or two small changes in their methods, in order to break the logjam. I may give examples, almost always blends of past clients, of people who had severe, or similar, problems and who were able to get better and stay better.

I attempt to increase the optimism and real reasons for hope that clients have by teaching some of the philosophy of REBT as a foundation. I bring out at least three points about REBT in the context of cultivating optimism.

One reason for optimism is REBT's viewpoint about the past. We cannot change the past; it is gone forever. But we *can* change how we let the past influence how we act today and how we want to act tomorrow. The more we see the past as all important, the more we may limit our growth and ability to change. According to REBT, I explain to clients, we keep the past alive in the form of our *present* beliefs and habits. REBT zeroes in on beliefs and habits harmful to us currently, no matter how long ago they developed.

A second key reason for optimism in REBT is that it promotes personal growth and actualization through self-reliance. REBT teaches us to become less impressionable, to consider what others think and feel but to learn to think for ourselves, and to minimize our dire needs for approval and success that may lead us into constrictive conformity (Velten, 1998).

A third reason for optimism in REBT is its philosophy of *unconditional self-acceptance* as opposed to conditional self-esteem. The latter may lead to one's unknowingly feeding fears about growing, to defensiveness and getting stuck blaming others and the past, and to feeling anxious, hostile, and depressed.

Motivational re-direction

A second side to motivation neglected in the REBT literature is ambivalence. Some people have motivational problems based on ambivalence ('Do I want to change or do I want to stay the same?') rather than defeatism ('Can I change, or can't I?'). More often than not, this is the case in my clients who have addictive problems. They seek therapy when in crisis or as a result of some rude awakening, and at the start they are firm in their desire to change. As time passes, they may forget the urgency, and the tide may then begin to flow toward a resumption of the past addictive behavior. I don't think of this as a situation in which the client lacks motivation. It's more a question of the balance of motivation. (Low-ambivalence people are not in therapy because they are uninterested in change or they have already changed by themselves.)

Therefore, I take into consideration the 'stage of change' of the client, and integrate 'motivational interviewing' into my work (Miller & Rollnick, 1991).

With clients who are ambivalent about a targeted problem, I find it helpful for us to analyze and tackle their problem using the succinct chart developed by Jonathan von Breton, an REBTer in Rhode Island (von Breton & Velten, 2000a, 2000b).

1. The bad things about staying the same are:
2. The good things about changing are:
3. The good things about staying the same are:
4. The bad things about changing are:

This chart, which I call the 'von Breton Chart,' is a graphic way for me and clients to lay out what it is about their own behavior they would like to change. *Does* the client want to change something about his or her own feelings or actions? Without clarity about that, sustained progress is unlikely.

The von Breton Chart identifies what clients want to reach toward, as well as the 'shitlist' of problems they want to leave behind and no longer cause themselves. Moreover, the chart makes it clear that change is a double-edged sword. Leaving behind a problem behavior, such as substance abuse, means welcome relief from negatives, but unwelcome loss of some pluses. It also means facing new situations without old coping methods, and if that weren't bad enough, new situations inevitably bring new hassles.

Another possible source of ambivalence may arise if the client thinks that acceptance strategies (unconditional self-, other-, and situation-acceptance) mean permanent passivity and doing nothing to change what *can* be changed. Therefore, I always make it clear that REBT is a two-pronged approach: (1) work on yourself so you aren't freaked out; (2) *then* see what you can do to sensibly solve the practical problem or to reduce its impact.

Another frequent downfall in therapy that can pass for a motivational problem is lack of concrete outcomes that the client and I are working toward. Often, when stuck or drifting, I can unstick therapy and steer it back onto course by looking again at the outcomes we are working toward.

Healthful versus unhealthful negative emotions
Failure to distinguish clearly between unhealthful and healthful negative emotions is a good way for me to stumble in REBT. This failure may lead clients to think that I am advising them to feel neutral, or perhaps even to feel 'OK' about the bad things in their lives. Thus, the client will resist changing. The central idea for me in avoiding this stumble is to convey to the client that *it is rational to feel bad about bad events in one's life*. Therefore, we specify what the 'bad' feelings are that the client wants to work *toward* in therapy, as well as those the client wants to work away from. In addition, clients sometimes have dysfunctional feelings, which I assume we'll target, only to learn belatedly the client does not want to change them. I find it advisable to ask.

Do I understand the context and the meaning of the client's problems?
In my young and foolish days as a therapist with clients who had addictive problems, I often stumbled by laboring under one of the delusions prevalent to

this day in the American therapy subculture. It holds that addictions are inexorable primary diseases quite independent of the person's beliefs, values, life experiences, environment, gender, age, culture, education, and ethnicity (Fingarette, 1988; Fox, 1993). Belief in that fiction almost guarantees wholly missing the meaning of the addictive behavior in the person's life, and it goes a long way toward guaranteeing disservice to the client (Peele, 1989; Peele, Brodsky, with Arnold, 1989; Peele, Bufe & Brodsky, 2000). For one thing, the American disease theory dictates that you wield a hammer to 'break through the denial,' which often inadvertently strengthens sections 3 and 4 of the von Breton Chart above.

Knowing now how counterproductive the Disease Theory is, I am very conscious that it is important for me to glimpse the world — parts of it at least — through the client's eyes. How any of us acts would be no mystery if we had sufficient information about the causes. Thus, if the client wants to change something about himself or herself, and it is not happening, I renew our efforts to identify the factors maintaining the behavior in question. Thus, I make a special effort to see not just addictive experiences and behaviors, but other kinds of problems as well, in the context of what they do for and mean to the individual. Further, I spend some time thinking about ways in which getting better and staying better could upset the client's apple cart, and I ask clients to think those issues through with me.

Do I distinguish between practical problems (activating events) and personal reactions (consequences)?

I carefully distinguish between the practical problem, such as an upcoming test for which study is required, and the client's personal reaction, such as procrastination. I say, for instance, 'Well, you've actually got two problems. One is the fact that you have an important test coming up, and how you do on it depends on how much you study, right?' The client assents. 'In a sense, you chose this problem when you decided to return to school and get your degree, because tests, lots of them, go with the territory. You didn't have to choose it, but you did. So, that's OK. However, you are giving yourself a second problem, namely agony and procrastination, which you don't have to choose at all. That one's optional.' Assuming the client goes along with these words of wisdom, I then remark, 'Let's figure out ways for you to refrain from choosing that second option.'

I explicitly teach clients an REBT general rule of thumb, to which we often return in the course of therapy: once one has diminished, conceivably even eliminated one's disturbances, then it's easier to tackle practical problems.

One practical problem with which all of us grapple throughout our lives is that we are human and limited and fallible. This being the case, most of us have a lifetime supply of botched possibilities and missed boats. These are activating events. As if this weren't bad enough, the universe, life, gives us many unpleasant activating events. We are dealt a hand of cards, but how we play it is something we can learn to have some degree of control over (Ellis & Velten, 1998).

What do the 'A', the 'B', and the 'C' stand for?

In previewing a draft of Windy Dryden's chapter for this book, I was reminded that there is an unresolved issue in REBT regarding what is considered an 'A', an activating event. Regrettably, the same thing seems true of 'C' and 'B'! My take on this subject — no surprise here — is idiosyncratic. It differs from Dryden's, and from Ellis's, and perhaps from everybody's. My view, however, is not written in stone. In fact, until this chapter came along, it was not written anywhere.

I think of 'B' in the ABC formulation as comprising three levels. These levels are continuous, rather than categorical. I separate them here for simplicity's sake.

The primary level of 'B'

At the biological bottom of 'B', behind it all, its taproot, is what I think of as the prime mover of musturbation and desire. The prime mover is the foundation and the font of one's belief system. I define beliefs as emotional evaluations, of which there are two kinds, demands and desires, and these demands and desires can refer to the past, present, or the future, and they can refer to facts or to one's inferences and conclusions about facts. A belief:

- is an emotional cognition;
- evaluates or rates the goodness or badness of whatever it refers to at 'A';
- contributes to one's emotional and behavioral consequences at 'C';
- has or implies action tendencies, whether explicit or implicit;
- contributes to what one notices and to what one makes into activating events;
- contributes to one's inferences and conclusions about activating events at 'A', including the paramount activating event: one's self.

The secondary level of 'B'

The secondary level of 'B' comprises solid schemas, with their supporting documentation and operating manuals. I think of schemas as accumulations at 'B', which are deposited through the interaction of our prime movers with experiences. These schemas are ready-made templates for viewing important aspects of life, and they direct us through schema-ordained patterns.

I see the critical schemas as crystallized rather than fluid, to use Raymond B. Cattell's terms about intelligence; the prime mover is fluid. After sufficient experience, the person who has *needed* love and acceptance will encounter quite a few situations, perhaps extremely important ones, such as with parents, where love and acceptance are not forthcoming. That process led (I hypothesize with the client), to her/his beginning to conclude solidly something like 'I'm unlovable,' 'No one will ever care about me,' or whatever it is that characterizes the client's 'worthiness schema.' Thus, the schema is a crystallized viewpoint that rose into existence, deposit by deposit, due to the interaction between the preexisting 'need' to be loved, on the one hand, and the realities of the world, on the other. Enough such interactions, and the individual builds up an automatic world view that reflects his or her conclusions based on the results of those interactions.

I use handouts and flip charts with clients to illustrate the idea of musturbation x experience → schemas, and I often refer to the targeted schema as built up over the years, very much like pigeon poop on a window, and with the same effect. Another way I may refer to a targeted schema is as a pet theory held by the client through thick and thin and in the face of contrary evidence (Barber, 1976). I say this treasured pet theory leads to approaching situations *expecting* to be disliked or not really cared about, and thus seeing it that way: believing is seeing.

The tertiary level of 'B'

At this level of 'B' lie the person's inferential activating events as well as the chatter of cognitions paramount in the person's awareness. It was at this tertiary level that Beck's Cognitive Therapy got its start, whereas Ellis began at the primary level of 'B'. Ellis saw, correctly, that there is a prime mover behind it all. It is at this tertiary level that the individual experiences repetitive inferences and conclusions, often beginning in childhood, which go on to crystallize and form solid schemas — that is to say, advance themselves in crystallized form as the secondary level of 'B'.

It is also at this tertiary level that the client experiences fallout from disputing the secondary-level schemas. Like shrapnel in a minefield, I may explain, but not so deadly; like bees from their B-hive, these blasts and buzzing words of negativity automatically spring to the defense of the old belief system as the client begins to contradict it. Disagreeable clamor and uncomfortable feelings are part of the trip. Sometimes I instruct clients to think, and even to say such things to the automatic negative thoughts and feelings as, 'You guys can bitch all you want, but your days are numbered,' or 'Sticks and stones may break my bones . . . '

I often refer to 'B' in the ABC framework as one's 'being.' We bring our whole beings to the situations we encounter. Our beings face the world and construct our activating events, some more hardwired, others less, but all of them relying on hardwiring in the sense that without being in existence and having a body, very few activating events would bother us! Everything that happens to us, every experience we will ever have, is biologically-based.

An example of 'A', 'B', and 'C'

I use various examples, tailored to the client, to illustrate the 'ABCs' as I see them. An example I often use is that of a person who did not get invited to a party. 'They didn't invite me because they don't like me' is a potential 'A', an activating event. A person could feel disturbed (at 'C') in reference to that activating event, or could feel disappointed, and the different reactions depend on different emotionally evaluative beliefs.

I teach the differences among facts, inferences, and solid pet theories. 'Would *everyone* who says "They didn't invite me because they don't like me" feel *disturbed* about it?' I ask clients. If they say no, I ask why not, and then move into IB versus RB. If they say yes, I ask, 'But what if the person only believes "I'd *like* to be invited, but it's not an utter necessity for happiness now and forever"?' I suggest that the conclusion, 'they don't like me,' may be an *inference* about a fact rather than a fact confirmed by a survey of the opinions of the inviters. Even if it is an inference, and possibly inaccurate, it is an activating event, and it fits with the client's pet theory, 'I'm a boring person.'

'They don't like me' *may* be accurate, whether it is an inference or a known fact. If the client has an activating event about some situation that may or may not, from its description, be a real rejection, I say, 'Well, let's assume for now that they really did reject you and don't like you and think you are a bum and completely boring. We don't know for sure what they thought, if anything, but they definitely may have thought that. In fact,' I go on to say, warming to the theme, 'there are times when we *think* someone likes us, and in the person's head it's quite a different matter. They *do* think we are bums! That's the truth, but we don't know it's true and therefore we don't even have the option of making ourselves miserable about it!' The client usually laughs at that line of 'reasoning,' as it obviously opens up a whole vista of unrealized rejections — so vast a vista that it might seem too much trouble to keep obsessing about rejection.

I usually follow Ellis in positing for the sake of argument the worst case scenario, and then bringing out and disputing irrational beliefs. 'OK, as an activating event you didn't get invited to the party and they don't like you. Now, what are you telling yourself at 'B', to depress and enrage yourself at 'C', as an emotional consequence?'

I also show clients that irrational beliefs lead one to be more likely to *infer* negative activating events, and, over time, to form solid conclusions (schemas, pet theories) about activating events. Thus, I explain to clients that they bring a preparedness to situations and may create some activating event as well as their reactions to them.

Key questions for our beliefs
When or before I see clients initially, I have them complete an assessment of irrational beliefs, a biographical information form, and an application for treatment/ informed consent. I have the client keep a copy of the latter, and I keep a signed copy for the file. The biographical information form is extensive, and it rapidly gives me information about the individual's background, past therapy history, medication, and the like.

I use a great many handouts with clients. I ask them to read these handouts and to comment on them. I also give them an Albert Ellis Institute catalog and suggest they consider various materials, and occasionally I loan a tape to a client. The two books I am most likely to recommend are *Optimal Aging* (Ellis & Velten, 1998) and *When AA Doesn't Work for You* (Ellis & Velten, 1992). Occasionally I will give a client one of these books, because I want to strike while the iron is hot, or at least lukewarm.

One form I nearly always use with clients, 'Three Key Questions To Ask about Your Beliefs,' asks these questions:

1. Does my Belief help me *over the long run* in attaining my goals and realizing my values, without causing needless trouble and personal conflict with others, or does it hinder me?
   If my Belief hinders me, that is, it's irrational, then what Rational Belief would help me reach my objectives better and realize my values better?

2. Is my Belief consistent with known facts and reality?
   If my Belief is inconsistent with reality, that is, it's irrational, what Rational Belief would be more consistent with reality?

3. Is my Belief logical? Does my Belief follow logically from my preferences or from known facts? If certain things in my life are bad; does it follow that *therefore everything* in my life is bad and *always* will be bad?
   If my Belief does not make sense logically, that is, it's irrational, what Rational Belief would make more sense?

The 'Three Key Questions' form also has quotes from such luminaries as Epictetus, Shakespeare, the Bible, and Pogo.

My own irrational beliefs

In a seminal paper, 'The Biological Basis of Human Irrationality,' Ellis (1976) presented 27 content categories of irrationalities, with 259 subcategories, and said his list 'in no way pretends to exhaust the field'! As a bonus of sorts, he then expanded *one* of the 259, namely 'The strong tendency of applied social scientists — such as clinical psychologists, psychiatrists, social workers, counselors, and clergymen — to behave self-defeatingly and unscientifically in their personal and professional lives.' This expansion resulted in 14 irrationalities pertaining to psychotherapists. From time to time — usually not on an hourly basis, but often enough — I notice some of these in myself. Those to which I am most prone to fall prey are (1) narrowness of emphasis and (12) striving for vaguely defined, utopian goals of therapy.

Narrowness of emphasis, as one of my fallibilities, most often turns up in the form of the client's having mentioned some problem other than the one we initially targeted, and I forget about it. To sidestep this fallibility, I often review my notes from early sessions. As for 'vaguely defined goals of therapy,' I push myself to figure out with the client what an actual observable behavior would be that we would shoot for.

Those two irrationalities hardly exhaust my supply. They do, however, exhaust my allotted space, so the reader will have to stay tuned for future and fuller confessions.

References

Barber, T. X. (1976). *Pitfalls in Human Research: Ten Pivotal Points.* New York: Pergamon.

Ellis, A. (1976). The biological basis of human irrationality. *Journal of Individual Psychology, 32,* 145–68. (Reprinted: New York: Institute for Rational-Emotive Therapy.)

Ellis, A. & Velten, E. (1992). *When AA Doesn't Work for You: Rational Steps to Quitting Alcohol.* Ft. Lee, NJ: Barricade Books.

Ellis, A. & Velten, E. (1998). *Optimal Aging: Get Over Getting Older.* Chicago: Open Court.

Fingarette, H. (1988). *Heavy Drinking: The Myth about Alcoholism as a Disease.* Berkeley, CA: University of California Press.

Fox, V. (1993). *Addiction, Change & Choice: The New View of Alcoholism.* Tucson, AZ: See Sharp Press.

Hester, R. K. & Miller, W. R. (eds.) (1995). *Handbook of Alcoholism Treatment Approaches: Effective Alternatives* (2nd edn.). Boston: Allyn & Bacon.

Horvath, A. T. (1999). *Sex, Drugs, Gambling and Chocolate: A Workbook of Overcoming Addictions.* San Luis Obispo, CA: Impact.

Horvath, A. T. & Velten, E. (2000). SMART Recovery®: Addiction recovery support from a cognitive-behavioral perspective. *Journal of Rational-Emotive & Cognitive-Behavior Therapy, 18,* 165–91.

Miller, W. R. & Rollnick, S. (1991). *Motivational Interviewing: Preparing People to Change Addictive Behavior.* New York: Guilford.

Peele, S. (1989). *Diseasing of America: Addiction Treatment out of Control.* Lexington, MA: Lexington Books.

Peele, S., Brodsky, A., with Arnold, M. (1989). *The Truth about Addiction and Recovery.* New York: Simon & Schuster.

Peele, S., Bufe, C. & Brodsky, A. (2000). *How to Resist 12-step Coercion.* Tucson, AZ: See Sharp Press.

Persons, J. B., Burns, D. D. & Perloff, J. M. (1989). Predictions of dropout and outcome in cognitive therapy for depression in a private practice setting. *Cognitive Therapy & Research, 12,* 557–75.

Velten, E. (1986). Withdrawal from heroin and methadone with rational-emotive therapy. In W. Dryden & P. Trower (eds.), *Rational-Emotive Therapy: Recent Developments in Theory and Practice* (pp. 228–47). Bristol, England: Institute for RET (UK).

Velten, E. (1993). Self-help and self-directed change. *Annual Review of Addictions Research and Treatment, 3,* 199–220.

Velten, E. (1996). The rationality of Alcoholics Anonymous and the spirituality of Rational Emotive Behavior Therapy. *Journal of Humanistic Education and Development, 35,* 105–16.

Velten, E. (1998). Acceptance and construction: Rational emotive behavior therapy and homosexuality. In C. Shelley (ed.), *Contemporary Perspectives on Psychotherapy and Homosexualities.* London: Free Association Books.

Velten, E. (2000a). Introduction to the special issue on addictive experiences and behavior, Part I. *Journal of Rational-Emotive & Cognitive-Behavior Therapy, 18,* 125–6.

Velten, E. (2000b). Introduction to the special issue on addictive experiences and behavior, Part II. *Journal of Rational-Emotive & Cognitive-Behavior Therapy, 18,* 195–6.

von Breton, J. & Velten, E. (2000a). *Advanced techniques: 8 tools it's SMART to use.* Phoenix, AZ: 2000 SMART Recovery Training Program (September).

von Breton, J. & Velten, E. (2000b). *Rehearsing the coordinator's role.* Phoenix, AZ: 2000 SMART Recovery Training Program (September).

7

Monica O'Kelly

In this chapter I elaborate on the following characteristics that I believe are important in my idiosyncratic style of REBT. I have come to realise that I:

i.   commence with an introductory session;

ii.   follow a clear structure for the sessions;

iii.   develop and attempt to maintain a collaborative relationship;

iv.   clearly set goals;

v.   thoroughly evaluate the emotional consequences;

vi.   make the most of the client's situation;

vii.   if appropriate use a systems or developmental perspective;

viii. place an emphasis on disputation of evaluations;

ix.   focus on one 'ABC' at a time;

x.   anchor the thoughts to the feelings;

xi.   philosophically respect that people have equal worth;

xii.   try to be patient and control my own low frustration tolerance.

Introduction

The understanding of an idiosyncratic style of therapy is enhanced by an appreciation of the influences that contributed to that style. These influences are broader and deeper than merely exploring the theoreticians that influenced the therapist. I hold that the development of therapeutic skills, attitudes and style are not readily achieved by reading a book alone. There are in fact many developmental influences that contribute to the formation of a therapist and the therapist's style. These influences may include the social, cultural, and family climate that influenced the therapist's value system, the general academic climate or school of thought prevalent during their university education, and the many experiences and training opportunities they may have explored and exposed themselves to as a practising therapist.

With this in mind I have reflected on the influences that have contributed to my style. Being raised within an Australian–Irish culture with a love of life, strong family values emphasising social cohesiveness and a deep respect for the equality and value of people has undoubtedly contributed to the foundations of my value system that influences my style. My undergraduate training in psychology in the late 1960s and early 1970s in a young university was behavioural in nature with a sound training in rats and stats psychology. The name Freud was hardly mentioned and the idea of labelling and diagnosing people was abhorrent. As a young graduate

I had a good knowledge of learning theory and highly developed skills in behavioural observation and applied behavioural analysis and the ability to write a report. At that time the cognitive revolution had not hit Australia. The behavioural training stood me in good stead in my first position working as a psychologist with intellectually disabled children and adults. It was there that I developed an appreciation for what I regarded as milieu therapies, such therapies being those through which the behaviour of an individual is changed by changing the environment. Both behaviour modification and family therapy fall into this category. Hence I embarked on a number of years of study, team therapy and supervision in family therapy, developing skills and knowledge in systemic approaches.

The acceptance of cognitive behaviour therapy as a worthwhile therapeutic tool was becoming evident in Australia in the 1970s and 1980s. My first introduction to this approach, other than reading about it in books, was when I attended a Primary Certificate Training programme offered by the Australian Institute for Rational-Emotive Therapy under the leadership of Michael Bernard and Robert Dawson. I found it blended nicely with my behavioural background and gave me tools that I could use with the mostly adult population that I was then dealing with in general private practice. Whilst my family therapy training gave me an understanding of system dynamics I was frustrated by limitations in techniques of change. I found rational emotive behaviour therapy gave me a powerful change technology. I had a thirst to learn more and subsequently completed the then-called Intermediate Programme. A trip to New York with a visit to the Albert Ellis Institute led to the completion of the Associate Fellowship course in rational emotive behavior therapy before completing my doctorate within a rational emotive behaviour therapy framework. These trips gave me first-hand exposure to the styles of Albert Ellis, Janet Wolfe and others at the New York Institute.

Teaching pressures led to further exploration of cognitive behaviour therapy. With trips to Philadelphia I was able to complete the Extra Mural training programme at the Beck Institute. Observation of therapists and videotapes gave me exposure to interventions by Aaron Beck, Judith Beck, Leslie Sokal and others.

Through observation and supervision at both the Albert Ellis Institute and the Beck Institute I believe I have developed an appreciation of the similarities and differences as well as the strengths and weaknesses of each of these major approaches. Both have had an impact on my idiosyncratic style of rational emotive behaviour therapy, which I regard as one of the several schools of cognitive behaviour therapy.

What follows are elaborations on twelve characteristics that I consider are important in my style of rational emotive behaviour therapy. These factors are not mutually exclusive but frequently overlap and interweave.

Commence with an introductory session

Those of us lucky enough to have seen Albert Ellis in action, at one of his regular Friday night sessions at the Albert Ellis Institute using rational emotive behaviour therapy with a volunteer from the audience, are aware that he launches straight into an ABC sequence and gets straight to work. He efficiently gets the 'ABCs' and starts disputing the volunteer's nutty beliefs. It is probably the most efficient and economical therapy in Manhatten. Ellis is world-renowned and his audience on such occasions is usually well versed in REBT principles. With those of us working in clinical practice where a new client does not know us, does not know who Albert Ellis is, and what REBT is, such an approach is likely to be off-putting. This is even more so if the new client is unfamiliar with and possibly reluctant to consult a therapist or psychologist. I agree with the view that it is the aim of the first therapy session to get the client to come again (Haley & Hoffman, 1967). I believe that time needs to be spent in building a therapeutic relationship.

The relationship between a therapist and client is like any other relationship between two people. There needs to be a get-to-know-you period. With this in mind I rarely rush in with the classical rational emotive behaviour therapy technology on the first session. The exceptions might be when a client has a discrete problem or if they came to me because they were aware of my reputation as a rational emotive behaviour therapist and were familiar with the approach.

My first session usually starts with a personal introduction followed by a clarification of how I see my role as a psychologist as distinct from a psychiatrist. My hope here is to demystify psychology and therapy. I then attempt to develop an understanding of how they feel about being there, asking questions such as who referred them and why.

I consider it essential in this first session to build rapport. Like a farmer tilling the soil preparing to sow the seed, building rapport in the initial phase of therapy prepares the client to trust the therapist and to be open to the more challenging rational emotive behaviour therapy techniques such as disputing that I use in later sessions. I place importance on developing a warm and empathic climate. As in other approaches to therapy, 'We must learn to understand the world *as seen and understood by the individual* and to communicate that understanding, if we wish to teach, influence, or even talk to another in an effective way' (Egan & Cowan, 1978, p. II-7). I attempt to use basic techniques of active listening, reflecting back feelings and thoughts and at times checking out that I have understood through paraphrasing.

There are many client characteristics that influence therapy, including rational emotive behaviour therapy. To rush in without exploring the myriad client variables in an initial session could lead to unethical and harmful therapy. Research on client variables (Garfield, 1994) outline many factors that need to be taken into account. Although this is not an exhaustive list they include diagnosis, presence of co-morbidity, severity of disturbance, motivation, responsibility regarding change, expectations, feelings of self-efficacy, socioeconomic status, cultural, religious and ethnic factors, sex, age, developmental stage, education, intellectual level and flexibility. An example of how such information influences which of the smorgasbord of rational emotive behaviour therapy tools I use initially is evident in my response to clients who I assess to have depression of different levels of severity. With extremely depressed clients I commence with behavioural interventions. With clients who are less severely depressed I am more inclined to use cognitive interventions.

I remember that clients are active participants in the therapy process and consider that this initial session gives the client time also to get to know me. This initial session is successful if I have been able to establish a therapeutic relationship with the client, with a therapeutic contract established and a commitment to return, thus enabling an opportunity for traditional approaches to rational emotive behaviour therapy to take place.

Follow a clear structure for the sessions

In the 30 years that I have been working with clients I have become very aware that the majority of clients are not aware of what is involved in therapy. Those that have experienced therapy other than rational emotive behaviour therapy may come with expectation based on their past therapy experience. Some think that therapy is where they just come and talk aimlessly, others think that you will tell them what to do, whilst others think that you will explore the details of their childhood. I find that having a clear structure that I follow for each therapy session helps to develop an effective working environment.

Judith Beck's (1995) work has influenced my therapy style in this context. She refers to the notion of socialising the client into therapy and also recommends structuring sessions. I believe that a clear structure enables the client to quickly catch on to how the therapy will proceed. In many ways the structure that I use in my therapy session sessions can be likened to the structure of a committee meeting in which procedures are followed to ensure that the necessary work is effectively and efficiently done. Some may think that the use of a structure to sessions leads to a regimental, boring approach. This does not need to be the case. The structure is more like the skeleton of the therapy process with the varying content giving each session a unique external appearance. Of course, I deviate from the structure if necessary.

The structure that I usually use is similar to that used by Judith Beck (1995). An example of a structure that I might use is shown in Figure 1.

---

1. General review of the week since the last session.

2. Check how the client is feeling today.

3. Review homework tasks.

4. List the agenda for the session.

   Item 1

   Item 2

   Item 3

5. Work through each item.

6. Summarise significant points learnt.

7. Summarise homework.

8. Check how the client felt about the session.

Figure 1. Example structure for a session

The structure allows for any number of agenda items. Frequently there is only one agenda item. At other times the client and I might list a number of agenda items but there might be time to only address one or two. If this is the case items are carried over to the next session.

When addressing each agenda item again a structure is followed, the structure being the rational emotive therapy sequence. The sequence that I use is similar to that outlined by Dryden & DiGiuseppe (1990) and is shown in Figure 2.

1. Establish the activating event

2. Establish the emotional consequence

3. Evaluate the emotional consequence

4. Check for secondary emotions

5. Elicit the unhelpful beliefs

6. Draw the thought–feeling connection

7. Check the goals for this sequence

8. Dispute the unhelpful beliefs

9. Elicit more effective beliefs

10. Establish relevant homework tasks

Figure 2. The rational emotive behaviour therapy sequence

I believe that following a clear structure for the rational emotive therapy sequence facilitates the clients' learning of the rational emotive therapy process. They are then in a better position to generalise this knowledge to other problems and settings independent of a therapist's involvement.

Develop and attempt to maintain a collaborative relationship
Initially in therapy I focus on establishing a collaborative relationship with my client and continue throughout therapy working to maintain that position. I am aware of the perceived power differential between therapist and client but attempt to work from the philosophical position that therapy is a meeting between two equals. I encourage my client to be an active participant in the therapy process and to take responsibility for their therapy with the personal goal of making myself obsolete in the client's life.

This position has a number of practical implications. In the initial phase and throughout therapy, goals are set collaboratively. I ask my client what they want to work towards changing in therapy. Keeping in mind that therapists, including rational emotive behaviour therapists, can have a profound impact on their clients' lives I consider it imperative to listen to the client and collaborate with every aspect of goal-setting mentioned elsewhere. Not only does this approach lead to ethical counselling but also ensures that I work in harmony with my client.

Throughout the sessions I paraphrase and summarise to give feed-back to my clients regarding what I understand they are saying. I seek feedback from them to check that my perceptions are correct.

When disputing beliefs I avoid didactically telling the client that their thinking is wrong. Whilst from a theoretical position this may be considered to be so, I believe that such an approach is judgemental, assuming a position of superiority. I do not believe that such a didactic approach helps me to work collaboratively with my client. I prefer to use a Socratic style, asking questions to explore the client's beliefs, weighing up the evidence both for and against a belief, exploring the logic of a belief and questioning whether the belief is helpful. I encourage the client to generate their own alternative beliefs, rather than telling them what to think, and help them to see that they have a choice. It is frequently the case that the client's beliefs are understandable given their past experience. I acknowledge that if it is the situation before Socratically disputing them. Throughout the disputing process I attempt to get the client to do as much work on changing his/her beliefs as I do.

At the end of a therapy session I review the session with the client. We summarise the session and the client is specifically asked if there was anything in the session they didn't like or were uncomfortable about.

Set clear goals

I use a goal-oriented approach in therapy. I keep in mind that the goals need to be the client's goals, not mine. There may be times, however, when therapy needs to focus on facilitating the client's ability to articulate the goals. Client's problems can be like a can of squirming worms, over which the client feels no sense of control. Setting goals and working on one goal at a time is like squashing one worm at a time. Eventually there are none left.

There need to be goals for the therapy overall. I attempt to establish and articulate these at the end of the first session. Such goal-setting is an important part of establishing the therapeutic contract. I usually contract to work with the client towards the goals verbally. There may be times, however, when I consider it necessary to develop a written contract with the client. General principles of goal-setting are used, ensuring that the goals are feasible, achievable, and articulated if possible with a clear outcome measure.

I establish goals for each individual session. This involves articulating what is going to be the focus of the session. Setting the agenda items is considered goal-setting with regard to the individual sessions.

I establish goals for each agenda item when working with the rational emotive behaviour therapy sequence. I seek consensus with the client regarding how they would rather feel and/or behave and seek agreement that thoughts need to be changed in order to change the feelings and behaviour.

I continually check goals and if necessary renegotiate them. Periodically throughout therapy I check with the client that the initially established goal is still what they want to work towards. There are times when the client changes or the client's situation changes with the need for there to be a renegotiation of the therapy goals. Such is commonly the case when the depression in a woman starts to lift as a result of therapy and she consequently develops dissatisfaction with the marriage, or alternatively I might be working on anxiety management in a worker who is anxious in the workplace only to find in the next session that they had just been fired. Their thoughts and feelings about being fired and re-establishing themselves in another job then need to be the focus of therapy. I find that there are times when either myself or my client gets off the track within a therapy session. On such occasions I reiterate the goals and explore with the client whether they wish to still work towards that goal or whether they wish to change the goal. Such checks against the established goal enables the therapy to be refocused. Alternatively new goals are set.

Thoroughly evaluate the emotional consequences
For a number of reasons I have developed the habit of thoroughly evaluating and exploring the emotional consequences. Clients are often naïve about emotions. Some are not in touch with their emotions. They may block their emotions because they consider them too painful or be reluctant to acknowledge the presence of an emotion because they have been socialised to consider a particular emotion, such as anger, unacceptable. Others are aware that they are distressed but have difficulty labelling or naming the emotion. They simply do not have an emotional vocabulary. Yet others label the emotion but their understanding and use of the term may differ greatly from the way the therapist uses the label. When asked for example if they are depressed they say, 'No' because, in their mind, to be depressed means that they are in the depths of despair, unable to get out of bed. They are not aware that the degree of depression can vary greatly. An additional factor is that clients might understate or overstate their emotions. They might, for example, say that they are a bit annoyed. As we know in rational emotive behaviour therapy parlance, annoyance can be an appropriate emotion that does not need to be changed through therapy. Further assessment of the emotion, however, might indicate that they are in fact extremely angry and therapy is warranted. Clients can have more than one emotion in response to an activating event. Such is the case when a person who reports that they are depressed also suffers from anxiety although they may not report it. This becomes apparent when the emotional consequences are thoroughly evaluated.

Thorough evaluation of the emotional consequences, if done well, exploring specific behaviours and at times quantification, enables the assessment of the baseline intensity of the emotion, which can be compared with emotional intensity during and after therapy. Therapeutic change can as a result be evaluated.

Such assessment might include all or a number of different strategies. If the problem is one of a lack of emotional vocabulary I find lists of emotional labels as well as pictures of faces with a variety of emotions depicted useful therapy aids. I consider the use of the SUDS scale developed by Wolpe (1969), a useful tool. Using this scale the client is asked to give a rating of the intensity of the emotion on a 100 point scale. I also rely heavily in my assessment of the emotional consequence on assessment using the BASIC ID approach which was developed by Lazarus (1981). This acronym outlines the significant areas that I obtain information about: behaviour, affect, sensations, imagery, cognitions, interpersonal and drugs/biology or lifestyle. With regard to the assessment of emotion, however, I do not explore the cognitions. It is significant for there for be congruence and consistency between each of these areas. If congruence is not present then further exploration with the client regarding the emotion is warranted. For example if the client reports emotionally that they are depressed but reports sensations such as dizziness, palpitations and muscle tension, such sensations being clinically consistent with anxiety, then the additional presence of anxiety is explored with the client. If the client reports that they feel a bit annoyed but also reports behaviours such as throwing plates at their partner, yelling and screaming, such behaviours being consistent with anger, then the more appropriate labelling of the emotion as anger is explored.

The assessment of secondary emotional consequences that may block emotional expression or potentiate distress, although not idiosyncratic to my style, is at times necessary. Such secondary emotions may need to be the initial focus for intervention.

Make the most of the client's situation

When using rational emotive behaviour therapy with clients I rarely didactically teach the 'ABCs' of REBT. My style is in contrast to that of Woods (1991), who espouses a mini lecture approach to teaching therapy clients the theory of rational emotive behaviour therapy. I consider that clients come to therapy to seek help to solve their problems, not to be given a theory lesson.

I keep in mind knowledge regarding how adults learn. When clients come to therapy, which is a learning situation, they bring with them a wealth of knowledge and experiences. New perceptions can be achieved though drawing out that knowledge into the client's conscious awareness.

Rather than teaching the 'ABCs' in an abstract manner, I use the client's problem situation, thoughts and feelings to give them an understanding of the fundamental principles of rational emotive behaviour therapy. I use different approaches to help them see that it is their beliefs that lead to their distress rather than the situation. The following is an example of what I might say to a client after the activating event, beliefs and emotional consequence have been established in order to teach the connection between the 'ABCs'. I might say, 'Now that you are off work with stress, you are thinking to yourself that it is you're fault, that you shouldn't be off work, that you are weak and that you are worthless and you feel depressed. Do you think there is any connection between how you are thinking and how you are feeling? I wonder if you need to think that way?' Alternatively I might say, 'Could you imagine someone being off work with stress and they are thinking, "Just as well I'm off work. I need a good rest." How do you think they would be feeling? Then someone else in a similar situation thinking, "Those rotten bastards. They shouldn't have done this to me." How do you think they would be feeling? But you're thinking, "It's my fault. I shouldn't be off work. I'm weak. I'm worthless," and you're feeling depressed. Do you think it is the situation that leads to how you are feeling? If it is, why do you think those people feel differently?' By questioning in this manner I try to get the client to see the ABC connection in their own distressed experience.

If appropriate I use a systemic or developmental perspective

I am aware that there are two ways in which my style of rational emotive behaviour therapy is influenced by taking a systemic perspective. Firstly, when I work with an individual client I keep in mind that that person is a member of a number of systems. They may, for example, be a member of a couple, a family or a workplace. Each of these systems has its own culture and influence on the individual, which is frequently internalised.

This perception has a significant influence when exploring the client's beliefs. I consider that the client's unhelpful/irrational beliefs fall into different categories with corresponding implication for intervention. They are as follows:

1. Individual irrational beliefs

These are the inferences, demands and evaluations that have been outlined by Ellis (1962, 1994). It is my assumption that many of the techniques I use to challenge and change these beliefs are similar to those used by other rational emotive behaviour therapists.

2. Familial/systemic irrational beliefs

These are beliefs that the individual client shares or holds in common with members of the close family. They may be beliefs that each person in a couple believe, such as 'Sex should be perfect' or 'It is terrible if we argue'. Alternatively there may be beliefs that parents and siblings in the same family also believe, such as 'Mum is weak. We have to protect her' or 'We must not do anything that will upset dad' or a pattern of low frustration tolerance or I-can't-stand-it that all family members share. In family therapy/systemic terms such beliefs are regarded as family myths.

When intervening with an individual who has such systemic beliefs there is a danger that therapeutic interventions focused on changing such systemic beliefs will be corroded and sabotaged by family or systemic influences. The client needs to be fortified to withstand this pressure. To do this I might explore why other family members think that way and challenge whether they need to agree. I also explore what it means to them if they disagree with family members and consolidate their sense of individual worth so that they can feel comfortable holding beliefs that differ from those in their close environment.

3. Cultural irrational beliefs

There are times when it is relevant that I explore with my client some of the many unhelpful/irrational beliefs that permeate our culture in general. By questioning societal values I encourage them to have a healthy scepticism for attitudes and opinions that many others take for granted but are not helpful. Examples of cultural unhelpful beliefs is the tendency to believe that well dressed people are more honourable and trustworthy than those that are dishevelled in their appearance or that high achievers are better people than those who have not had the opportunity to achieve.

The second way that my therapy is influenced by a systemic perspective is that I do not restrict myself to working only with individuals. There are times when I work with couples and families. When working with families in particular I use systems theory to conceptualise problems. I might explore the presence or absence of boundaries, the existence of an enmeshed or over-emotionally-involved relationship or the lack of an executive structure to set limits for children. With all family members present I then use the technology of rational emotive behaviour therapy to target the activating events and emotions of individual family members that are blocking the change to a more functional family system. During this process not only does the 'targeted individual' move towards more helpful beliefs but the observers frequently learn and consolidate the rational emotive behaviour therapy principles. This can be to the extent that they may function as co-therapists, a role that continues between therapy sessions.

There are also times when I use a developmental perspective with my clients. In order to consolidate more helpful beliefs I frequently ask the client where they thought the unhelpful beliefs came from. In doing this we often explore childhood experiences. I consider that it is constructive to reassure the client that it is understandable that they think the way they do given their experience but question whether the belief is still helpful given that their situation has changed. I may even use an age regression strategy. An example of such an approach would be when I ask the client to close their eyes, focus on relaxing and then picture a typical scene in their childhood when they thought in the unhelpful way. This may have been when they were being badly treated by others. I then encourage them, whilst holding the same image in their mind, to think the more constructive thoughts that we had previously generated using traditional rational emotive behaviour therapy strategies.

Place an emphasis on disputation of evaluations

When elegantly disputing unhelpful beliefs I place an emphasis on disputing evaluations rather than demands. Together with two of my rational emotive behaviour therapy colleagues, I have questioned that shoulds are the primary source of disturbance (O'Kelly, Joyce & Greaves, 1998).

It has been a central tenet of rational emotive behaviour therapy that demands expressed in the form of shoulds, musts and oughts are the basic cause of emotional disturbance (Bernard & DiGiuseppe, 1989; Campbell, 1985; Bond & Dryden, 1996; Wolfe & Naimark, 1991). Ellis states forcefully that:

> *REBT almost uniquely holds that when people become – or* make themselves – *emotionally disturbed, they almost always have unconscious and conscious, overt and tacit absolutistic musts that spark their other disturbance-creating irrationalities.* (Ellis, 1994, p.142)

A practical result of holding this tenet is that therapists invariably focus on disputing the shoulds.

Ellis (1994) accepts that to date there is no evidence to support this claim. Concerns regarding the primacy of the should have been raised by others (DiGiuseppe, 1996; Bond & Dryden, 1996). In addition other writers in the general field of cognitive therapy do not emphasise the importance of rules or shoulds (Beck, 1989; Padesky & Greenberger, 1995; Hawton, Salkovskis, Kirk & Clark, 1989).

In the summary of research studies exploring the relationships between unhelpful beliefs and disturbance that I have done with my colleagues (O'Kelly, Joyce & Greaves, 1998), Demandingness did not correlate higher with disturbance than the evaluation processes of low frustration tolerance, awfulizing and generalized rating. In addition demandingness did not discriminate between normal and disturbed groups. The data suggested that the evaluation processes were more significantly associated with disturbance.

From a practical viewpoint when engaged in therapy I find that many clients do not interpret the word should in the absolutistic sense that Ellis uses it. Few clients regard the word should as a moral imperative. Shoulds may also be considered conditional, for example, 'You should study if you want to pass your exams.'

For the reasons above when initially eliciting the beliefs I probe deeply, past the inferences and demand, and explore what it means to the client if the demand is not met. For example, 'If your husband does not come home at 6 pm, as he should, what does that mean to you or what does it mean about him?' I attempt to draw into conscious awareness the low frustration tolerance, the catastrophising, the negative rating of either self or other. When I am disputing it is the evaluation that is the major focus.

There are at times exceptions to this approach. It is frequently the case that angry people are adamant that the other person . . . *should not have done it!* but are reluctant to damn the other person. In this case the demands are the focus.

Focus on one 'ABC' at a time

When working with clients it is my experience that they can be unfocused in their thinking. Whilst they might start talking about one situation they are distressed about, they can easily slip into talking about another, and then yet even another. Alternatively when discussing the emotional consequences associated with an activating event they might have a number of different feelings that they initially mention, or they might start with one feeling then slip into talking about another feeling. I prefer to focus the client to work on one 'ABC' set at a time, keeping it clear in my mind and that of the client what we are both working on at any particular time.

I particularly find it helpful, when using the client's experience in drawing the connection between their beliefs and their feelings, to have elicited and summarised the beliefs that are associated with just one feeling. When this is done I find that the link between the thoughts and feeling is readily apparent and the client catches on quickly to the belief–feeling connection, thus enhancing emotional responsibility.

I consider that it is, however, the client's choice regarding what activating event or feeling they wish to work on. I keep in mind the activating event being discussed. If I become aware that the client starts to discuss another activating event I point that out and ask the client which of the activating events they want to continue to work on. For example, a client might indicate that they want to talk about losing their job due to a back injury then, whilst talking about that, slip into talking about their distress regarding how their boss treated them. In such a case I would say, 'It seems that you are also upset about how your boss treated you. Would you rather talk more about your feeling and thoughts about that or stick to talking about losing your job?' I respond in a similar manner if a client starts to talk about another feeling. For example, the client might be talking about his anxiety regarding losing his job then start talking about feeling angry. In this case I might say, 'It seems to me that you are also angry about losing your job in addition to feeling anxious. We can do some work on both feelings. Which one would you like to work on first?'

I consider that it is particularly important for both therapist and client to be clear regarding which 'ABC' is being discussed when there are secondary emotional problems. If not, confusion can set in regarding the thought–feeling connections.

Anchor the thoughts to the feelings

Throughout the rational emotive behaviour therapy sequence I attempt to anchor thoughts to the feelings. In doing so I believe that the thought–feeling connection is being continually reinforced.

When observing a number of therapists working within a general cognitive behaviour therapy framework I have noticed them exploring the client's beliefs. They ask the client what they are thinking but frequently pay little attention to the feelings. In such a scenario thoughts are explored in isolation to the feelings. Little if any attention is in fact paid to how the client is feeling. The thought–feeling connection is therefore not evident. In addition the therapist can be perceived as cold and lacking in empathy if the feelings are not identified and acknowledged.

When I identify and elicit the client's beliefs, phrases that I might initially use to anchor the thoughts to the feeling include:

• When your mother tells you to be home early you feel angry because?
• When you are feeling down what's going in your head?
• What are you thinking when you are feeling anxious?

When probing for further thoughts and evaluations I often summarise the beliefs already elicited and again anchor them to the feelings. I might say, for example, 'When your mother tells you to be home early and you're thinking, "She's always on my back. She should stop nagging," and you're feeling angry, what are you thinking about her, what does it mean about her?'

By using such phrases the client readily comes to see that a particular feeling is connected to a specific group of thoughts. Throughout therapy I summarise the specific 'ABCs', continually checking out with the client that I have understood them correctly and reinforcing the rational emotive behaviour therapy model.

Philosophically respect that people have equal worth

Throughout the writings of Ellis and his followers (Boyd & Grieger, 1986; Ellis, 1962, 1976, 1985, 1994; Ellis & Harper, 1975; Franklin, 1993) the concept of self-acceptance is espoused rather than the concept of self-confidence or self-esteem. In the words of Ellis (1994), rational emotive behaviour therapy:

> *emphasizes the harm of self downing, but it takes the somewhat special position that all ratings or evaluations of the self tend to be mistaken and illegitimate. It holds, instead, that although people biologically and socially strongly tend to rate themselves as well as their acts and performances, they can learn to omit the first and stay mainly with the second rating.* (pp. 249)

The notion of self-esteem based on achievement or approval by others is challenged since it is thought to be neither philosophically sound nor psychologically helpful.

Two alternatives to self-rating have been outlined in the rational emotive behaviour therapy literature (Ellis, 1976; Ellis & Harper, 1975; Boyd & Grieger, 1986). The less elegant position is for people to consider they have worth, are esteemable and good, because they exist. The implication of this position is that people have equal worth. This view is in accord with the philosophy of many religions that consider that people have worth because they are children of God or because God made them. The more elegant position is to recognise that people are complex with many traits and behaviours. Any attempt at rating has no scientific basis. This position considers that people have no worth but rather aliveness.

When working with clients I am more inclined to work towards the less elegant position regarding worth. Using Socratic dialogue I explore the meaning of personal worth and the factors that contribute to it, asking question such as, 'What makes a person worthwhile?' From a pragmatic viewpoint, I find it is rarely the case that clients can appreciate the more elegant view. In addition I am aware that the notion of individuals having equal worth is more consistent with my own personal philosophy.

A technique that I find useful in this context is to describe three people, for example, a drunk or prostitute, a very handicapped person and then someone they might admire, such as Mother Theresa or Nelson Mandela. Socratically we explore if each of these have worth and if so which has the most worth. I make the point that I am not asking them which does the most worthwhile things.

Another useful technique is to suggest that a very dear friend is sitting in the empty chair. This friend I describe as having the same problems as the client. I then ask them if they would say the same things to their friend as they had been thinking about themself, actually paraphrasing the exact sentences. Clients are usually horrified to think they would talk to anyone else in the same manner. They are then encouraged to think more 'lovingly' about themself and generate more constructive self-talk.

I consider that working on the concept of self-acceptance is vitally important, as I believe self-acceptance is the foundation of a person's emotional well-being.

Try to be patient and control my own low frustration tolerance

Having studied and practised rational emotive behaviour therapy for many years I am well aware of the basic principles involved and versed in identifying, challenging and changing unhelpful beliefs. I repeatedly remind myself that my clients are not as well versed as myself. Others may not catch on and learn quickly. Yet others may have had extremely unpleasant experiences in the past so that their unhelpful beliefs are well entrenched. There are therefore some clients who are slow to change. With such clients I remind myself to be patient.

I can clearly remember one occasion when I was having supervision with Albert Ellis. I thought that given that I had gone half way around the world for the experience that I would take a tape of myself doing therapy with a woman whom I regarded as a difficult client. After listening to the tape with Dr Ellis, I waited for words of advice regarding how I could help the process of therapy proceed more effectively and quickly. The response still resounds in my mind. Dr Ellis said to me in his well-known New York accent, 'What you are doing sounds fine, but watch your own low frustration tolerance.' To be effective with many clients I believe I need to use a style in which I go slowly, patiently and be persistent. Not only do I need to be aware of my clients' unhelpful beliefs but I also keep in mind that I need to be aware of and work on my own unhelpful beliefs that will impede the therapy process (Ellis, 1985).

References

Beck, A. T. (1989). *Cognitive Therapy and the Emotional Disorders*. New York: Penguin Books.

Beck, J. (1995). *Cognitive Therapy: Basics and Beyond*. New York: Guilford Press.

Bernard, M. & DiGiuseppe, R. (1989). Rational-emotive therapy today. In M. E. Bernard & R. DiGiuseppe (eds.) *Inside Rational-Emotive Therapy. A Critical Appraisal of the Theory and Therapy of Albert Ellis* (pp. 1–7). New York: Academic Press.

Bond, F. W. & Dryden, W. (1996). Why two central REBT hypotheses appear untestable. *Journal of Rational-Emotive & Cognitive-Behavior Therapy, 14,* 29–40.

Boyd, J. & Grieger, R. (1986). Self-acceptance problems. In A. Ellis & R. Grieger (eds.) *Handbook of Rational-Emotive Therapy Volume 2* (pp. 146–61). New York: Springer.

Campbell, I. (1985). The psychology of homosexuality. In A. Ellis & M. E. Bernard (eds.) *Clinical Applications of Rational-Emotive Therapy* (pp. 153–80). New York: Plenum Press.

DiGiuseppe, R. (1996). The nature of rational and irrational beliefs: Progress in rational emotive behaviour therapy. *Journal of Rational-Emotive and Cognitive-Behavior Therapy, 14,* 5–28.

Dryden, W. & DiGiuseppe, R. (1990). *A Primer on Rational-Emotive Therapy*. Champaign, IL: Research Press.

Egan, G. & Cowan, M. (1978). *Human Development in Human Systems: A Working Model*. Monterey, CA: Brooks/Cole.

Ellis, A. (1962). *Reason and Emotion in Psychotherapy*. Secaucus, NJ: Citadel.

Ellis, A. (1976). RET abolishes most of the human ego. *Psychotherapy: Theory, Research and Practice, 13*(4), 343–8.

Ellis, A. (1985). *Overcoming Resistance: Rational-Emotive Therapy with Difficult Clients*. New York: Springer.

Ellis, A. (1994). *Reason and Emotion in Psychotherapy: Revised and Updated*. New York: Birch Lane Press.

Ellis, A. & Harper, R. (1975). *A New Guide to Rational Living*. Hollywood, CA: Wiltshire Books.

Franklin, R. (1993). *Overcoming the Myth of Self-Worth: Reason and Fallacy in What You Say to Yourself*. Appleton, WI: Focus Press.

Garfield, S. L. (1994). Research on client variables in psychotherapy. In A. E. Bergin & S. L. Garfield (eds.), *Handbook of psychotherapy and behavior change* (4th edn.) (pp. 229–69). New York: Wiley.

Haley, J. & Hoffman, L. (1967). *Techniques of Family Therapy*. New York: Basic Books.

Hawton, K., Salkovskis, P., Kirk, J. & Clark, D. (1989). *Cognitive Behaviour Therapy for Psychiatric Problems*. Oxford: Oxford University Press.

Lazarus, A. (1981). *The Practice of Multimodal Therapy*. New York: McGraw-Hill.

O'Kelly, M., Joyce, M. & Greaves, D. (1998). The primacy of the 'shoulds': Where is the evidence? *Journal of Rational Emotive and Cognitive-Behavior Therapy, 16*(4), 223–34.

Padesky, C. & Greenberger, D. (1995). *Clinician's Guide to Mind Over Mood*. New York:

Guilford Press.

Wolfe, J. L. & Naimark, H. (1991). Psychological messages and social context: Strategies for increasing RET's effectiveness with women. In M. E. Bernard (ed.), *Using Rational-Emotive Therapy Effectively: A Practitioner's Guide* (pp. 265–301). New York: Plenum Press.

Wolpe, J. (1969). *The Practice of Behavior Therapy*. New York: Pergamon Press.

Woods, P. (1991). Orthodox RET taught effectively with graphics, feedback on irrational beliefs, a structured homework series and models of disputation. In M. E. Bernard (ed.) *Using Rational-Emotive Therapy effectively: A Practitioner's Guide* (pp. 69–110). New York: Plenum Press.

8

Nando Pelusi

Following Windy Dryden's example of focusing on one's idiosyncratic practice of REBT, I examine how and why I practice it in the way that I do. I discuss the importance of:

i. explaining the approach and coming to agreement;

ii. separating the practical problem from the emotional problem;

iii. understanding the nuances of the 'ABCDEs';

iv. the three main musts;

v. constructing 'Bs' from emotional and behavioral 'Cs';

vi. creating a trial-and-error philosophy for risk-taking;

vii. seeing that behavior results from controlling one's perceptions;

viii. human nature and biological effects;

ix. the role of subconscious processes;

x. cultivating a philosophic and scientific mind-set;

xi. understanding semantics;

xii. identifying goals and pursuing desires.

While this list overlaps with classic REBT in many ways, I notice some unexpected differences.

Introduction
One of my favorite activities as a psychologist is to conduct the unique Friday Night Workshop at the Albert Ellis Institute in New York City. I aspire to emulate and sometimes imitate the deceptively simple beauty of orthodox REBT, à la Ellis. I learned some good REBT in part by watching Ellis conduct this weekly demonstration. I also realized that there is no real 'orthodoxy' — for many reasons. Inherent in REBT is antidogmatism, and I have seen it mutate before my eyes at the Institute where fellows debate. However, as Justice Potter remarked about obscenity, 'I know it when I see it,' there exists clear consensus about what constitutes REBT, and even 'good' REBT among experts (Ellis and Dryden, 1987). My own therapeutic approach seems orthodox in that I specifically use Ellis as mentor and model, minus the Bronx accent. Therefore, it continues to amaze me that the participants and other members of the audience, along with some regulars, tell me how I so differ from the way Ellis would do things.

Following Windy Dryden's example of identifying one's idiosyncratic practice of REBT, I lay out what I consider representative of the things I do which follow the classic, principled REBT I aspire to do, and how that may differ from the way Ellis would do it. While REBT consists of certain essential aspects, there are novel approaches that still can reside within the theory (Ellis, 1962). Some of those essential aspects include efficiency, both therapeutic and emotional, and attributing disturbances not to events, but to the views taken of them. We teach a method of self-help via identification of irrational beliefs. Many REBTers identify irrational beliefs and dispute 'the main musts' and the derivative inferences that emerge from them, also known as cognitive distortions.

Among the many ways therapists copy or imitate Ellis are some non-REBT things such as gestures, vocal inflection, and attitudes. These may prove to be sub-clinical and irrelevant, but I describe them as study of Ellis the therapist rather than merely theorist.

There are three main sources for feedback that I get. First, knowledge about idiosyncrasies comes from the audience at the Friday Night Workshop in New York. The second source is almost two decades of experience listening to and watching the way Ellis conducts therapy and comparing. The third source is the feedback of fellows, trainees and colleagues. My idiosyncrasies are well described as an evolution, with perhaps some random drift from Ellisian REBT.

Explaining the approach and coming to agreement

The initial sessions are didactic and include about one to five visits. This phase involves explaining the causes of emotional problems and the methods to overcome them. We may call this standard REBT. The first goal consists of clearly distinguishing practical problems from emotional problems. This includes discussing the methods, tone, and expectations of collaboration in REBT. We then discuss the fact that subsequent sessions involve more thoroughly working through the problems. Various multimodal REBT methods come out in this working-through phase. We explore the philosophy of REBT and how it may be applied during the week between sessions. In these sessions, I speak less, and encourage more, and ask more details about 'As' and 'Cs'.

Some amount of discussion goes into the therapeutic process itself. I convey my enthusiasm and confidence for the methods that I possess. I like to find agreement and I make an offer of collaboration, saying, 'I propose, you dispose.' This is a preamble that constitutes the offer of collaboration. I describe to new clients the ways in which I may differ from previous therapists that they may have encountered, such as the active and directive approach. I request that the client assert when and how we disagree. I show interest by active listening, which consists of asking questions. This shows that I am not the passive, inductive, data-gatherer they may expect.

The encouragement of disagreement is designed to encourage expression and collaboration. Also, it guides me in making hypotheses about 'Bs'. I occasionally suggest that their disposal is premature, and offer reasons. I offer suggestions on logical grounds and demonstrate that better hypotheses still exist. The hypothesizing phase is seen as such: I do not claim mystical wisdom, but show we have a good theory (REBT), experience with clients, and confidence in the method.

Explanations regarding how I conduct the session refer to content and style, making explicit what Ellis leaves implicit. For example, I inform the client that I may use humor, bring up ideas that may be wrong, state something tentatively, etc. Ellis gets right in, interrupts, and often directs the session while the client holds on and finds his way through an intellectual ride. Ellis does that magnificently, and we can speculate that he can do that for several reasons: that he's the famous Dr Ellis, he's older, he's wiser, he's a diagnostic genius, and he's got a loud voice.

The collaborative concept that I prefer and use typically is well received, since it shows interest and encourages a workshop atmosphere for trial and error. It seems to convey a useful scientific mind-set for experimentation. We rid the therapy of some magic and mysticism. The ethic in session is in keeping with REBT's experimentalist, hypothesis-and-deduction style.

I differ from Ellis in deferring more to the client with respect to speed and force of disputation. I also work more to assess our agreement on problem formulations.

Separating the practical problem from the emotional problem

REBT breaks problems down into the famous 'ABCs', where the emotional problem, the 'C', is not attributed to the 'A', the practical problem, but to 'B', the beliefs a person holds. I explicitly show that the problem can be separated with what Edelstein and Steele (1997) call the Problem Separation technique. I explicitly describe how inferred 'A' *leads to* 'C' connections, and correct them with how hypothesized 'B' *leads to* 'C' connections. In standard REBT a client's language of causality for disturbance-creation can be: 'He made me so mad,' as though someone's acting unfairly towards the client caused the anger. That one is an obvious case of 'A' causes 'C' type thinking. However, more subtle attributions come in sneaky forms. For example, 'He's allowed to act any way he wants, but *not* after I've treated him so well.' The practical problem here is harder to define, and the explicit problem separation technique makes it easier to think in terms of finding the 'B' that really causes 'C'. I separate the practical from the emotional problem as a general rule more emphatically than general REBT advocates. This seems a clinical judgment call.

Understanding the nuances of the 'ABCDEs'

I use and describe the 'ABCDE' profile explicitly. Separating the 'A' and 'C', identifying the real culprit 'B', and setting the stage for a bold dash of 'D' are my goals for the first session. Clients entering therapy may not know their 'A' from their 'C', and may thus experience the concomitant hopelessness, demoralization, self-downing, and awfulizing.

My enthusiasm for REBT causes me to consider the average client a potential REBTer. I like to discuss the nuances of the theory with clients who evince any psychological insight and interest in their own cognitive processing. I find that most distinctly do.

I keep a list of the clients' personal 'classic' irrational beliefs, and a disputation and new philosophy log. The new philosophies constitute the 'E' in the 'ABCDEs'. Clients often get assigned a formal 'ABCDE' to write out. Two main methods of disputing seem to get clients over initial emotional disturbance. The first is the formal Ellis 'ABCDE'. The second consists of making a list of the chronic 'Bs' a client holds, and then coming up with several reasons why the ideas prove false. Thus, we collaborate on illuminating the important irrational beliefs, but the client is assigned the task of finding the evidence against the various beliefs during the week. He is also encouraged to come up with several disputations for each belief.

By setting the 'ABCDEs' in a context of goals, we highlight specific and general goals. In general, the goals a client has may be quite implicit. Besides acting in ways that enhance survival and contentment, we examine the goals of self-actualization, flexibility, creativity, and productivity. It turns out that seeking contentment per se may actually lead to discontentment.

Succumbing to the effects of emotional disturbances does not aid in daily living. Thus, clients are implored to identify their secondary 'Cs'. We discuss of the importance of identifying and working on the secondary disturbances. Often, primary disturbances are much alleviated when attention is given to the secondary problem. The word 'secondary' might incorrectly convey an impression of secondary importance. Thus, the discussion of secondary disturbance is identified as often having the major importance in resolving the disturbance.

We discuss the role of force, vigor and repetition in disputing 'D', and reinforcing 'E'. Ellis has often written on this topic. Edelstein and Steele (1997) add several other ideas that seem clinically relevant: dispute 'Bs' immediately, and enumerate the various ways a demand is false.

The three main musts

Ellis has distilled the essence of most human emotional disturbance as stemming from core beliefs that seem to fall into three categories. They are demands on oneself, others, and the conditions of one's life. This is a staple of the therapy. A variation or a supplement is to categorize the main emotional reactions that also seem to fall into predictable categories. They are shame, self-downing, anger, and discouragement.

Next, we discuss the 'B' leads to 'C' connection. I offer the example of looking at how a population of 100 people might react differently to the same event. Clients quickly understand this once it is made explicit. Responsibility for disturbed emotions is gently but persistently highlighted by 'B' leads to 'C', and that 'A' cannot cause 'C'.

Along with the classic 'Bs', we look for the salient 'B' in this situation. Usually, the salient 'B' is in the client's own words. A variation on Ellis's traditional question, 'What are you telling yourself?' is, 'How would you translate this belief into your own words?' This question seems poised midway between telling a client their salient belief, and asking them to grope in a void for their 'B'.

Avoidance of responsibilities can be described as pursuing ease and comfort and not going for difficulty. However, we speculate that clients perpetually or determinedly going for ease (a) *view* responsibility as more onerous than it really is, and (b) it is really onerous, plus *I can't stand it*. REBT elegantly goes for the idea that a task really is onerous, while we can also question the prediction that it truly would be all that onerous.

REBT is not a theory of personality, but of personality *change*. The three main musts can seem to constitute shorthand for a personality theory useful to the client. Eysenck's three factors, Extraversion, Psychoticism (aggressiveness), and Neuroticism, seem to fit within the REBT musts (Blau, 2002, personal communication). Self-damning affects extraversion, other-damning affects aggression, and world-damning affects neuroticism. Hopelessness and discouragement are examples of LFT. Shame is an example of ego, and it illuminates for the client the salient 'Bs' for us to dispute.

Constructing 'Bs' from emotional and behavioral 'Cs'

A focus on what can be called insidious 'Bs' helps clients zero in on unusual or unexpected 'Bs'. These beliefs are hidden or nested within more obvious beliefs: 'Since I have treated him so well, he shouldn't have treated me unfairly.' Or, 'Because I go out of my way to try, I should succeed, and I'm a failure.' To highlight the salient nested belief is to identify more clearly the values and desires that are beneficial, and the musts that are not.

Crawford and Ellis (1989) have skillfully constructed a dictionary of common 'Bs' associated with 'Cs'. Clients are helped to discern their 'Bs', and to identify their undesirable emotional and behavioral 'Cs'. In addition to the main 'Cs', such as anxiety, depression, guilt, and anger, that cause clients to come to therapy for help, we can examine unusual 'Cs'. These unusual 'Cs' can be subtle, or unexpected, but may be the source of chronic problems for clients. A sampling of the subtle 'C' with concomitant 'Bs' follows:

i.   *Boredom:* I must enjoy myself, this should be more exciting or I can't stand it.
ii. *Compulsions:* I must ensure safety and must feel certain, and must get what I want or I cannot stand it.
iii. *Defensiveness:* I must have no flaws, and I need your approval, and you have no right to critique me.
iv. *Dependency and love needs:* I need your approval and love, or no one else will ever love me, and that would be horrible.
v.   *Mental fixation:* I can't stand focusing on what I had better do.
vi. *Grandiosity:* I must be superior, and therefore I really am, otherwise I'm a rotten person.
vii. *Self-pity, other-pity:* Poor me (or other) for not getting what I need. Life is made awful.
viii. *Impatience:* I can't stand waiting or any inefficiency.
ix. *Indifference and detachment:* It is too hard to discover and assert my desires.
x.   *Loneliness:* I need others to validate me.
xi. *Obsessions:* I must do something perfectly and any other thinking is too boring.
xii. *Phobias:* I can't stand the fear and panic I feel when confronted with this object.
xiii. *Avoidance:* It's too hard to face my desire and risk. I need certainty.
xiv. *Shame:* I must have no serious flaws, or I become an inadequate person.

Creating a trial-and-error philosophy for risk-taking

I advocate an experiment-taking approach to problems, with cumulative trial and error. I redefine the notion of failure for the client as a necessary component to growth. I will discuss the various ways this is true with a client. Thus, failure is actively to be sought out, rather than avoided. I base this on the Popperian notion of knowledge acquisition gleaned from the expositions of Campbell (1990) and Cziko (1995). The issues here relate to the process of 'cumulative blind variation and selective retention.' Blind variation refers to trying things with no need for certainty and no need for a guarantee. Blind variation (trial) yields information, some of which is useful and selectively retained. This is the selective retention of knowledge gained by blindly varying behavior.

This seemingly radical approach actually denotes the mechanism by which all knowledge comes about and accumulates. However, few of us would willingly experiment with risky behaviors, if we believe 'I must not fail, and I must be accepted.'

The process I use within therapy of proposing hypotheses and allowing for corrective error is the same model espoused by general REBT on how to live between therapy sessions. The difference with REBT is my emphasis on the accumulated knowledge that such trial-and-error (experimentation plus failure) brings. The insight to avoidant or depressive clients is that failure makes one stronger not weaker. REBT espouses this, but the *mechanism* for such growth has not received much attention. The main mechanism explored with clients is the one of accumulating information, learning several important things:

i.   That failure at a task does not equal failure as a person.
ii.   Failure at attaining a goal is not complete failure. One has still learned much of value. For example, that nothing awful has occurred.
iii. Failure means we close in on the general goal. If I fail with this job or that potential mate, I gain skill at the pursuit.
iv.   Clients can keep a record of their accumulated insights.

The halo effect may seem to come into play here. The weekly chipping away at dysfunctional beliefs seems to have a cumulative effect eliciting a sense of self-efficacy in the client, whereas previously they felt some degree of helplessness.

Trial and error is a form of Darwinian or selection thinking. Cziko (1995) describes this as universal selectionism. This includes Trials and corrective Errors. Both phases of Trial and Error are integral to finding good fit (with a mate, job, or practically anything) and the phases work reciprocally.

Feedback loops, vicarious learning, risk-taking and imagery explain emotional advances by advocating a flexible attitude towards the Trials phase. Thus, demanding perfection, or refusing to risk failure, negates the Trials part. Self-downing and demands for ease may be another inhibitor of Trials. Population thinking and selection thinking forcefully endorses the Trials part as a good thing, a means of finding fit, or finding out whether something proves good enough. As Ellis remarks to clients when a member of the opposite sex rejects them: 'That's a good thing, because you quickly get rid of people who aren't for you!'

There are several advantages to using this metaphor. Clients quickly respond to this way of thinking. It normalizes failure as corrective Error instead of providing fodder for self-downing or giving up. It also advances the risk-taking, self-directing philosophy of REBT in simple but forceful imagery.

This method has proponents making a potent case for it. Perkinson (1993) builds upon the work of Karl Popper and takes this evolutionary epistemology seriously. He advocates a radical conception of how individuals learn. I deviate from Ellis in emphasizing the trial and error approach and in building error into the growth stage, but mainly in stressing the cumulative aspect. One gets stronger by accumulating experiences from which to base further growth. REBT shows we can stand failure, and in addition, I emphasize that failure is actually good.

I employ 'vicarious learning' techniques. Vicarious learning is what Cziko (1995) refers to as using thoughts and thinking as a means of 'risking' safely, in your head. REBT uses a form of this in Ellis's version of Rational Emotive Imagery. Vicarious learning differs from actual experience in that emotional coping with failure is not the main focus. The main focus is practical coping with failure. This does not supplant the elegant goal of REBT, but adds to it an imagery-based procedure for practical problem solving.

Behavior results from controlling one's perceptions

Ellis and other REBTers sometimes use Skinnerian operant conditioning. This is done as a means of 'reinforcement.' I do not because it unintentionally endorses that the environment (the 'A') can control the client's emotions and behaviors (the 'C').

Behaviorism is based on the principle that the environment causes behavior. Ellis occasionally applies this when assigning homework, but I believe it is an error. In fact, Ellis has noted this in his own experience. Chronic rejection and getting turned down for dates in the Bronx Botanical garden should have 'extinguished' his talking to women. Instead, he pushed himself to talk (whereas he historically remained silent) despite lack of reinforcement and pleasure. Operant conditioning has never worked for my adult clients and has not worked in my personal experiences.

William T. Powers provides a much more useful model for rearranging behavior and understanding learning. Gary Cziko (1995) fully describes the failures and poverty of Behaviorism based on Powers' concept of perceptual control, and the benefits of instead identifying the purposes and goals of the individual actor.

Control theory (Powers, 1973) solves the problem of the observation that behavior can actually increase despite diminishing reinforcement. Like Ellis's experience in the park. Ellis *told himself his purpose* in continuing to talk to attractive women despite his getting rejected. His *purpose* was twofold: first, to meet attractive women, and second, to get better and less upset about rejection. Ellis's genius lay in seeing this second part. You get less upset as you pursue your purpose and deal with obstacles (such as a number of uninterested women in the park).

Perceptual control theory overlaps with REBT in that the purposes of the individual get highlighted and put into place as references. The environment provides varying challenges to overcome (such as recalcitrant women, bad weather, and poor economy). REBT theory looks at the 'B' (ideas, beliefs) that derails purposive behavior. It is not the 'A' (activating event, environment) that causes behavior and determines reactions. Using any aspect of behaviorism with clients confuses the issue. The question is not: which external, environmental conditions cause your behavior? The salient questions are: what are your goals and how are you blocking yourself from their pursuit, and how do you get closer to your goals?

Human nature and biological effects

I openly discuss biological bases for why we tend to do and want things, and why we demand, or doing that bad thing Ellis calls *musterbation*. Along with human nature I introduce evolutionary psychology and Darwinian thinking about problems in an REBT context. We see that certain emotions and habits of mind evolved because they provided utility to our ancestors in the service of survival and reproduction. Those qualities that aided survival and reproduction then may not serve our needs and goals in today's environment. Knowledge of a distinct human nature aids in self-understanding. It answers questions about why we do and feel certain things, while REBT answers the more proximate how questions.

Ellis (1976) acknowledges human nature by noting the biological basis of human irrationality, but without distinguishing male and female propensities as explicitly as I do. He is correct in stressing the many similarities between the sexes. It often doesn't matter whether one is a male or a female, pretty or homely, young or old when it comes to disturbances. But sometimes it does. Ellis has acknowledged biology somewhat by asserting that the origin of disturbance 'isn't because your mother looked at you cross-eyed — you were BORN an arrant screwball, because you're human.' I more distinctly abandon the 'standard social science model' (SSSM) as described by Barkow, Cosmides & Tooby (1992). REBT follows the standard social science model. The SSSM attributes emotions and behaviors largely to culture and experiences. This negates the influential role of human nature, as understood in evolutionary psychology and biology. Most recent studies demonstrate that human cognitive plasticity is not infinite, and is fairly circumscribed in predictable ways (Pinker, 1997).

The topic of human nature, human universals, and why we tend to have difficulties in uprooting musts is actively discussed in my sessions. We talk about how certain 'Cs' (anger, anxiety, jealousy, guilt and depression) made sense and served our genes in the ancestral environment where we evolved in present form over 100,000 years. We no longer live in that ancestral environment, and those emotions may not serve us well today.

The discussion includes often-made errors such as the naturalistic fallacy, which says, 'If it's natural it must be good.' The modern evolutionary psychology view is that we can make an informed decision to deliberately put our genes second to our wishes (such as putting on a condom). Those in the social sciences assert biological means genetic, which in turn means determined. Dawkins (1989) and Buss (1999) note that genetic does not necessarily mean determined, since some traits are obligate (like blue eyes), but some traits are not (like musical talent). Also, genetic does not necessarily mean good. Cancer and obesity have genetic influences, and few would consider those good. REBT does not espouse determinism, and neither does evolutionary psychology.

The constructivist and post-modern view of the mind implies a blank-slate mind. Current evidence from evolutionary psychology shows that the mind is not a blank slate. Modern investigation into the mind suggests that mental and cognitive activity is the product of the brain – no brain, no mind (Pinker, 1997). Also, it seems that the mind contains modules that evolved to solve problems. These modules consist of specific algorithms designed by natural selection to aid in our survival. I have explored this issue more fully on the junction of REBT and evolutionary psychology (Pelusi, in press).

With a self-downing client, the assignment was to distinguish her traits from her self, using Darwinian population-thinking. The population in question referred to her traits and characteristics. She intensely disliked several traits, such as procrastination, and tendency to get hurt and angry. She correctly saw these as flaws. She concluded that she was thus a 'flawed human being.' We then defined a human being as having a catalog of traits, some positive, some flawed. By incorporating into the definition of a human being 'a person with flawed traits,' she became not a flawed human being' but merely a human being.

The role of subconscious processes
One of Ellis's main contributions is igniting a powerful case against psychoanalysis. He correctly and presciently identified many of the false assumptions underlying psychoanalysis. In a paper showing errors (Ellis, 1968) he highlighted a few. Psychoanalysis promotes sidetracking, dependency, conformity, submission to authority, affirming irrationality, and worst of all, misidentifying the cause of most human disturbance.

Self-deception is a topic we discuss, not as a psychoanalytic unconscious, but as a part of our evolved psychological makeup. As Trivers (1977) noted in a seminal work, 'One of the important things to realize about systems of animal communication is that they are not systems designed for the dissemination of the truth.' Self-deception is an effective part of deceiving others. Beneffectance, the biased positive interpretation of our actions, when we succeed or fail, helps to deceive oneself, and thus, others. This tendency has adaptive value for manipulation. Exaggeration, minimizing, and selective retention are all adapted cognitive processes. Awareness of this tendency of selective perception is no guarantee of truthful assessment. Clients more readily accept disputation after a discussion of self-deception.

With a good scientific theory (such as evolutionary biology) we may find discussion of subconscious processes useful. With a nonscientific theory we get a psychodynamic garden path. For example, I will give an explanation that someone craves sugary and fatty foods because his ancestors for the last hundred thousand years evolved to adapt to nutritional scarcity. This makes infinitely more sense than looking for unresolved 'oral fixations'.

Cultivating a philosophic and scientific mind-set
There are commonly three possible approaches in therapy: (a) helping a client feel better, (b) helping a client get less disturbed, and (c) helping a client get less disturbable in general. REBT seems alone among therapies to specifically target the third approach in therapy.

Ellis (1986) distinguishes elegant and inelegant REBT by noting that disputing the derivatives of the must neglects the salient absolute thinking. Regular cognitive therapy seems to dispute the various probabilities of the clients' Activating Events. REBT goes for disputation of the philosophy that makes one prone to disturbance (Ellis, 1986). Imparting an overall philosophic approach is part of the goal of REBT (by not merely helping clients get less disturbed, but less prone to disturbance). My work with clients includes making this third approach explicit.

Clients easily see the merits of each of the approaches, and many continue therapy to get the 'philosophy' clearer.

I attempt to impart the wide application for the principles. I give little or no advice. One goal for a client looking for direction on what to decide is to help a client discern and choose a goal.

Regarding the therapeutic change process, I attempt to place responsibility for change squarely on the shoulders of the client. I definitely enter into a discussion and highlight pros and cons of an issue, but ultimately defer to the client, 'What is your goal, and what do you want and prefer?' I help clients choose for themselves, but almost never would strongly advocate what I believe would be better for the client. I tip the scales one way if a client truly has ambivalence about an issue, and if I clearly see a benefit.

I endorse explicitly and abstractly the canons of science, and then make them accessible to individuals in quandaries. For example, suspending judgments until the facts are in, experimenting with concrete steps towards goals, and finding alternative explanations for phenomena in one's life.

We discuss Popper's idea that an idea is scientific when stated in a manner that allows falsification (at least in principle). However, we also discuss the thinking process and how easily we succumb to faulty reasoning. What constitutes fallacies or sound argument?

Understanding semantics
General semantics examines the effects words and language can have on thinking. It provides an explanation for how words and language can rigidify thinking, and make biases more difficult to uproot. Ellis has adapted general semantics into REBT in some creative ways. He uses 'referenting,' the notion that some words, such as smoking or working, may actually mean several different things. For example, 'smoking' means pleasure, but also expense; fiddling with a cigarette, but also brown teeth. His adventurous use of E-prime in several books has illuminated our overgeneralized language, especially when carelessly using words such as 'be' and 'is.' E-prime consists of the English language with the verb 'to be' excised. This word can violate the principles of sound thinking and denote unrealistic descriptions of what actually occurs. Thus, if I say, 'I am a musician,' I globalize myself, and when I fail to do well musically I may tend to put myself down as a failure. To eschew the *capula* 'to be' we say, 'I play music.' This more accurately, and less dangerously, depicts reality (Bourland, 1999).

I also discuss general semantics when examining a client's self-talk. Again, I focus much more carefully on slights, and highlight a client's usage of words I believe denote his beliefs. I will not compulsively correct any usage implying that 'A' causes 'C', but will keep it in mind, and then offer it later as a hypothesis based on a client's expression.

Some words more accurately describe phenomena than others. For example, the neologisms, 'anxietizing, hopelessizing, and shameizing,' more accurately describe the phenomenon experienced in REBT philosophy than Standard English. This is an extention of Ellis's famous terms 'catastrophizing' or '*must*erbating.'

Clients immediately understand the concepts of general semantics, and often adopt the neologism without realizing that we are using them. It seems we easily understand neologisms when the concept describes familiar phenomena in human nature. If I say, 'Let's go after your 'shameizing' in yesterday's exchange with your boss' the client immediately understands the word and uses it in his own descriptions.

Identifying goals and pursuing desires

Ellis (1962) has written out his ideas on attaining personal happiness. REBT aims to reduce disturbance. I emphasize the principle of finding long-range goals and issues larger than oneself about which to get passionate. Many clients lack an overarching passion in life, and one distinct goal of therapy consists of finding that passion. Areas of disturbance may include not finding a passion, or resisting the work or the risk involved in finding it, or indeed, making the passion a must.

In making goal-setting a part of therapy, we usually consider moderate-range goals. In looking directly at long-range pursuits we give context to shorter-range goals.

REBT advocates an informal, anti-authoritarian stance for the therapist to take. I go a bit further, in order to give credence and authority to the concepts I espouse, I answer queries about what I believe and what I have experienced in my own personal growth. I disclose my personal values, like individualism, rationality, and skepticism. I also disclose my own idiosyncrasies. This includes foibles and failures, and not just bragging about some accomplishment. The main reason is that I want to model self-acceptance, but also, I assume that the client accepts me, and may adopt a more self-accepting stance.

Summary

In the initial stages of therapy, I emphasize teaching of REBT, applying it to the problems brought in by the client. I indicate that I will propose what I think, and ask them to correct me. The offer is, 'I propose, you dispose.' I also attempt to foster an alliance, something like coaching and cheerleading, indicating confidence, 'You can achieve it.' I clearly try to distinguish the practical from the emotional problems, the 'A' from 'B' and 'C'. I more fully and explicitly discuss human nature than REBT normally does. I look at biology, evolutionary aspects of disturbance, and sex differences. I ask the clients to accept the formula for trial and error. I advocate an experimentalist approach to problems, with an emphasis on the cumulative aspects of trial and error. Another way to look at this is to define it as selection thinking.

In the subsequent sessions, I concentrate on working through the various problems, with little didactic emphasis. We discuss general semantics, and the role of self-talk and words in creating and maintaining disturbance. We do this more explicitly and intensively than normally espoused in REBT. Another difference from REBT in my practice is that I do not use any operant reinforcement, nor do I use any kind of behaviorist language that supports the idea that 'A' causes 'C'.

Albert Ellis has conveniently provided me with a therapeutic Weltanschauung that so suffuses my approach that the main differences in therapy consist mainly of emphasis. There are a few omissions and deletions that have emerged over the years.

Now, you go work on that.

References

Barkow, J. H., Cosmides, L. & Tooby, J. (eds.) (1992). *The Adapted Mind: Evolutionary Psychology and the Generation of Culture*. New York: Oxford University Press.

Bourland, D. (1997). *E-prime III: Third Anthology*. Concord, CA: International Society for General Semantics.

Buss, D. (1999). *Evolutionary Psychology: An Introduction*. New York: Allyn & Bacon.

Campbell, D. T. (1990). Epistemological roles for selection theory. In N. Rescher (ed.), *Evolution, Cognition, and Realism*. (pp.1–19). Lanham, MD: University Press of America.

Crawford, T. & Ellis, A. (1989). A dictionary of rational-emotive feelings and behaviors. *Journal of Rational-Emotive & Cognitive-Behavior Therapy*. 7(1).

Cziko, G. (1995). *Without Miracles: Universal Selection Theory and the Second Darwinian Revolution*. Cambridge MA: MIT Press.

Dawkins, R. (1989). *The Selfish Gene* (new edn.). New York: Oxford University Press.

Edelstein, M. & Steele, D. R. (1997). *Three Minute Therapy: Change Your Thinking, Change Your Life*. New York: Open Court.

Ellis, A. (1962). *Reason and Emotion in Psychotherapy*. Secaucus, NJ: Lyle Stuart.

Ellis, A. (1968). Is psychoanalysis harmful? *Psychiatric Opinion, 5*(1) 16–25.

Ellis, A. (1976). The biological basis of human irrationality. *Journal of Individual Psychology, 32*, 145–68. Reprinted by the Albert Ellis Institute, New York.

Ellis, A. (1986). A sadly neglected cognitive element in depression. *Cognitive Therapy and Research, 1*(2).

Ellis, A. & Dryden, W. (1987). *The Practice of RET*. New York: Springer.

Palmer, J. A. & Palmer, L. K. (2002). *Evolutionary Psychology: The Ultimate Origins of Human Behavior*. Boston MA: Allyn & Bacon.

Pelusi, N. (2002). In Press: *Evolutionary Psychology and REBT*.

Perkinson, H. J. (1993). *Teachers without goals/students without purposes*. New York: McGraw-Hill.

Pinker, S. (1997). *How The Mind Works*. New York: Norton.

Powers, W. T. (1973). *Behavior: The Control of Perception*. Greenwood, NY: Aldine/de Gruyter.

Trivers, R. (1977). *Social Evolution*. Menlo Park, CA: Benjamin Cummings.

9

Michael Neenan

My idiosyncratic practice of REBT focuses on the following twelve areas but it is not limited to these areas. In this chapter, I discuss:

i.   moulding the therapeutic relationship;

ii.   establishing SMART goals;

iii.   clarifying the meaning of commitment;

iv.   simplifying the 'ABCs' of REBT;

v.   finding convincing arguments to dispute clients' irrational beliefs;

vi.   encouraging clients to put rational beliefs into their own words;

vii.   understanding how change occurs;

viii.   combating 'I don't know';

ix.   looking for ways to encourage clients to take responsibility for their problems;

x.   looking for ways to increase homework compliance;

xi.   encouraging change: not necessarily profound or philosophical;

xii.   tackling verbosity.

Introduction
Do REBT therapists practise in the privacy of their counselling rooms what they publicly say they do or state in print? I certainly have been guilty, at times, of not practising what I preach, teach or write about with regard to REBT. My idiosyncratic practice of REBT resembles general REBT, i.e. broad-based cognitive-behaviour therapy rather than authentic or preferential REBT, i.e., based on the centrality of the musts in emotional disturbance (Ellis & Dryden, 1997). Why this is so is explained in this chapter.

Moulding the therapeutic relationship
I routinely ask my clients if they have had previous experiences of therapy and what was helpful (e.g., 'He didn't judge me') and unhelpful (e.g., 'He didn't give straight answers to my questions') in order to build on the helpful elements and avoid repeating the unhelpful elements. In addition, I ask my clients what they expect from my role as their therapist (e.g., 'You sort me out') and what they see as their own role (e.g., 'I sit here and listen and do what you tell me to do'). Such information allows me to correct immediately clients' misunderstandings of their role in therapy and explain that the therapeutic relationship is based on collaboration — not necessarily or usually 50-50 at the start of therapy — and both of us need to put on our thinking caps if problem-solving solutions are to be

found (e.g., 'If I do all your thinking for you, what will happen when I'm no longer around to consult?'). From the first session onwards, I look for ways of giving more responsibility to the client for the running of therapy, as the essence of REBT is self-help.

I also build up a learning profile of my clients in order to create an optimum learning environment for them. For example, a client might say, 'I like things explained in a straightforward way, no jargon or big words', to which request I will do my best to purge my vocabulary of such encumbrances for the client; another client might want a 'get on with it' approach which means doing just that, while a third client prefers a more reflective approach to tackling his problems which involves allowing time for 'digesting one's thinking', i.e. creating a milieu in which 'thinking things through' is given sufficient time and attention (Neenan & Dryden, 2002).

I am also aware that forming a relationship needs to take into account a client's personality style in order for a productive 'fit' to emerge. For example, with a passive client I avoid being overly active-directive as this may increase his passivity instead of encouraging greater activity on his part; with a reactant client, who values autonomy and dominance, I offer lots of options so she feels she is in control of therapy and, following Dowd's (1996) advice, put her in charge of her own homework rather than engage in negotiation about it (the usual procedure in REBT).

A therapeutic relationship is not always a smooth one, so when alliance ruptures threaten or impasses emerge, I suggest to my clients that we should step back from the relationship and discuss what is happening within it. Safran & Muran (2000) call this process metacommunication, i.e. the relationship itself becomes the focus of collaborative exploration and discussion. It is my job to initiate and maintain this metacommunication but I encourage my clients to call 'time out' when they detect strain in the relationship.

Establishing SMART goals

Clients frequently state their goals in vague terms (e.g., 'I want to feel happier') or suggest ones that are outside of their control to achieve (e.g., 'I want my boss to treat me better'). In order to focus clients' minds on what is required in goal selection, I use SMART criteria for this purpose (Neenan & Dryden, 2000):

- Simple and specific
- Measurable
- Agreed
- Realistic
- Timescale

With regard to Realistic goals, these can be unrealistically ambitious (e.g., 'To always give perfect presentations') or unrealistically unambitious (e.g., 'Just to scrape by in my exam'). The former goal is probably unachievable (perfect presentations are given by imperfect people which means that presentations are unlikely to always be perfect) while achieving the latter goal is likely to be seen by the client as inconsequential or having no real sense of accomplishment (Cormier and Cormier, 1985). Goal theory suggests that people will be likely to work harder and thereby pull a better performance out of themselves if the goal is a challenging one (Butler and McManus, 1998). Therefore, in order to make a realistic goal become a reality, I follow Dryden's (1994) principle of challenging, but not overwhelming, goal-directed tasks, i.e. assignments that are sufficiently stimulating, given the client's present psychological state, to promote constructive change, but not so daunting as to inhibit her from carrying them out.

I point out to my clients that goals established at the outset of therapy are likely to change over the course of therapy as more information about their problems is obtained. I usually remind my clients in each session of their goals in order to determine if we are still on track to achieve them or if they are having second thoughts about them; this reminder also reinforces in clients' minds the purpose of therapy — what we have come together for — and helps to reduce client meandering and verbosity (see later section).

Clarifying the meaning of commitment

When goals have been agreed, the next step is to ascertain if the client is committed to achieving them. I ask the client for her definition of commitment (e.g., 'I'll try and give it a go') and compare it with my own ('Doing whatever it takes to achieve the goal'). Some clients are shocked or surprised by the stark differences in our respective definitions, but it does lead to a fruitful discussion of the likelihood of success when commitment to change is full-blooded, half-hearted or barely detectable.

I do not go as far as to encourage clients to sign a commitment contract (see Grieger, 1991), but just bringing up the idea indicates to the client the seriousness of the enterprise we are embarked upon. I also outline my commitment to the client: doing my professional best for her which may include fieldwork such as going into situations with her in order to help her overcome her agoraphobia. If clients are not committed to thinking and acting differently on a sustained basis, then enduring change is unlikely to occur. It is as simple as that.

Simplifying the 'ABCs' of REBT

I have never been in favour of using elaborate examples to teach the ABC model (see Dryden, 1995a, for such example using money and lateness) or explaining the complex interrelationships within the model (Ellis, 1991) and later refinements of the model (Ellis, 2001). I think such examples and explanations are complicated, turn REBT into a technical treatise and do not bring much enlightenment for clients about REBT. This conclusion is based on my own clinical experience of supervising countless session audiotapes of REBT therapists, both experienced and novice, struggling to teach 'complex' REBT to frequently bewildered clients. I like to teach the 'ABCs' of REBT in a straightforward manner, eschewing complexity whenever I can. For example, referring to an ABC example I have written on my whiteboard regarding two men who have been rejected by the same woman, I might say:

> The situation or 'A' is the same for both men but one of them believes 'B': 'I absolutely shouldn't have been rejected by her, but as I was, this means I'm worthless.' The second man believes 'B': 'It is unfortunate to have been rejected but there is no reason why I cannot be rejected. I will not reject myself because

she has.' Now, which man is likely to feel depressed and which one disappointed at 'C' and why?

I am usually Socratic to start with in teaching the ABC model as I want to see what beliefs the client suggests each man holds and then compare these with the REBT view in my didactic presentation. This approach engages clients in discussing the ABC model including their objections to it or misunderstandings about it (e.g., 'If they both felt depressed at 'C', then 'A' must have caused it'; possible reply: 'They're probably thinking something very similar at 'B' if they are both depressed at 'C'). The key point to get across to clients is that 'B' represents a choice regarding how they want to respond emotionally and behaviourally to 'A': irrational (self-defeating) beliefs and ideas maintain their emotional problems whereas rational (self-helping) beliefs and ideas ameliorate them.

We then apply the ABC model to a specific example of the client's target problem and further feedback is sought to see if he agrees that the model can help him to understand his current difficulties and show him a way of tackling them.

Finding convincing arguments to dispute clients' irrational beliefs
Disputing clients' irrational beliefs using logic, empiricism and pragmatism is to be found in many REBT texts (e.g., Dryden, 1995b; Ellis, 2001; Ellis & Dryden, 1997; Neenan & Dryden, 2001). While these three criteria provide guidance for clients (and students learning REBT) on how to dispute their irrational beliefs, it is easy for the client and/or therapist to slip into formulaic disputing (e.g., 'How does it logically follow?', 'Where is it written or where's the evidence?' and 'Where's it going to get you holding on to that belief?'). The client may see the sense in these arguments but is not convinced or aroused by them to the extent that a significant cognitive shift gets underway. To overcome this mechanical and somewhat dull approach to disputing, I like and follow Paul Hauck's advice:

> *Since brief counseling is largely a matter of getting the client to change irrational beliefs to rational ones, those points which the counselor makes and which turn the tide in the client's thinking are most powerful tools. Learn, therefore, which arguments are ignored by clients and which are respected [as] they open new views to an issue, views the client may never have been exposed to before* (1980, p.117).

For example, a client believed that she was worthless without a man in her life and standard REBT disputes were not making much of an impact upon her until I changed tack and asked her if she would teach this belief to her teenage daughter. Her reply was, 'Of course not.' Exploring why she would not do this (e.g., 'I don't want my daughter to be screwed up like me') and why she continued to teach it to herself (e.g., 'I suppose because I never thought about it any differently') started the process of belief change. She later said that the 'teenage daughter question was a shock that really got me thinking differently not only about my relationship with men but also what I was doing with my life'.

Another example is a client who says he does not have the time to carry out his homework, so I ask him whom he would like to meet most (e.g., 'David

Beckham') and would he find the time to meet him ('Yes')? Then I reply: 'He won't be coming, but you can now use the time to do your homework.' The point is not lack of time but of commitment (see above). David Beckham, even if he did turn up, is not likely to help the client overcome his panic attacks; the client is the agent responsible for his own change and this change will not occur if he does not find the time to execute his homework assignments. He has the time to maintain his problems but, apparently, not the time to overcome them. Whenever the client dragged his feet over carrying out his homework, he reminded himself that 'I can make time for David, so I can make time for myself' and carried out the assignments. Having many arguments to deploy in the disputing process, instead of relying on the standard ones, is one of my key interests as an REBT therapist (see Neenan & Dryden, 2002).

Encouraging clients to put rational beliefs into their own words
In my experience, textbook rational responses to irrational beliefs never sit easily with clients or myself. For example, a client who is challenging her approval needs might say (with prompting by or coaching from the therapist), 'I would prefer to have your approval, but there is no reason why I must have your approval. If I don't receive your approval this does not mean that I'm inadequate, but what it does mean is that I'm a fallible and unrateable human being who can accept herself irrespective of how others view me.' While I agree with the rational principles in this response, I certainly do not talk like that nor do my clients or probably the rest of the population. In order not to turn out 'rational robots', I ask clients to put rational statements into their own words — this makes such statements meaningful and easier to recall in problematic contexts. In the above example, the client's response to being disapproved of was 'Too bad' which, when explored, contained REBT's view of rationality (a desire but not a need for approval and self-acceptance in the face of disapproval) but in a highly condensed and idiosyncratic form.

Understanding how change occurs
Do clients instinctively understand how change occurs? Hanna observes that one of the fundamental mistakes made in therapy 'is to assume that clients understand change processes. If they did, change might be accomplished much quicker and easier on a routine basis' (2002, p.43). I ask clients how they think change occurs. Some typical replies are: 'Hard work', 'I don't know' (see below), 'Time heals', 'It just happens, doesn't it?' and 'That's what I'm paying you for!'

In order to clarify what change involves, I may ask the client to carry out an in-session experiment such as trying to write with his left hand when he has been right-handed all his life. The awkwardness and unnaturalness of this action is compared with developing a rational outlook when the client's irrational beliefs seem natural to him. In order for the client to become proficient with his left hand and gradually stop writing with his right hand, what does the client need to do? The client usually acknowledges that a lot of practice is required as well as tolerating the strangeness of becoming left-handed until he accepts it as a normal part of his repertoire. This process can be linked to internalising a rational outlook and attenuating his long-standing irrational beliefs.

Spending time on discussing what change involves prepares the client for what lies ahead as well as coping more successfully with blocks to change like cognitive-emotive dissonance (Grieger & Boyd, 1980), i.e. the clash or tension between old and new ways of thinking, feeling and behaving.

Combating 'I don't know'

Such a reply is to be expected but should be challenged. 'I don't know', if left unexplored, helps to perpetuate the client's problems by keeping her in a state of ignorance about what maintains them or what to do about them. The client has not found helpful answers to her problems outside of therapy, so I help her to find answers within it (after all, that is what I am being paid for). When I ask a client, for example, 'What do you get anxious about in that situation?' and she replies 'I don't know', my next question is: 'Would you like to find out?' Clients usually readily agree and they say something like, 'That's what I'm here for'. Thereafter, the number of 'don't knows' steadily declines over the course of therapy, as clients are more active in searching for answers to their problems.

However, some clients seem to be on automatic pilot and many of my questions are met with an 'I don't know'. With these clients, I unobtrusively time the latency period between asking a question and receiving a reply — sometimes a reply is received as soon as I have finished asking my question. To which I respond: 'Have you given my question due care and consideration before delivering your reply?' When I ask the original question again, the client may now wait a couple of minutes, seemingly absorbed in exploring my question, but then says, 'See I told you, I don't know.' Then I ask for a detailed account of how he processed my question, which often reveals that the client's mind was elsewhere, e.g., thinking about what he will be doing that evening.

'I don't know' is often a form of mental laziness, i.e. the reluctance of some clients to expend mental effort in exploring questions in order to gain knowledge about their problems which will ultimately help them to find solutions to these problems. The bottom line for such clients is this: their mental life in therapy (and beyond) should be effortful, not effortless, if constructive change is to occur and be maintained.

Looking for ways to encourage clients to take responsibility for their problems

When clients blame others or events for their emotional problems, they have, in effect, relinquished control over how they feel, e.g., 'I didn't upset myself: it was my wife who made me angry when she forgot to take my suit to the dry cleaners.' If others can make you feel a certain way, I try and 'make' my clients feel how I would like them to: 'Now, I want you to feel happy that your wife forgot to take your suit to the dry cleaners.' Clients usually protest that this is not how they feel about a particular situation and, therefore, I am unable to 'give' them feelings. When clients eventually agree that it is how they evaluate a situation or the actions of others that is the key factor in determining how they feel, then the first glimmerings of responsibility emerge. If responsibility means not blaming others for one's feelings, then it also means not blaming oneself for one's feelings and problems. A therapeutic definition of responsibility that I suggest to my clients is 'response-ability' (Glover, 1988): 'You have the ability to respond in different ways to this situation once you claim ownership of the problem.'

With clients who were on the receiving end of others' actions (e.g., sexual abuse, being mugged) and insist there was nothing they could do at the time, how they think and act in the aftermath of these events is within their control. To get this point across I might say:

> Imagine a car crashing into your car and your car then bursts into flames. Will you expect the other driver to rescue you because he crashed into you or will you try to free yourself? Or someone throws a brick through your window; do you expect that person to repair your window and clean up the mess on your carpet or will those tasks be undertaken by you?

If some clients still refuse to take responsibility for their problems because 'I didn't cause this situation, others did', I often use the famous example of Viktor Frankl's experiences in Auschwitz. Despite the appalling situation he was in, he stated that the Nazis could not deprive him of 'the last of the human freedoms — to choose one's attitude in any given set of circumstances, to choose one's own way' (1985, p.86). I sometimes suggest survivor literature to clients who seemingly refuse to budge on this issue of responsibility and point out to them that by continuing to blame others, they perpetuate their perceived powerlessness to find solutions to their problems or effect any constructive change within their present circumstances.

When clients do claim ownership of their problems, it does not automatically follow that they will undertake a programme of work to tackle these problems (known as therapeutic responsibility) or 'How to undisturb myself'. I can assist clients in this process but I cannot do it for them; that is their task.

Looking for ways to increase homework compliance

Burns suggests 'that compliance with self-help assignments may be the most important predictor of therapeutic success' (1989, p.545). In order to increase homework compliance, I do my best to negotiate homework assignments that clients will find interesting. I might suggest several of them and ask the client to take his pick or add his own to give a wider spread of options. For example, a client called herself a 'freak' because she was unhappy with her appearance and did not like walking down her local high street as she thought others would stare at her. She knew she was 'being silly' but could not convince herself that her beliefs were false. I suggested she could:

1. Walk slowly down the high street with her head up to observe what was actually happening instead of rushing with her head down and thereby imagining what was going on (e.g., people staring at her and making unkind comments).

2. While out walking, ask several people the time and monitor their reactions.

3. Bring attention to herself by sitting on a bench outside the library for ten minutes.

4. Get into a queue in the local supermarket so she would be close to people for several minutes.

5. Make smalltalk with the person behind the counter when buying a newspaper (her suggestion).

She chose option two and reported that no one ran away, fainted or vomited when she asked them the time; this reaction from others, which contradicted her catastrophic predictions, encouraged her to be more ambitious (she next chose option four).

When negotiating homework, I remember that the client has a life outside of therapy and therefore the assignment has to be fitted into his other activities rather than take precedence over them. I emphasise to my clients that homework is about learning, *not* success or failure — learning occurs whatever the outcome of homework. Following Padesky's and Greenberger's advice (1995), I do not ask clients to do assignments they are unwilling to do or that I would not be willing to do myself.

Greater homework compliance can be encouraged by starting the homework in the session, e.g., if a client is procrastinating over beginning an essay for college, I usually suggest that he starts the essay twenty or thirty minutes before the session ends. This not only uncovers blocks to task initiation which can be tackled there and then but also boosts the client's efforts to complete the essay in his own time. As Judith Beck observes, initiating a task is usually harder than continuing it because 'patients often describe the hardest part of doing homework as the period *just* before they start it — that is, motivating themselves to get started' (1995, p.256; emphasis in original).

When a client refuses to do a homework assignment, I avoid getting into an argument over it (e.g., 'Look, how do you expect to make progress if you don't do any work outside of therapy?'), and suggest that not doing homework can be seen as an experiment: what will be the impact on the client's problems — stasis or progress? The results of the experiment can be reviewed in a week's time. In my experience, such clients often say I am being ridiculous and then assign themselves some homework. If this does not happen, I will stick by the experiment. If a few clients consistently do not carry out their homework, I explore the likely consequences for them (e.g., remaining emotionally disturbed) and, if they have children, why do they insist on their children doing their school homework while not undertaking their own therapeutic homework?

Encouraging change: not necessarily profound or philosophical
The REBT literature heavily emphasises philosophical change, whether situationally or generally, and ridding oneself of all musturbatory (musts) thinking and its derivatives is a profound change indeed. As I have written elsewhere (Neenan, 2001), much valuable therapy time can be wasted as therapists attempt to encourage clients to strive for profound change while clients' interests lie elsewhere (e.g., more modest change). Sometimes musturbatory thinking plays little, if any, part in my work with my clients. For example, helping clients with panic disorder to learn how to non-catastrophically interpret their symptoms through experiment, exposure and education usually

brings good results; it would seem absurd to me to dispute the presumed belief, 'I must not have a heart attack and die', when developing benign explanations for a pounding heart are both more helpful and convincing for clients (Clark, 1996).

I believe that REBT should emphasise a broad range of problem-solving approaches (as I do in my work) rather than focus narrowly on uprooting rigid musts and shoulds because REBTers have to face the possibly unpalatable fact that 'there are no empirical studies to support the claim that absolute musts are causal factors in any form of psychological disturbance' (Wessler, 1996, p.46) and that the primacy of the musts hypothesis is currently untestable (Bond & Dryden, 1996). Some clients do reject the musturbatory hypothesis and, when this occurs, I then focus on the ideas that these clients *do* find disturbance-producing (e.g., 'Everyone is against me'; 'I never do anything right'). Insisting to clients that the 'musts are there' if only they would work harder (or be more compliant) to find them would suggest evidence of a closed mind that seeks to prove REBT theory right.

The musts and shoulds are supposed to be primary in emotional disturbance and the derivatives, flowing from these premises, to be secondary. Like so much else in REBT, this is a matter of conjecture rather than fact. What I am concerned about is to engage the client — I work on the assumption that the current session could be the last one — and work where her focus is. In my experience, clients more readily reveal derivatives, particularly self-depreciation, than musts or shoulds. If a client believes, for example, she is a failure for making mistakes, I advance the hypothesis, based on REBT theory, that this negative self-evaluation occurs because she demands that she must or should not make mistakes. If the client sees that REBT theory makes sense to her and agrees to work on both parts of her irrational belief (demand and derivative), then all well and good.

However, a significant number of my clients insist that what they actually say is, 'I don't want to make mistakes.' In the past, I have spent considerable time trying to convince such clients that what they were actually doing (because REBT theory says so and, therefore, I knew best) was converting wants into demands and thereby disturbing themselves about making mistakes. As with Wessler above, the research tells a different story:

> As scientist practitioners, empirically investigating theory to guide practice, REBT practitioners need to practice what they preach to their clients. It would be an act of hypocrisy to believe that the shoulds are the primary source of emotional disturbance if there is poor evidence to support it. To date there is a paucity of empirical evidence to support the axiom that DEM [demands] are the primary source of disturbance. Is it appropriate then for the practitioner to be primarily looking for the shoulds? Based on the evidence it seems not. Until there is reason to believe to the contrary, it appears to be more appropriate for the practitioner to also look for, and dispute, the other REBT evaluations of AWF [awfulizing], LFT [low frustration tolerance] and SD [self-downing] to be effective (O'Kelly, Joyce and Greaves 1998, p.232).

In my experience, it is self-downing that seems to be at the core of so many clients' problems and self-downing statements usually ring loud and clear in their minds in contrast to the frequent silence of the musts and shoulds. A lot of my time is spent on teaching clients self-acceptance. I believe that teaching self-acceptance is one of the greatest services that REBT offers to its clients. Generally speaking, I find that I spend more time working on derivative beliefs than on premise beliefs. Furthermore, if some clients are not persuaded they are subscribing to any derivative beliefs, then we elicit the ideas they are troubled by (this approach minimises the besetting sin of REBT therapists which is to put words into clients' mouths). Therapy should not become stalled or strained because some clients do not agree with the REBT framework.

Tackling verbosity

'The ability to speak succinctly is a problem for many patients' (Walen, DiGiuseppe and Dryden, 1992, p.79). If clients are to become their own therapist, it is essential that they train themselves to detect, dispute and act against the key maintaining factors (beliefs and behaviours) that largely determine their emotional problems; in other words, cutting to the chase (therapy is not an extension of their social life where their minds can roam wherever). It is true that clients want to tell their stories but not every aspect of the story is equally important — the emotional hot spots in the story are the main focus.

As soon as I have gained an understanding of the client's presenting problem, and the client agrees that I have this understanding, I encourage him to shift from unstructured to structured self-exploration through the use of the ABC model (Neenan & Dryden, 2001). Some clients object to their stream of consciousness style being channelled through the model as too constricting but, as I usually point out to them, 'endless talk' has not proved helpful so far in ameliorating their problems. It is the 'B' that is at the centre of our clinical attention, not the narrative or 'A' (e.g., 'What exactly were *you* angry about with your partner's behaviour? Put it in a sentence for me').

I endeavour to make my questions and didactic presentations clear and concise in order to encourage my clients to reply in kind. I ask them to interrupt me if I ramble on or my communication is unclear — we have an interruption agreement. Cutting to the chase helps the client to concentrate her mind and efforts on becoming an effective problem-solver and this means, among other things, that she will spend less time in therapy.

I have explained my idiosyncratic practice of REBT which, in turn, requires an idiosyncratic understanding of the client, so that he or she is not fitted into the REBT model but, instead, REBT is tailored to the uniqueness of the client (Neenan & Dryden, 1999).

References

Beck, J. S. (1995). *Cognitive Therapy: Basics and Beyond.* New York: Guilford.

Bond, F. W. & Dryden, W. (1996). Why two, central REBT hypotheses appear untestable. *Journal of Rational-Emotive & Cognitive-Behavior Therapy*, *14* (1), 29–40.

Burns, D. D. (1989). *The Feeling Good Handbook.* New York: William Morrow.

Butler, G. & McManus, F. (1998). *Psychology: A Very Short Introduction.* Oxford: Oxford University Press.

Clark, D. M. (1996). Panic disorder: From theory to therapy. In P. M. Salkovskis (ed.), *Frontiers of Cognitive Therapy* (pp. 318–44). New York: Guilford.

Cormier, W. H. & Cormier, L. S. (1985). *Interviewing Strategies for Helpers: Fundamental Skills and Cognitive Behavioral Interventions,* (2nd edn.) Monterey, CA: Brooks/Cole.

Dowd, E. T. (1996). Resistance and reactance in cognitive therapy. *International Cognitive Therapy Newsletter 10* (3), 3–5.

Dryden, W. (1994). *Progress in Rational Emotive Behaviour Therapy.* London: Whurr.

Dryden, W. (1995a). *Preparing for Client Change in Rational Emotive Behaviour Therapy.* London: Whurr.

Dryden, W. (1995b). *Brief Rational Emotive Behaviour Therapy.* Chichester: Wiley.

Ellis, A. (1991). The revised ABC's of rational-emotive therapy. *Journal of Rational-Emotive & Cognitive-Behavior Therapy, 9* (3), 139–172.

Ellis, A. (2001). *Feeling Better, Getting Better, Staying Better.* Atascadero, CA: Impact.

Ellis, A. & Dryden, W. (1997). *The Practice of Rational Emotive Behaviour Therapy,* (2nd edn.) New York: Springer.

Frankl, V. E. (1985). *Man's Search for Meaning.* New York: Washington Square Press.

Glover, M. (1988). Responsibility and therapy. In W. Dryden & P. Trower (eds.), *Developments in Cognitive Psychotherapy* (pp. 106–127). London: Sage.

Grieger, R. M. (1991). Keys to effective RET. In M. E. Bernard (ed.), *Using Rational-Emotive Therapy Effectively: A Practitioner's Guide* (pp. 35–67). New York: Plenum.

Grieger, R. & Boyd, J. (1980). *Rational-Emotive Therapy: A Skills Based Approach.* New York: Van Nostrand Reinhold.

Hanna, F. J. (2002). *Therapy with Difficult Clients.* Washington, DC: American Psychological Association.

Hauck, P. A. (1980). *Brief Counseling with RET.* Philadelphia, PA: Westminster Press.

Neenan, M. (2001). REBT 45 years on: Still on the sidelines. *Journal of Rational-Emotive & Cognitive-Behavior Therapy, 19* (1), 31–41.

Neenan, M. & Dryden, W. (1999). *Rational Emotive Behaviour Therapy: Advances in Theory and Practice.* London: Whurr.

Neenan, M. & Dryden, W. (2000). *Essential Rational Emotive Behaviour Therapy.* London: Whurr.

Neenan, M. & Dryden, W. (2001). *Learning from Errors in Rational Emotive Behaviour Therapy.* London: Whurr.

Neenan, M. & Dryden, W. (2002). *Cognitive Behaviour Therapy: An A-Z of Persuasive Arguments.* London: Whurr.

O'Kelly, M., Joyce, M. R. & Greaves, D. (1998). The primacy of the 'shoulds': Where is the evidence? *Journal of Rational-Emotive & Cognitive-Behavior Therapy, 16* (4), 223–34.

Padesky, C. A. & Greenberger, D. (1995). *Clinician's Guide to Mind over Mood.* New York: Guilford.

Safran, J. D. & Muran, J. C. (2000). *Negotiating the Therapeutic Alliance.* New York: Guilford.

Walen, S. R., DiGiuseppe, R. & Dryden, W. (1992). *A Practitioner's Guide to Rational-Emotive Therapy,* (2nd edn.). New York: Oxford University Press.

Wessler, R. L. (1996). Idiosyncratic definitions and unsupported hypotheses: Rational emotive behavior therapy as pseudoscience. *Journal of Rational-Emotive & Cognitive-Behavior Therapy, 14* (1), 41–61.

10

Kristene A. Doyle

This chapter will focus on my idiosyncratic practice of Rational Emotive Behavior Therapy (REBT). Although I am relatively young in the field, I have devoted much of my time to chiseling out a unique style of practising REBT, doing my best to incorporate my personality into such practice. After reviewing my caseload, both past and present, I have narrowed down the list of idiosyncrasies to the following:

i.   deeming the client as expert from the start;

ii.   incorporating social psychology into my practice;

iii. encouraging my clients to assertively speak up during sessions;

iv.   use of self-disclosure;

v.   referring back to client goals;

vi.   listening to the client's language;

vii. use of client background in the development of homework assignments;

viii. the high-energy therapist;

ix.   the use of reinforcement;

x.   the formal/informal issue;

xi.   the session as a television series;

xii. the use of humor.

While many REBT practitioners probably utilize many of these strategies throughout the course of treatment, I have determined that these twelve points are most important in my practice. Due to space limitations, I have only touched on each point and done my best to emphasize the key points.

Introduction
In preparation for an interview at the Albert Ellis Institute for their internship program, I borrowed the Masters Therapist videos from a professor and watched them assiduously, afraid even one trip to the refrigerator would leave me in 'REBT darkness.' What I distinctly recall from each of those tapes is Raymond DiGiuseppe's speech on the varying styles of REBT practice, as well as the importance of incorporating your own personality into your practice. I have taken those words seriously. For the last seven years I have worked on developing my personal style of REBT — ever so aware that my style was in fact at times somewhat different from those around me.
   Almost immediately it becomes clear that the theory of REBT is one that

was designed with the intention of *teaching* it to clients; teach it to clients for their use outside of therapy sessions. REBT, in my opinion, resolves the problem often seen in psychoanalysis of 'lifers' — clients who engage in therapy for thirty or so years. With that in mind, the theory of REBT is not complicated, not mysterious, not something that only a trained clinician can use. It is a simple theory that makes sense and is easily adaptable. Therefore, I believe that there are other distinctive qualities that unravel in the therapy session; qualities that separate one REBT therapist from another. The focus of this chapter will be to demonstrate what I believe to be the twelve idiosyncrasies of my practice of REBT.

Deeming the client as expert from the start

Building a therapeutic alliance with my clients is one of my most important goals. Research has indicated that the therapeutic alliance is one of the most important, if not the most important, factors in outcome (Safran & Muran, 2000). In fact, the therapeutic alliance has been described as 'the quintessential integrative variable' (Wolfe & Goldfried, 1988). At the onset of therapy, I treat the client as the expert in terms of his/her cognitive, emotive, and behavioral experiences. In fact, I often will say to my client, 'You are the expert here. You tell me what you were thinking and feeling.' The purpose of this is to build a collaborative relationship whereby my client assumes responsibility for change. I make a distinction between being an expert in psychological theory and disorders and a client being an expert on him/herself. I have found that by doing so, as a therapist I appear more on the same plane as my clients and they are less threatened by me. Clients with a background of psychoanalysis especially react to this approach. A sense of empowerment evolves for the client that is often a strong motivator throughout the change process.

I must stress, however, that there are times when clients are uninformed or uneducated about varying emotions, at which point I assume some role as expert for the sake of explanation. Even so, while doing this, I consistently refer back to the client to assist me in teasing out which emotions are experienced most frequently and which emotions are hardly ever experienced. Using personal examples from the client's life help to make this exercise quickly understood. There is never an assumption on my part that I know more than the client in terms of his or her experiences.

Approaching clients as the expert has been quite helpful with clients who have a history of neediness and dependency, as well as a lack of assertion. Shifting the responsibility from therapist to client for determining what irrational beliefs and dysfunctional negative emotions they are experiencing at any given moment models a more adaptive way of operating for the client. Furthermore, a collaborative relationship is fostered by taking such an approach. I tell my clients to view me as a facilitator who may be utilized to help discern *what* the client is telling him/herself at various times, rather than *that* the client is telling him/herself something.

Incorporating social psychology into my practice

In the more recent years, I have developed an interest in the experimental findings of social psychology. Given that REBT therapists dedicate much of their sessions to disputing irrational beliefs, the social psychology research findings on persuasion may be applicable. Richard Petty and John Cacioppo's (1986) theory of the Elaboration Likelihood Model can be useful when working with clients on disputing irrational beliefs. According to the model, we are inclined to think deeply about a persuasive argument if the issue is one that is relevant and important to us. The theory posits that there are two major routes to persuasion, the central route and the peripheral route. The central route relies on solid arguments based on relevant facts and figures and involves the prudent, thoughtful deliberation of *message content*. The central route gets people to think about their issues. High elaboration indicates the central route, and requires that the receiver have both motivation and the ability to process the message carefully. On the other hand, the peripheral route involves simple cues (e.g., an attractive source), and takes short cuts in cognitive processing. Therefore, rather than attempting to engage a person's thinking, cues are provided that stimulate acceptance of the argument without much thinking (Fraser & Burchell, 2001). Low elaboration indicates the peripheral route and is likely in the absence of motivation and ability. When I first begin working with a client, there are several important pieces of information that I obtain to help determine which route to take. I gather information on the type of job or employment they have, as well as whether or not they were self-referred for therapy or they have been coerced (e.g., adolescents). Depending on this information, I will purposefully choose one route over another.

I also take into account communicator variables when conducting therapy. Based on the finding that a communicator can be effective if it is clear that the person has nothing to gain (and perhaps something to lose) by persuading someone, after presenting an empirical dispute (i.e., where is the evidence for this belief?), or logical dispute (i.e., how does it logically follow that because you *want* something it therefore *must* be that way?), I will very casually and almost apathetically state something like the following to my client: 'Look, go ahead and continue thinking the way you are. I'm not losing *anything* by you maintaining your belief on this issue or continuing to engage in this behavior. In fact, it's hard work for me to challenge your beliefs — so let's move on to another area, okay? What else would you like to work on?' I have clients who at times dedicate more of their session to disagreeing with me and trying to prove that they are correct, rather than listening to my words and arguments. It is often when I stop the back-and-forth banter and appear to 'give in', that my clients get concerned and actually begin to listen to disputes and entertain the idea of incorporating them into their behavioral repertoires. Some critics of this approach may find it to be manipulative, and in fact I would argue that being manipulative is precisely what I set out to do when it comes to helping my clients. I manipulate (i.e., persuade) them into seeing that their current way of thinking and feeling is self-defeating. I must emphasize that it is not *I* who decides what beliefs and feelings are self-defeating, but rather my clients who make such a decision. If, however, during the course of therapy, I see that other irrational beliefs or self-defeating behaviors exist for the client that he/she has not identified during goal formulation, I discuss this with my client and determine whether or not we should work on them.

Encouraging my clients to assertively speak up during session

One of the most important practices I engage in is encouraging all clients to indicate when they do not understand something I have said, or when they disagree with something I propose. I believe a dangerous assumption therapists can make during session is that a silent client is one who is 'taking it all in.' I make it a special point to periodically check in with clients, asking them to tell me what it is they believe they heard me say, or their opinion on a topic or statement I have made. When clients speak up during the session and challenge something I have said, it becomes clear that a collaborative relationship is either being established or has been established. I suggest that this assertive communication in conjunction with treating the client as expert are key ingredients to a client working on his/her irrational beliefs and self-defeating behaviors. In addition to checking in during a session, I will often follow up with clients after a particularly 'hot' session, and ask for feedback or thoughts. One reason for doing so is to shape the behavior of thinking about and reflecting on issues that arise during the session throughout the course of the week. Most of my clients, with the exception of those who have a dire need for approval (a point I will return to in a moment), will comment on a particular behavior or statement I made in a previous session that offended them. I believe that this speaks to the therapeutic relationship and the sense of trust between clients and myself. One area that I have worked hard at improving is not becoming defensive when a client brings up feeling offended by something I have said or done. Listening to what the client says and accepting responsibility for my behaviors is one way in which I try to model an adaptive response. Returning to those clients with a dire need for approval, one assumption I operate from during session with such clients is that they probably won't speak up during a session due to their irrational belief(s). As such, after teaching them disputations and seeing that progress has occurred at some level, I make a special effort to *in fact* offend them, as a means of providing a forum for them to practice out their newly acquired skills. By no means do I take this exercise to an extreme level, but rather just enough to push the client to try out a newly formed behavior.

Use of self-disclosure

Self-disclosure can be one of the most powerful strategies in facilitating change with your clients. Of course, knowing why you disclose what you do (i.e., having a rationale for disclosing particular information) preferably should be a prerequisite for self-disclosure on the part of the therapist. Many of my clients know about key events in my life that have shaped my thinking, emotions, and behaviors. I will often draw upon a personal event to help make a point. Furthermore, I have found through informal assessment of my clients that by self-disclosing, clients feel more comfortable with me and see me in less of a mysterious manner. Through my self-disclosures, clients have come to see me just as fallible as they are, and in fact are encouraged to change. Many report feeling optimistic that I have experienced some very negative activating events and have managed to move beyond them. In fact, I will often incorporate an exercise into my self-disclosure, with the goal of maintaining the session on an REBT level. For example, after self-disclosing a particular behavior in response to a very aversive activating event, I might ask my client to identify what I might have been telling myself during that time to contribute to my dysfunctional negative emotions and self-defeating behaviors. I then go on to ask how I might have gotten myself out of the situation to a point where I am right now. This exercise has been effective in the past, perhaps because it demonstrates that even 'shrinks' have problems, and that most problems can be overcome via disputation and a commitment to change.

It is not uncommon for clients to refer back to a vivid experience that I have spoken about months prior, and use that as a springboard for their own progress.

The strategy of self-disclosure may be especially helpful for clients in individual therapy because they do not have the opportunity to experience the therapeutic factor of Universality (i.e., the disconfirmation of a client's uniqueness in their horrible nature) the way they might in group therapy (Yalom, 1994).

Referring back to client goals

During the initial session, formulation of specific goals is essential. Once this is done, together we will break down each goal into smaller sub-goals. When possible, I will have the client operationally define the terms they use. If, after gathering background information and listening to what the client is presenting, I determine that additional goals would be constructive, I bring this up at this point, explaining the reasons for such additional goals. Together with the client, we rank the goals in order of importance, taking into consideration the importance of achieving some symptom relief and some experience of success. Doing so increases the likelihood that the client will return the following week and will complete homework assignments.

The formulation of goals is important not only for symptom relief and philosophical change, but also for minimizing the occurrence of 'lingerers' — individuals who stay in therapy beyond its utility and simply 'report' on the weekly or daily occurrences. When I find this to be the case, it is helpful to be able to return to the goals and determine whether or not they were accomplished. If it is discovered that indeed the goals were in fact met, then the client has to make a decision: either formulate new goals to work on, or terminate therapy. This may sound harsh to the reader, but I believe that this approach keeps both myself as the therapist and my client focused and working during sessions.

Listening to the client's language

One technique I employ rather diligently is that of paying close attention to the client's use of language as they speak. Furthermore, I train my clients to do the same, often giving homework assignments involving tuning in to their internal and external dialogue. When and if they do detect any all-or-nothing thinking, overgeneralizations, or global ratings, they are to alter their language immediately. At times my clients find this in-session behavior irritating, but at the risk of sounding therapist-centered, too bad! I consistently stop them as they are speaking and do one of two interventions:

1. correct their use of language
   a. client: . . . and I've *never* had a successful relationship . . .
   b. therapist: . . . and I've *not yet* had a relationship that I deem successful . . .

2. ask them to stop and think about what they just said
    a. client: . . . I'm totally unassertive and I hate that about my self . . .
    b. therapist: . . . just stop for a moment, look at what you just stated, and see if you could change it a bit . . .
    c. client: I'm unassertive at work, a behavior I am dissatisfied with, but there are areas where I am assertive, such as in my relationship . . .

The first time I carry out this type of intervention, I explain its rationale to clients. What I have found is that, for the most part, this procedure becomes an accepted aspect of my practice of REBT. Clients become accustomed to it, and adopt it for their own use. Occasionally, a client will find such an intervention more of a disruption than helpful. This point should be taken into account, and timing of the intervention is crucial. If a client is in the heart of recounting a highly charged emotional event, or identifying his/her beliefs about a particular activating event, you may best be served to wait until he/she has finished speaking to highlight the language issue. I have found that immediate intervention works optimally after you have been working with a client for some time and have identified their core underlying irrational schema.

Use of client background in the development of homework assignments
Homework assignments, being a crucial component to REBT practice, require thought and effort on the part of the therapist. It is too easy, though not a bad idea, to assign clients to identify and dispute irrational thinking as it occurs throughout the course of the week. I believe homework assignments should be idiosyncratic to each client, and should be as creative as possible to increase the likelihood that they are actually completed. Some of my most successful assignments have been those that actually mean something to the client. One way to achieve this is to incorporate the client's background in terms of employment or hobbies into the design of the assignment. For example, one client I have been working with on and off for a number of years is employed as an advertiser. His main function is to work at ad agencies and come up with catchy persuasive commercials to sell products. One of his main irrational beliefs is that 'I must be with a woman (and an attractive one at that) for me to be worthwhile as an individual.' After sessions of disputing this irrational belief and out of session homework assignments to do the same, I came to the conclusion that this client, who knew REBT theory better than some of the therapists in the building (the author of this article excluded of course), was, simply put, bored. He had been doing REBT for many years, and had seen, heard, and done just about every homework assignment known to REBTkind. So I was forced to be creative. This client was given the assignment to create a commercial with the theme of the rational alternative for his irrational belief. I had him 'show' me the commercial at our next session, as if I was the audience he was trying to convince. He was very energized by this assignment, and indicated to me that he began to look at his thinking in a new light.

Another example of utilizing a client's background/employment is demonstrated with a 21-year-old college student majoring in creative writing, with a dire need for approval from men. She indicated during the first session that she loves drama in her life, and often seeks it out, even though most of the time it was self-defeating. In this instance, I had this client create a story beginning with her irrational beliefs, develop several characters through a series of dramatic events, and have the story end on a more rational level. Once she completed this assignment, she agreed that she could live out her desire for drama through the characters in her stories that she created, and that she no longer needed the approval of men to feel okay about herself. She left that crazy idea to the fictional characters in her stories.

Although I may be the one who initially develops idiosyncratic homework assignments for my clients, like the rest of my REBT practice, I eventually make it the client's responsibility to create their assignments. This transfer of responsibility solidifies any philosophical changes occurring in and out of session, and further ensures that clients will continue to work once therapy has terminated. Furthermore, it demonstrates to me that the client has actually incorporated REBT theory into their everyday existence.

The high-energy therapist
One of my distinct traits as an individual as well as a therapist is being highly caffeinated (I prefer 'high on life'). Besides letting me squeeze a few more hours out of every day, being caffeinated or energetic serves me as a therapist as well. When working with clients who are depressed, and consequently lethargic or simply 'down', my activity level balances us out. I have found in the past that clients who are quite depressed have actually brought me down in the session as well, and we are both dragging. Disputation is never as forceful under those circumstances, and being totally honest, time seems to go by at a depressed pace. This can't be good for the client, myself, or our work together.

In addition to bringing up the energy in the room, being caffeinated and consequently energetic has had the effect of providing many of my clients hope in their own lives. Clients have indicated that seeing me so 'bouncy' and 'up' helps them to believe that they too can reach that point some time. I reinforce this idea, but add to it the importance of working hard at challenging their beliefs and completing homework assignment. I play off of the idea 'act how you want to feel' and discuss this with my clients. If you want to feel up, energetic, and positive, act that way (and in the course of doing so, drink lots of Diet Coke and coffee).

The use of reinforcement
Reinforcement, a concept vastly discussed throughout the psychology literature (Goldfried & Davison, 1994), is taken very seriously in my practice of REBT. When a client reports on making some progress in any area that they are working on, verbal praise and, at times, a standing ovation (see 'The high-energy therapist' above) is given. Even if a client does not complete an entire assignment, some praise is in order, in an effort to increase the probability that he/she will continue to work towards the goals outlined during the initial session. Reinforcement of the progress is made, and almost immediately following this, a discussion occurs regarding the obstacles or impediments that got in the way of full completion of the assignment. In my perspective, this is a modified version of the method of successive approximations.

   In addition to verbal reinforcement, it is a little well-known fact throughout the Albert Ellis Institute among staff as well as my clients, that I have an impressive stash of candy available at all times. Let me say right away that I am sensitive to my clients who have eating disorders and remove such temptations and symbols of self-defeat prior to their sessions. However, for the majority of my clients (most of whom are adults), they reward themselves after a session with a KitKat or some tootsie rolls. In fact, many have commented that they worked hard in the session and that 'they deserve it.' While I am well aware that some of the psychoanalytic literature admonishes clinicians to avoid using food as a reinforcer, I have found that my clients look forward to coming to session. Many will come charging in to the session and head straight for the candy, indicating that they can't talk until they have a piece. Some will go for a piece as they are discussing a topic or issue that is very difficult for them. This reminds me of working with children who will often use some toy as a distraction when talking about something they perceive to be overwhelming. Food has been described as having a consoling, comforting effect for people. It is no surprise that a person would call upon it if available when discussing 'hot' issues. However, I would like to emphasize that if I notice that a client is discussing a particular unhealthy negative emotion, or describing an especially aversive activating event, and in the process goes for a piece of candy, I will make it a point to bring this up to the client. Socratically I will attempt to have the client make a connection between perhaps Low Frustration Tolerance for a particular feeling and the subsequent distraction of food.

The formal/informal issue
Overall, I would argue that my style of REBT practice is quite informal. I never bought into the idea that I am an expert in a particular area, but rather, I have certain specialty areas. I ask that my clients refer to me by first name (unless they have a particular reason for not wanting to do so), and allow my clients to do whatever they want during their session (i.e., lay on the couch, pace back and forth as they are thinking, take their shoes off, etc.). However, this style certainly does not preclude taking on a more formal approach when the necessity arises. Because I look quite young, it is not uncommon for some older clients to question whether or not I can be of any help to them due to what they wrongly believe as limited life experience. In such cases, I have found that what works best is to present myself according to my educational background, discuss my credentials, and then agree that if they believe that they will not be able to be helped by me they probably should see someone older (due to their expectational set). Upon doing this, most have decided to 'give me a shot' at therapy and see what happens. Most end up staying, some end up leaving. Regardless, it is not being defensive when a client presents this issue that is the key to keeping such clients. By appearing as if I don't 'need' a client and am not desperate for the experience, clients begin to get curious as to what that all means. Their curiosity often keeps them returning to therapy.

   When working with kids, I especially take on a more informal role, being aware of the negative connotation the word 'doctor' can mean for children. Being seen in a different light from teachers, parents, and other adults is important for the work to be done in therapy to actually get done. By 'normalizing' who I am for children, and acting more like a 'cool adult', disputes and other interventions may be more credible. Having children and their parents call me by my first name is one way to alleviate anxiety. On the flip side, if I find that parents are being somewhat resistant to treatment and interventions and believe it is my job to 'fix their child' and all the problems are the child's, a more formal approach is warranted. At this point, being backed by my credentials helps convince some parents that although I might not be a parent, I have been trained in issues regarding discipline and child management strategies that they have not. This is not to create a back-and-forth power contest, but rather to assist parents in assuming some responsibility (even if it boils down to supporting their child) in their child's problems.

One final note about the formal/informal issue; when I am working with a client of a different ethnic background, I leave it up to them on how formal/ informal they would prefer me to be. I will also not hesitate to ask such clients what is typical/acceptable practice in their culture in terms of this issue.

The session as a television series
In general, I approach my practice with the viewpoint that I have the luxury of not being emotionally involved in my client's issues, and have the ability to be an excellent listener with a very good memory for details. At the risk of totally delegitimizing my reputation, or of minimizing client pain, I will confess that I approach each of client sessions as a 45 minute comedy/drama depending on the problems targeted for change. By doing so, I have been able to recall particular names and events that clients have mentioned in passing while discussing an activating event, and use such information several sessions later when I check up on particular issues or during a disputation. This use of personal information as well as the timing of it has served well in terms of the therapeutic alliance. Clients tend to appreciate such attention to detail and perhaps believe that they are really being understood. Some other REBT therapists may dismiss this approach as being too overly focused on detail. My response to such potential criticism is that it is just enough detail to convince a client that you are listening. In addition, on some level I believe such attention and recall of the details makes the therapy experience all the more 'real' for clients and brings issues home for them. While I am not in the habit of, nor do I endorse the idea of, external motivation, I don't have much problem with the idea that a client may work a little harder in the beginning of the course of therapy because he/she believes that I am working hard at paying attention to them and remembering details that they consider to be important in their personal lives. My hope is that somewhere along the way, external motivation (if that is actually what is happening) transforms into internal motivation. Viewing and treating clients as expert, as well as designing homeworks specific to clients, may help facilitate this transformation.

The use of humor
One intervention that Ellis writes about and utilizes is the use of humor with clients (Ellis, 2001). I find this to be an especially helpful strategy with clients who come to therapy with a 'psychologically heavy' attitude; in other words, those clients who are so entrenched in their problems that they fail to see the humor in some aspects of it. Of course, I stress to my clients when using humor that I am not laughing at them, per se, but rather, at some of their thinking or some of the events that they experience. It is rare that a client reacts negatively to

this behavior, although it does indeed occur. In such instances I immediately stop everything and clarify what is going on. For some clients, humor is not the way to go. For many clients, humor can be the most helpful therapeutic technique, if I dare call it that. However, I must stress that I have found humor as an intervention to be *most* powerful *after* I have taught the B→C connection and have worked with the client to identify and dispute irrational thinking and dysfunctional negative emotions. Humor during the initial sessions is used tentatively, so as not to appear as lacking empathy and being insensitive. Furthermore, by modeling the use of humor to my clients, they are better equipped to use it throughout the week in their 'real world' when they may typically make themselves angry or depressed about a situation.

A common exercise I will do with my clients is to have them find something humorous in what they are reporting, to have them see the lighter side of their reality. If nothing else, humor has proven to provide temporary relief for clients who experience more continual pain in their lives. In no way am I suggesting that humor as an intervention is deep and elegant, nor is it the primary choice in terms of strategies. I am suggesting that in conjunction with the cognitive, behavioral, and emotive techniques used, humor can be an additional source of relief.

So there you have it, twelve idiosyncrasies as an REBT therapist. What I have found to be most appealing about the theory of REBT is its flexibility and adaptability. My wish is that after reading these chapters from various REBT therapists, the idea of REBT theory as being flexible and versatile is highlighted.

References

Ellis, A. (1994). *How to Control Your Anxiety Before It Controls You*. New York: Kensington Publishing Corp.

Ellis, A. (2001). *Overcoming Destructive Beliefs, Feelings, and Behaviors*. New York: Prometheus Books.

Fraser, C. & Burchell, B. (2001). *Introducing Social Psychology*. Cambridge, UK: Polity Press.

Goldfried, M. R. & Davison, G. C. (1994). *Clinical Behavior Therapy*. New York: John Wiley & Sons, Inc.

Petty, R. E. & Cacioppo, J. T. (1986). The elaboration likelihood model of persuasion. In L. Berkowitz (ed.), *Advances in Experimental Social Psychology* (pp. 123–205). Hillsdale, NJ: Erlbaum.

Safran, J. D. & Muran, J. C. (2000). *Negotiating the Therapeutic Alliance: A Relational Treatment Guide*. New York: The Guilford Press.

Walen, S. R., DiGiuseppe, R. & Dryden, W. (1992). *A Practitioner's Guide to Rational-Emotive Therapy*. New York: Oxford University Press.

Wolfe, B. E. & Goldfried, M. R. (1988). Research on psychotherapy integration: Recommendations and conclusions from an NIMH workshop. *Journal of Consulting and Clinical Psychology, 56,* 448–51.

Yalom, I. (1995). *The Theory and Practice of Group Psychotherapy*. New York: Basic Books.

11

Ann Vernon

In this chapter I will describe my idiosyncratic practice of REBT with children and adolescents by elaborating on the following twelve points:

i.   the CARE model that outlines four important elements in the relationship-building process;

ii.   the importance of developmental assessment in terms of both problem conceptualization and intervention;

iii.   assessing the 'C': specific adaptations and considerations in working with children and adolescents;

iv.   assessing the 'B': specific adaptations and considerations in working with children and adolescents;

v.   disputing irrational beliefs: creative, developmentally appropriate strategies;

vi.   the appropriateness of the inelegant solution with younger populations;

vii.   age-appropriate techniques for helping young clients develop an effective new philosophy and REBT values;

viii.   the goal-setting process with children and adolescents;

ix.   using contracts and letters of introduction to help engage reluctant customers;

x.   developing an anticipatory set to entice young clients into therapy;

xi.   age-appropriate homework assignments;

xii.   the termination process and how to maintain change.

Since its inception in 1955, REBT has been practiced throughout the world with adults as well as children, and has been successfully applied to individual, group, marital, and family therapy in a variety of settings (Ellis & Dryden, 1997). The versatility of this theory is demonstrated by the fact that it has been used to treat a wide array of problems such as fears and phobias, depression, anger, underachievement, acting out, perfectionism, interpersonal relationship issues, low self-esteem, anxiety, aggression, procrastination, and job performance (Bernard, 1991; Vernon, 2002; Wilde, 1992). As Yankura and Dryden (1997) noted, REBT can be effectively applied to different populations and therapeutic modalities, but how it is practiced varies (Warren & McLellarn, 1987).

In this chapter, I will be describing how I practice REBT, with specific emphasis on applications to children and adolescents. This population has been under-represented in the REBT literature until recently (Vernon, 1997, in press; Wilde, 1992; Ellis & Wilde, 2002). Given the fact that special adaptations are critical in applying REBT to younger populations, my approach, based on years of clinical and educational practice, will hopefully prove helpful to other practitioners.

The CARE model

Children and adolescents are often reluctant consumers of psychotherapy, for several reasons. First, they may not understand what counseling is or have misconceptions that cause them to think that they are 'sick' or 'crazy' if they have to see a therapist. Furthermore, they often resent being labeled as the 'problem,' especially when they may not think anything is wrong with them. They also may be skeptical, wondering if they will ever feel better. All of these factors contribute to resistance that can have a negative impact on the client–counselor therapeutic relationship.

Over the years there has been considerable discussion and controversy among REBT practitioners and scholars regarding the nature of the therapeutic relationship. According to Ellis and Dryden (1997), giving clients considerable warmth and caring may be detrimental because it may inadvertently reinforce their need for love and approval, but they acknowledged that under certain conditions, therapist warmth may be appropriate. Dawson (1991), however, stressed the importance of the relationship between client and counselor, and practitioners working with children agree that the client–counselor relationship is very critical (Bernard & Joyce, 1984; Vernon, 1997, 1999, 2002; Wilde, 1992). A significant aspect of my idiosyncratic practice of REBT involves establishing a good relationship, which I do in a variety of developmentally appropriate ways.

Because I see the relationship as a very integral aspect of counseling, I developed the CARE model to describe elements of the relationship-building process. Although I will be describing the model as it applies to children and adolescents, many of the concepts may also be used effectively with adults.

C — Connect

There are a variety of ways to connect with young clients, including using self-disclosure, having a sense of humor, and being warm and genuine. Because children and adolescents are often uncertain or fearful about what this experience will be like, I think it is imperative to 'hook' them in the first session by being friendly and personable and showing a genuine interest in them as individuals. I also sometimes find myself being a sort of 'salesperson' with adolescents in particular, pointing out to them the advantages of counseling and how this approach can help them get better and feel better. Because they are often reluctant to self-disclose, normalizing their problems, assuring them that they are not 'sick or crazy,' and not being overly serious and formal are key ingredients to a good relationship. It sometimes helps to share that you had a similar problem at their age or indicate that you work with other young people who have comparable issues.

Because children and adolescents may not always be able to express themselves verbally, employing other strategies such as activities, art, or games may be necessary in the rapport-building process and certainly represents a departure from more conventional ways to build rapport. Several specific suggestions are subsequently described.

Activities

With young children, a good but simple 'get acquainted' strategy is to play *Who Are You*? (Vernon, 2002). To initiate this process, I invite the young client to play this game so that we can learn more about each other. I instruct the client to ask 'Who are you?' and then I respond with something about myself, such as 'I am someone who loves to read . . . who are you? The client responds, and we go back and forth for several rounds.

Another effective game is *Alphabet Soup* (Vernon, 2002), where the client and I take turns drawing a letter of the alphabet out of a large soup can and sharing something about ourselves beginning with the letter they drew. It is surprising how much I can learn after a few rounds of this game, and this in turn increases trust and openness.

For adolescents, asking them to share three things from their purse, wallet, or back pack that reveal something about their interests or values is often effective, especially if I am willing to do this as well. Another activity for adolescents is a variation of the *Alphabet Soup* strategy where they write their first and last names down the side of a sheet of paper and identify something about themselves beginning with each letter. Again, this is more effective if I also participate in the activity.

Art

Drawing is often an effective way to connect with young clients. During the initial session, I invite them to share more about themselves by drawing a picture of their family, friends, of favorite hobbies and interests. Having them draw about their problem in the form of a cartoon or film clip is also a good strategy that may work better than having them verbally describe the issue.

Games

Most children, as well as many adolescents, enjoy playing games. There are many commercial games from companies such as *Childswork, Childsplay*, but it is also relatively easy and much less expensive to create your own. One that works well for both children and adolescents is to write feeling words on squares of a checkerboard. As you play checkers and land on a space, share about a time you have experienced that feeling. A variation is to write topics such as friends, interests, hobbies, favorite movies, fun times, or school subjects on the squares and share something about that topic as you land on the space.

Another game that can be a very engaging way to build rapport is to play a variation of the game *Twister*. To play this game, make a game board by dividing a thick plastic tablecloth into squares and labeling each square with a different color. Then make two sets of cards, one with directions such as 'left foot red, right hand blue, right knee yellow', and another set of cards that includes several cards for each color of the squares on the board. On these cards, write topics that would help you and the client become better acquainted, such as: 'things I get angry about, what makes me frustrated, things I like to do, things I don't like to do, things I am good at, things I am not good at'. As you and the client play the game by drawing a directions card, moving, and then drawing a colored card with topics, you are building a relationship in a way that is fun and non-threatening to the client.

Due to space considerations, it is not possible to go into further detail. Readers can refer to *What Works When with Children and Adolescents: A Handbook of Individual Counseling Techniques* (Vernon, 2002) for additional suggestions.

A — Appreciate the story

I often step back and think about what it takes for clients to 'tell their stories' to a counselor who is most likely a complete stranger. Oftentimes the problems relate to things they are ashamed or embarrassed about, or they think they are crazy or a misfit because of the way they think feel, or behave. I remind myself how vulnerable they are when sharing facts and feelings with me, and I communicate to my clients that I know this may not be easy to do. That's not to say that I think it *should* be easy, but rather, that I recognize what it might mean for them to put themselves in that position. I often let my clients know that I appreciate the fact that they were willing to self-disclose, and I emphasize certain REBT principles during this process, such as verifying that they are fallible human beings who, like all of us, make mistakes. I sometimes use self-disclosure which helps clients see that they are not alone, or I may simply use non-verbal methods of communicating empathy and appreciation for their self-disclosure through touch, a smile, or a nod.

Because I appreciate 'the story,' and know that many clients do not have people who will really take the time to listen to them, I do not rush into the problem-solving process immediately. Instead, I often take time during the first session to connect and build a solid relationship based on trust.

While I do not believe in Carl Rogers' (1961) assumption that clients are able to solve their own problems if the therapist is warm, genuine, and empathic, I do believe that a good relationship in which the practitioner demonstrates empathy and appreciation for the client's story contributes to the overall success of the counseling process.

R — Respect

I agree with Dryden's statement in the first chapter that the REBT literature has tended to underplay the importance of the relationship. In addition, I think REBT practitioners have unfortunately earned the reputation as being abrasive, with little respect for their clients. Having come from a humanistic background, I have always emphasized that in my approach, integrating REBT principles in a less directive way. Respect for the client as a person is important to me, and in my opinion, one of the 'gifts' of being a therapist is to be able to work with a variety of people from many different walks of life. Some of the adolescents who come through my door have a different hair color or pierced body part each time I see them, and many of the adults in my therapy practice have had life experiences very different from mine. I think it is important to respect these individuals for who they are, and in accordance with REBT principles, accept them unconditionally. I think respect is communicated by not being condescending, and I make it a point to never treat clients rudely. This respect and unconditional acceptance strengthen the therapeutic alliance, which in turn facilitates the problem-solving process.

E — Educate

A basic premise of this theory is that it is educative (DiGiuseppe, 1999; Dryden & Ellis, 2001; Ellis, 1994), and it would be rare to find an REBT therapist who did not educate clients about the nature of their emotional disturbance, the link between beliefs and emotional and behavioral consequences, and how to challenge their irrational beliefs and replace them with rational alternatives (Ellis, 1994; Walen, DiGiuseppe & Dryden, 1992; Yankura & Dryden, 1997). However, in working with children and adolescents, I need to adapt the concepts by using age-appropriate language and techniques that I will share throughout this chapter.

In addition, I usually find it necessary to educate young clients about what counseling is and clarify any misconceptions they may have, such as thinking that I will tell them what to do or tell their parents everything we discuss. I also emphasize that counseling is a problem-solving process and that it is a joint effort — we both collaborate to make change happen. With young clients I also find it helpful to speak in simple language about their problem so as to not overwhelm them, noting that they seem to be having some problems with school attendance rather than saying that they are here to work on school phobia, for example.

I oftentimes find that it is necessary to educate them about normal child and adolescent development — for example, that moodiness is characteristic of early adolescence, and they are not the only ones who experience this. I find that sharing this information seems to relax clients — they are not as anxious about being abnormal or sick. This same concept holds true for adults. For example, when working with parents of adolescents, I often acknowledge how frustrating this transition from childhood to adolescence can be for them and educate them about some of the normal developmental characteristics which I believe prevents them from overgeneralizing or awfulizing about what they are experiencing with their young teenagers.

As I educate them about what they can expect to experience in counseling, I emphasize that the process will be expedited if they are open and honest about their issues and also point out that they are in charge of changing their thinking, feeling, and behaving. This is often reassuring to clients who think that the therapist is going to 'tell them what to do.'

I employ the CARE model to help establish a good working relationship with clients and continue to integrate the basic concepts until we reach closure. Although I may spend more time in the first session developing the relationship, especially with children and adolescents, I agree with Walen, DiGiuseppe & Dryden (1992) that therapy actually begins with the first moment of contact and develops as you establish the therapeutic alliance. As I develop rapport, I also begin to formulate hypotheses about the client's problem and how to proceed, integrating the initial stages of the assessment process into the CARE model.

Developmental assessment

Working with child and adolescent clients necessitates some form of developmental assessment from two perspectives. First, it is important to assess whether they are in the preoperational, concrete operational, or formal operational stages of development (Vernon, 1993). These developmental stages influence how youngsters interpret their world, which has important implications not only for accurate problem diagnosis, but also for treatment. Especially from an REBT perspective, it is important to keep in mind how their level of cognitive development affects perceptions. For example, preoperational and concrete operational thinkers are limited in their ability to generate problem-solving alternatives. They also take things literally, so they are naturally prone to overgeneralizing and making assumptions (Vernon, 2002). Dichotomous thinking is very prevalent, and their perspective-taking abilities are limited. Because they do not begin to develop formal operational thinking skills until early adolescence, and then it is a very gradual process, most young clients will be limited in their cognitive abilities. Therefore, it is crucial for REBT counselors must take developmental levels into consideration as they do problem assessment, realizing that they should not jump to conclusions when a child says, 'My parents are always mean,' because their interpretation of what is mean and how often it occurs may very well be distorted. It is therefore important to ask extending questions to gather more detail in order to make an accurate diagnosis.

In addition, paying attention to social and emotional developmental levels is critical. Children in middle childhood, for example, are slowly developing better perspective-taking skills (Cole & Cole, 1996; Pruitt, 1998) and are therefore more adept at interpreting social cues, but their perceptions of social interactions may still be misconstrued. In terms of emotional development, feeling vocabularies are often quite limited for younger children, and although they are able to recognize and label basic emotions such as happiness, sadness, anger, and fear (Owens, 2002; Vernon & Al-Mabuk, 1995), they are not always able to accurately express how they feel. During adolescence, strong negative emotions can be overwhelming and will influence not only how young clients perceive an event, but also how they cope with it.

Second, developmental assessment is also important in tailoring interventions. For example, with younger children, practitioners need to use a variety of creative interventions that are more appropriate for their stage of development. Hands-on activities, games, stories, art, and music are very effective. While most adolescents respond well to verbal approaches, it is often very helpful to reinforce concepts through worksheets, activities, music, or art. Specific examples will be described throughout the chapter.

Assessing the 'C' — emotional and behavioral consequences

All REBT therapists assess the emotional and behavioral consequences, but in working with children and adolescents, it is often necessary to first teach young clients a feeling vocabulary since their ability to express themselves may be limited due to their level of emotional development. To increase their skills, I might use feeling flash cards, where clients define or act out the word described on the card, or play a game such as *Face the Feelings* (Vernon, 2002). To play this game, clients roll a dice and move along a board, landing on a colored circle that corresponds to a feeling face that depicts happiness, sadness, anger, or worry. As they share about a time they felt this way, they learn more about their feelings and consequently are better able to describe how they feel about their present problem.

Because young clients may not always accurately label their feelings, I make it a point to clarify how they are defining a term, which is something I do not normally have to do when working with adults. But with children, I usually probe further and try to uncover behaviors or beliefs in order to make certain that what they are communicating is what they really intend. For example, a sixth grader indicated that she was a little irritated about her parents getting a divorce, and I asked her to describe what was irritating about it. She identified several things that seemed quite minor, so I asked what she did when she felt irritated. She responded by saying that she shut herself in her room by herself for hours on end, which seemed to me that she was feeling more than a little irritated. I then asked her what she thought about when she was alone in her room, and she stated that it was during those times that she thought about how much she hated her parents for doing this. I conveyed to her that the vehemence in her voice and her use of the word hate, which is a very strong negative emotion, indicated to me that she might actually be quite angry. When she acknowledged that that is how she really felt, it confirmed for me the importance of not taking their words at face value.

Another aspect I stress when working with children and adolescents is the connection between what they feel and how they behave, which is something that I do with adults, but with young clients I find that I need to do this in more creative ways. I may, for example, ask them to act out how they behaved when they felt a certain way. Or, I might use an activity such as *Chain Reaction* (Vernon, 1998a), where clients identify an activating event and write it on the first link of a paper chain. Next, they identify how they felt about that event and put it on the next chain, followed by what they did when they felt that way on the next chain. They can also identify consequences of that behavior on the next chain, and so forth. This activity is very age-appropriate because it illustrates the connections between feeling and behaving in a very concrete way, which appeals to young clients' thinking patterns.

As I have attempted to point out, assessing the emotional and behavioral reactions is an integral part of REBT assessment but needs to be adapted when working with children and adolescents. Especially with younger children, an activity-based format that incorporates visual, auditory, and kinesthetic approaches works most effectively.

Assessing the 'B' — rational and irrational beliefs

Assessing beliefs is the major objective of the REBT assessment process (Dryden & DiGiuseppe, 1990; Ellis & MacLaren, 1998), but significant modifications need to be made when working with child and adolescent clients because they may not readily grasp the concept of rational and irrational beliefs and may not be able to accurately identify what they were thinking (Vernon, 1997, 1999). For these reasons, I use a variety of creative, age-appropriate techniques to assess cognitive distortions.

To begin with, I seldom use the terms *rational* or *irrational*, choosing instead to use *sensible* and *insensible*, or *helpful* and *unhelpful,* which children and adolescents can more readily identify with. I might also use words such as junk thoughts, muddy thoughts, or nonsense thoughts to describe irrational beliefs (Vernon, 2002).

Another point that I stress in working with young clients that I usually do not have to emphasize as much with adults is the difference between facts and assumptions. Even well into adolescence, it is common for them to assume things without checking out the facts. The reason this is so problematic for this age group is that because their sense of time is more immediate, they often react impulsively, and their actions often have negative consequences, some of which can be very detrimental and long term. For this reason, it is important to help them be 'fact detectives.'

There are several ways to do this. First, young children readily buy into the concept of being a detective, so playing with their imaginations by giving them a magnifying glass and having them use this as a symbol for 'looking for' assumptions and facts as a homework assignment is generally effective. Another engaging way to do this is to play a game called *Fact, Fact, Fact* (Vernon, 2002), where you draw a tic-tac-toe board on a sheet of paper and make fact and assumption cards such as: facts — milk comes from cows and goats, corn is a vegetable, lakes are smaller than oceans; assumptions — winter is the best season of the year, cats are better than dogs, all presidents do a good job. Designate the client as 1 and yourself as 2, and as you each draw a card, you determine if it is a fact or an assumption, writing an F or an A on the board, along with your number. The game is played like tic-tac-toe, so the first person who has three numbers in a row is the 'expert' on facts and assumptions. For other ideas, the reader is directed to *Thinking, Feeling, Behaving* (Vernon, 1989a,b).

Eliciting irrational beliefs is also a very different process with young clients. Simply asking 'what are you thinking?' usually does not get the response I am looking for. Once again, I use numerous age-appropriate, creative techniques to help them identify irrational beliefs. The following are examples specifically for children:

- Use thought bubbles as a visual way to elicit beliefs.
- Use activities such as *Does That Make Sense?*, a card game that helps children distinguish between rational and irrational beliefs (Vernon, 1998a).
- Engage children in *Really Rational* role play situations, where they learn to identify irrational beliefs based on school-related incidents (Vernon, 1998a).
- Play *Rational or Irrational*, a competition game that helps children distinguish between rational and irrational beliefs (Vernon, 1989a).

The following suggestions apply to adolescents:

- Use an activity such as *Rational Reasoning*, which helps adolescents identify cognitive distortions such as tunnel vision, overgeneralization, mind reading, and self-downing (Vernon, 1998b).
- Teach clients to distinguish between rational and irrational thinking with a *Rational Thinking* worksheet that asks them to identify irrational beliefs associated with typical developmental problems (Vernon, 1998c).
- After teaching clients about the core irrational beliefs and sharing examples, invite them to select a television show or video and identify irrational beliefs.
- Make a list of common cognitive distortions with age-appropriate examples, such as: all or nothing thinking (I'm either the best or the worst football player on the team). Invite clients to rate each distortion on a 1–5 basis to indicate how frequently they practice these irrational beliefs.

These techniques have proven effective in helping young clients understand the concept of irrational beliefs and identify them. In working with children as opposed to adults, I find that I need to do more educating about what these beliefs are and be more active and creative in helping them identify irrational beliefs relative to their specific activating events.

Disputing irrational beliefs

According to Walen, DiGiuseppe & Dryden (1992), 'Changing the beliefs is the real work of therapy and occurs at D, the Disputation' (p. 153). Ellis and MacLaren (1998) identified several types of disputes: philosophic, functional, empirical, and logical. However, as several authors (Bernard & Joyce, 1984; DiGiuseppe & Bernard, 1983; Vernon, 1989a; DiGiuseppe, 1999) noted, that children who have not yet reached the concrete operations stage will have difficulty with the concept of disputing. And although children develop the ability to think more logically as they enter this concrete operations phase at approximately age eight, I find that with children as well as with adolescents, it is imperative to be creative and versatile in how I help them through the disputing process. Specifically, I seldom use the philosophic dispute because it is often not effective given their level of cognitive development. I cannot hear myself saying to an eight year old, 'Well, suppose something horrible did happen to your parents and they died, would that be the worst thing that could ever happen to you?' Because parents are the center of their universe and source of support at this age, I think it would be insensitive to dispute in this manner. Instead, I would more likely to challenge the inference and help them look at the likelihood that something disastrous would happen to their parents.

Although functional, logical, and empirical disputes are more effective than philosophical disputes with school-aged children, DiGiuseppe (1999) pointed out that even adolescents will not always follow a logical argument, so we should not assume that they will engage in disputing. According to DiGiuseppe, adolescents in particular benefit more from functional as opposed to logical or empirical disputes. And, since there is such variation in the rate of cognitive maturity for this age group, it is often necessary to incorporate more creative, activity-based methods into the traditional forms of verbal disputing. For example, a young adolescent was getting bad grades. We had identified his irrational beliefs as the following: I shouldn't have to do things that are boring or a waste of my time; I shouldn't have to take work home or study since I have better things to do; I can't stand to do things that require effort. As a therapist, my response was, 'Lots of kids your age don't want to do things that are boring or a waste of time. I understand that — but how is what you are doing helping you if you intend to graduate from high school? Sure, it would be great not to have to take work home or study, but where in the school handbook does it state that you won't have to study in high school?' Although my client responded as if he understood that his beliefs were irrational, it wasn't until he did a survey of his classmates, asking them if they thought they should never have to study or do boring work but still graduate that he really saw the absurdity of his beliefs.

I have developed numerous games, stories, limericks, songs and puppet plays to facilitate the disputing process (Vernon, 1989a,b; 1998a,b,c; 2002). Because they are concrete interventions that appeal to visual, auditory, and kinesthetic learners, school-aged clients grasp the concepts more readily. An example I used with an adolescent who refused to give up her irrational belief that not being elected to an honor association was the absolute worst thing that could happen to her was to have her cut out newspaper articles that she thought described 'awful' events. When I had her place her event on a continuum along with the rest of her articles, she finally was able to see that this wasn't the worst thing that could happen, and from there deduced that she could stand it.

I also use rational coping self-statements with regularity, particularly with younger children, but I often have to generate the statements for them, whereas adults can usually develop them on their own. At times I am able to go to a deeper philosophical level with these statements, such as, 'I will work hard to get all my homework done, but if I don't, it doesn't mean I'm a bad kid.' The only thing to be cautious about is that children and adolescents as well tend to think dichotomously and may only focus on the 'If I don't get it done it doesn't mean I am a bad kid' and therefore not place much importance on completing the work instead of seeing that they should try, but if they fail, it doesn't make them a failure. Also, the concept of failing but not being a failure is a very abstract one for concrete thinkers, so it is important to remain cognizant of developmental levels in developing disputes and rational coping self-statements.

How I do disputing is a departure from what many REBT therapists do. With adults as well as with children, I am not very forceful and directive. I do not find that as effective as when I convey some empathy by acknowledging the difficulty in giving up the irrational belief (i.e., 'I understand that your life would be easier if you didn't have any rules, but how realistic is that?'). I also seldom raise my voice or speak in a forceful manner, and I never put clients down for holding irrational beliefs. I might, however, use a bit of humor or sarcasm to get the point across, saying something like 'I can just picture you floating in the pool on your raft forever and never having any demands or responsibilities placed on you, but how real is that?' However, concrete thinkers may have difficulty understanding some humor and sarcasm, so it is important to use it judiciously.

Although disputing is more of a challenge with children and adolescents, I find it more enjoyable because I have the flexibility to be inventive. In many instances I involve the clients in creating useful analogies, games, or homework assignments that help them with disputing. Due to space limitations, it is not possible to go into detail about other age-appropriate disputation techniques. Readers are referred to *Thinking, Feeling Behaving* (Vernon, 1989a,b), *The Passport Program* (Vernon, 1998a,b,c), and *What Works When with Children and Adolescents: A Handbook of Individual Counseling Techniques* (Vernon, 2002) for specific interventions that facilitate the disputation process.

The inelegant solution
In REBT, there are several levels of change, with the most long-lasting involving philosophic restructuring of irrational beliefs (Ellis & Dryden, 1997; Dryden & Ellis, 2001). Although it is far better to help clients change irrational beliefs at the philosophic level and arrive at the elegant solution, this is usually quite difficult with youngsters due to their level of cognitive development (Bernard & Joyce, 1984; DiGiuseppe, 1999). For this reason, I rely more on inelegant solutions and problem solving/coping strategies.

There are some compelling arguments for relying more on the inelegant solution with this population. First of all, their sense of time is more immediate, so what is a problem today may not be tomorrow. Therefore, they need specific ideas about how to address the problem now. Secondly, because their sense of time is immediate and they are prone to catastrophizing (Vernon, 1999), they frequently overreact to upsetting events and can behave impulsively, which can have negative long-term effects (Vernon, 2002). For example, a young adolescent was so distraught over the fact that her boyfriend started dating her best friend that she was contemplating suicide, thinking that her life would never be good again. She was not in a logical frame of mind to respond well to disputing, and certainly not at the philosophic level. However, helping her develop rational coping self-statements such as, 'I can survive this even though it is tough,' or 'I will eventually feel better, so it there is no reason to end my life now' and engaging her in a brainstorming activity where she listed people she could turn to for support and specific things she could do to cope day-to-day helped her get through the immediate crisis and reach a point where she was able to identify and dispute her irrational beliefs about herself, the relationship, and how this was affecting her life.

Effective new philosophy and REBT values
The ultimate goal of REBT is to help clients of all ages develop a more rational philosophy which includes the values that promote emotional adjustment and mental health (DiGiuseppe, 1999). Since these concepts are rather abstract, I have written rational emotive stories and designed activities to simplify these concepts and present them in a variety of ways that will help young clients develop an effective new philosophy and understand the values.

For example, one of the REBT values is for people to take responsibility for their own disturbance and not blame others for their thoughts, feelings, and behaviors. This can be a rather difficult concept for young people, so an activity like *Who's in Charge?* (Vernon, 1989b, p. 17–18) helps them understand, through age-appropriate situations such as 'failed a test,' whether this was someone else's fault or their own. After responding to other examples in the activity, it always becomes clearer to youngsters that they are in charge of their behavior. Other activities such as *Who's Responsible for Feelings?* (Vernon, 1989b, p. 25–26) helps them see that others aren't responsible for their emotional upset.

In trying to help them achieve a rational philosophy, I use a *do-review-teach* model. For example, in the therapy session I might engage clients in reading or writing a story that exemplifies the effective new ideas. Then I review the concepts in a different way such as through role-playing or rational role-reversal. Finally, with the client's permission, I ask them to teach their parents the concepts they have learned by having the parents join us at the end of the session. I oftentimes have them do a before-and-after poster to help them explain the concepts, writing words or drawing symbols to portray the before and after contrast in their thinking, feeling, and behaving.

Goal-setting
Goal-setting is an important part of the REBT therapy process, but the procedure must be modified for school-aged clients for several reasons. First, goal setting may be an alien concept — the word may not exist in their vocabulary, depending

on age. Therefore, I often have to educate them about what goals are and why they are important. With younger children I also may have to change the terminology, using a word such as *plan*, which seems to make more sense to them. Also, it is important to remember that their sense of time is more immediate so goals or plans need to be short term. Having realistic and achievable goals is also critical because it is easy for them to give up if they are unable to do something the first time or see the goal as unattainable. Finally, I stress to the client that the goal-setting process is a partnership, but with younger clients, I realize that I might have to be more active in suggesting appropriate goals or helping to modify them so they are more feasible. In contrast to working with adults who can develop their own goals, I am more collaborative and active in helping children and adolescents identify their goals.

Contracts and letters of introduction

As previously mentioned, children and adolescents are often not eager participants in counseling, especially when they do not think that they have a problem or see their parents as the problem. I find that contracts work well with reluctant customers. Therefore, when parents call to make the appointment, I always try to ask how the child feels about coming. If the parents indicate that they are hesitant and uncertain, I ask if it might help for me to write a short letter of introduction, telling a little bit about myself and what they can expect from counseling. I also have developed a brochure specifically geared to children and adolescents, and I include that with the letter. Or, if parents indicate that the child is oppositional and threatens not to say anything once they are in the office, I suggest to parents that I am willing to enter into a contract with them where they would agree to try it for three sessions and then we re-evaluate. Given that children's sense of time is more immediate, contracting for a few sessions is often a good idea — and then it is up to the therapist to make sure to 'hook' the client so the contract can be extended as needed.

The anticipatory set

Because children and adolescents are generally referred for therapy by their parents and teachers, their resistance is understandable. Not only do they resent the fact that others have the power to make decisions for them, but they are often confused and uncomfortable about the entire process. Therefore, I think it is important to create an atmosphere that makes them want to return. That is not to say that therapy has to be all fun and games or that they *shouldn't* have to learn to tolerate unpleasant things, but I think therapy is much more effective if I create an anticipatory set, which I do in several ways. First, younger children respond well to challenges, such as, 'I learned something really important about feelings, and I bet you can't guess what it is!' This challenge creates a type of anticipatory set that engages young clients in learning about the concept and discussing how it applies to them. Another strategy I use is to involve them in helping me make a game or write a story or create a puppet play that presents rational concepts and introduces some of the problems they are having. Since we generally do not have time to finish these projects during the session, they are encouraged to take it home to complete. I find that they are more excited to come back because they have the finished product to share.

It is more difficult to create the anticipatory set with adolescents, but I have found some things that work. First, I show interest in the significant people in their lives by asking them to bring in pictures or yearbooks to share with me. I have been surprised at how eager some are to do this, and they often continue this after the first invitation. Even though it takes a few minutes out of the session, it seems to be an effective way of getting them more involved in the therapy process. Having them bring in music that is meaningful to them is also a good strategy that helps connect them to therapy.

Homework

Homework, an integral part of REBT counseling, (Dryden & DiGiuseppe, 1990; Dryden & Ellis, 2001; Ellis & MacLaren, 1998) is done somewhat differently with young clients. First, I seldom use the term 'homework' since it can have an aversive connotation for children if they associate it with schoolwork. Instead, I suggest that they try an 'experiment,' to which they are much more receptive. It is also important to realize that since children's sense of time is more immediate, it is sometimes hard for them to remember what they did if you are only seeing them once every week or two. For this reason, homework assignments that involve drawing, writing, or audio taping are more effective because they can bring in the results to share and that helps them recall what they did. Even very young children are capable of doing this: I had a six-year-old talk into a tape recorder whenever she felt jealous and upset that her mother was giving her baby sister more attention. Then I had her pretend to be a counselor who was asking her questions to help her dispute her irrational beliefs. She really got into this and even switched voices when she was the counselor! I needed to model the process to help her understand the concept, but then she became quite adept at doing it on her own.

I also expect that a number of clients will not complete their homework because they may not be all that invested in therapy. For this reason, I try to make the experiments fun and engaging. I also often involve parents at this stage of the process so they can remind them to finish the experiments before the next session.

Termination

I generally collaborate with parents regarding termination since young clients may say they have changed, but in reality that is just their wishful thinking. If the young client is very resistant about returning time after time, I turn it into a challenge and we identify specific ways to prove to me and to their parents that they are thinking, feeling, and behaving more rationally. However, in other cases where this resistance is not present, I begin phasing out by having less frequent 'check up' visits, often asking for the child's input about how often those should occur. We then identify what they need to do to maintain their current level of effective functioning, often through some sort of art or writing activity. For example, adolescents make rational bumper stickers as friendly reminders and younger children create comic strips that convey the effective rational philosophy. During the check up visits we either create new reminders or work on other issues that may arise.

Conclusion

In this chapter I have described my idiosyncratic practice of REBT as it applies particularly to children and adolescents. As I work with this population, I think my biggest challenge is how to create lasting results, and I think the best way to do this is to acknowledge that as practitioners, we need to be flexible and creative as we educate young clients in rational principles. Furthermore, it is also important to teach the basic principles to parents and teachers so that they can not only model rational behavior, but can help their children learn how to think rationally and behave sensibly. The psychoeducational nature and solid principles of this theory contribute to its effectiveness with children and adolescents as described in this chapter.

References

Bernard, M. E. (1991). *Using rational-emotive therapy effectively: A practitioner's guide.* New York: Plenum Press.

Bernard, M. E. & Joyce, M. (1984). *Rational-Emotive Therapy with Children and Adolescents: Theory, Treatment Strategies, Preventative Methods.* New York: John Wiley & Sons.

Childswork, Childsplay: A Guidance Channel Company (winter/spring, 2002). Plainview, NY.

Cole, M. & Cole, S. R. (1996). *The Development of Children.* (3rd edn.). New York: Freeman.

Dawson, R. W. (1991). REGIME: A counseling and educational model for using RET effectively. In M. E. Bernard (ed.), *Using Rational-Emotive Therapy Effectively. A Practitioner's Guide* (pp. 112–32). New York: Plenum Press.

DiGiuseppe, R. (1999). Rational emotive behavior therapy. In H. T. Prout & D. T. Brown, *Counseling and Psychotherapy with Children and Adolescents: Theory and Practice for School Settings* (pp. 252–93). New York: John Wiley & Sons, Inc.

DiGiuseppe, R. & Bernard, M. E. (1983). Principles of assessment and methods of treatment with children: Special considerations. In A. Ellis & M. E. Bernard (eds.), *Rational Emotive Approaches to the Problems of Childhood.* New York: Plenum Press.

Dryden, W. & DiGiuseppe, R. (1990). *A Rational Emotive Therapy Primer.* Champaign, IL: Research Press.

Dryden, W. & Ellis, A. (2001). Rational emotive behavior therapy. In K. S. Dobson (ed.), *Handbook of Cognitive Behavioral Therapies* (2nd edn.) (pp. 295–348). New York: Guilford.

Ellis, A. (1994). *Reason and Emotion in Psychotherapy: A Comprehensive Method of Treating Human Disturbances* (Rev. edn.). New York: Birch Lane Press.

Ellis, A. & Dryden, W. (1997). *The Practice of Rational Emotive Therapy* (2nd edn.). New York: Springer.

Ellis, A. & MacLaren, C. (1998). *Rational Emotive Behavior Therapy: A Therapist's Guide.* Atascadero, CA: Impact Publishers.

Ellis, A. & Wilde, J. (2002). *Case Studies in Rational Emotive Behavior Therapy with Children and Adolescents.* Columbus, OH: Merrill Prentice Hall.

Owens, K. B. (2002). *Child and Adolescent Development: An Integrated Approach.* Belmont, CA: Wadsworth/Thomson Learning.

Pruitt, D. B. (Ed.) (1998). *Your Child.* New York: HarperCollins.

Rogers, C. (1961). *On Becoming a Person.* Boston, MA: Houghton Mifflin.

Vernon, A. (1989a). *Thinking, Feeling, Behaving: An Emotional Education Curriculum for Children.* Champaign, IL: Research Press.

Vernon, A. (1989b). *Thinking, Feeling, Behaving: An Emotional Education Curriculum for Adolescents.* Champaign, IL: Research Press.

Vernon, A. (1993). *Developmental Assessment and Intervention with Children and Adolescents.* Alexandria, VA: American Counseling Association.

Vernon, A. (1997). Applications of REBT with children and adolescents. In J. Yankura & W. Dryden, (eds.), *Special Applications of REBT: A Therapist's Casebook* (pp. 11–37). New York: Springer Publishing Company.

Vernon, A. (1998a). *The Passport Program: A Journey Through Social, Emotional, Cognitive, and Self-Development.* Champaign, IL: Research Press.

Vernon, A. (1998b). *The Passport Program: A Journey Through Social, Emotional, Cognitive, and Self-Development.* Champaign, IL: Research Press.

Vernon, A. (1998c). *The Passport Program: A Journey Through Social, Emotional, Cognitive, and Self-Development.* Champaign, IL: Research Press.

Vernon, A. (1999). Applications of rational emotive behavior therapy with children and adolescents. In A. Vernon (ed.), *Counseling Children and Adolescents* (2nd edn.) (pp.140–57). Denver, CO: Love Publishing.

Vernon, A. (2002). *What Works When with Children and Adolescents: A Handbook of Individual Counseling Techniques.* Champaign IL: Research Press.

Vernon, A. & Al-Mabuk, R. (1995). *What Growing Up is All About: A Parents' Guide to Child and Adolescent Development.* Champaign, IL: Research Press.

Walen, S., DiGiuseppe, R. & Dryden, W. (1992). *A practitioner's guide to rational-emotive therapy* (2nd edn.). New York: Oxford University Press.

Warren, R. & McLellarn, R. W. (1987). What do RET therapists think they are doing? *Journal of Rational-Emotive Therapy, 5,* 71–91.

Wilde, J. (1992). *Rational Counseling with School-aged Populations: A Practical Guide.* Muncie, IN: Accelerated Development, Inc.

Yankura, J. & Dryden, W. (eds.) (1997). *Special Applications of REBT: A Therapist's Casebook.* New York: Springer Publishing Company.

contributors

The Editor

Windy Dryden is Professor of Psychotherapeutic Studies at Goldsmiths College, University of London and is Programme Co-ordinator of the College's MSc in Rational Emotive Behaviour Therapy. He has written or edited over 130 books and numerous book chapters and journal articles. He first trained in REBT in 1977 and has practised it ever since. He is an avid supporter of Arsenal FC and an avid watcher of Frasier, the US comedy programme.

The Contributors

Dr Raymond DiGiuseppe, a native of Philadelphia, received his BA from Villanova University and his PhD from Hofstra University. He then completed a Post Doctoral Fellowship at the Institute for Rational Emotive Therapy with Dr Albert Ellis. Dr DiGiuseppe has published over 70 journal articles and book chapters and co-authored five books. His present work involves the assessment and treatment of anger, the therapeutic alliance with children and adolescents, the treatment of external disorders in children and adolescents, and the development of REBT theory and practice. He is Professor and Chair of Psychology at St John's University in New York City, and Director of Professional Education at the Albert Ellis Institute for Rational Emotive Behavior Therapy. He lives in Hempstead, NY with his wife and four children.

Kristene A. Doyle, PhD, is the Training and Development Coordinator and the Child and Family Services Coordinator at the Albert Ellis Institute in New York. She also is an Associate Adjunct Professor at St John's University, teaching courses in the psychology doctoral program.

Albert Ellis is President of the Albert Ellis Institute in New York, where he still conducts many individual and group psychotherapy sessions, supervises a number of therapists, and gives many public and professional talks and workshops in Rational

Emotive Behavior Therapy. He also presents many workshops and talks nationally and internationally and is consulting editor of a dozen psychological journals. He has published over 700 articles and 68 books on psychotherapy, relationships therapy and sex therapy, and some day hopes to catch up with Windy Dryden's phenomenal record.

Paul A. Hauck has been one of the early practitioners of REBT, dating back to 1964 when he attended a post-doctrinal seminar with Dr Ellis for one week at Temple University, Pennsylvania. It was the week that changed his professional life. Since then he was the inaugural editor of *Rational Living*, the first REBT journal, has had a very successful practice in all the years following the seminar and has published 18 books which have been translated into 16 languages. Paul has many interests including music, tennis, golf and skiing.

Michael Neenan is Associate Director of the Centre for Stress Management, Blackheath, London and Visiting Tutor at Goldsmiths College, University of London. He is co-editor of the REBT Association's (United Kingdom) journal, *The Rational Emotive Behaviour Therapist. His* books include (with Windy Dryden) *Essential Rational Emotive Behaviour Therapy* (2000), *Learning from Errors in Rational Emotive Behaviour Therapy* (2001), *Life Coaching: A Cognitive-Behavioural Approach* (2002) and *Cognitive Behaviour Therapy: An A-Z of Persuasive Arguments* (2002).

Monica O'Kelly, BSc (Hons), DipEd, MBSc, PhD, has worked as a psychologist for 30 years. For the past 20 years and at present she is in full-time private practice in metropolitan Melbourne, Australia. She works with people with a range of problems applying her skills in Rational Emotive Behaviour Therapy. She is the Director of the Australian Institute for Rational-Emotive Therapy and is involved in conducting training programs in affiliation with the Albert Ellis Institute. She is an Honorary Lecturer in the Faculty of Psychology, Psychiatry and Psychological Medicine at Monash University where she teaches in the Doctor of Psychology program. She has a research interest in Rational-Emotive Therapy and women and has presented papers and published a number of articles in this area.

Nando Pelusi holds a PhD in clinical psychology and is an adjunct professor at St John's University. He is a certified supervisor of REBT at the Albert Ellis Institute where he conducts various workshops. He is on the board of advisors for the National Association of Cognitive Behavior Therapists and is in private practice in New York City. He is co-author with Dr Michael Abrams of a musical about Machiavelli.

Emmett Velten holds a bachelor's degree from the University of Chicago and a PhD from the University of Southern California. His dissertation produced the Velten Mood Induction Procedure, which is widely used in research on mood states. Velten has been a clinical school psychologist, chief psychologist at a community mental health clinic, clinical development director at a substance abuse treatment agency headquartered in California and an assistant clinical professor at the University of California, San Francisco. He is a past president of the Association for Behavioral and Cognitive Therapy and serves on the Board of Trustees of the Albert Ellis Institute. He co-authored several books with Ellis, has published a number of articles on addiction, currently is working on three books (including Ellis's biography) and has a private practice in Phoenix, Arizona.

Dr Ann Vernon is Professor and Coordinator of Counseling at the University of Northern Iowa in Cedar Falls, Iowa. In addition to her university teaching, Dr Vernon has a private counseling practice where she specializes in working with children and adolescents and their parents. She is currently the Vice President of the Albert Ellis Board of Trustees and the Director of the Midwest Center for REBT.

Dr Vernon is the author of numerous books and articles, including *Counseling Children and Adolescents, Developmental Assessment and Intervention with Children and Adolescents,* and *What Do You Do After You Say Hello: Individual Counseling Interventions with Children and Adolescents.* Her Thinking, Feeling, Behaving and Passport curriculums are used in many countries throughout the world as mental health prevention programs. Dr Vernon conducts workshops on applications of REBT with children and adolescents, as well as on other topics relating to work with young clients.

Sue Walen was for many years an Associate Professor in the Department of Psychology at Towson State University, and Instructor in Psychiatry at the John Hopkins Hospital Department of Psychiatry. Her two major texts were *A Clinical Guide to Behavior Therapy* (1977) and *A Practitioner's Guide to Rational Emotive Behavior Therapy* (1980), currently in its second edition (1992). After a satisfying career of teaching, writing and editing on the national and international level, she now accepts such assignments only under duress. Currently, Dr Walden is busy in independent practice in Bethesda, Maryland, building a garden, and enjoying her grandchildren.

index

'ABCs' of REBT 18, 69, 78, 83–6, 97, 100, 108–9
  simplifying 122–3
Academy of Cognitive Therapy 64
activating events 83
active participant 94
activities 146
addictive problems 78
adjunctive therapies 62, 70
Adler, A. 19, 28
affect, acceptance of intense 67
  deepening 62
  importance of 66
  intense 62, 67
age regression 99
Al-Mabuk, R. 149, 158
Alberti, R. 54, 59
alexythymia 66
alliance, working 3
anchor thoughts to the feelings 101
Andreason, N. C. 64, 73
anger 52
anticipatory set 155
arguments, convincing 120, 123
art 146
assertion, three rules of 52
assessing
  the critical 'A' 8–9
  the 'B' 150–2

the 'C' 9–10, 149–50
assessment, developmental 144, 148
attentive listening 17
avoiding jargon 35
awfulizing 44
Ayllon, T. 62, 73
Azrin, N. H. 62, 73
Backx, W. 2, 14, 60
Barber, T. X. 84, 87
Barkow, J. H. 113, 117
Beck, A. T. 13, 55, 56, 59, 99, 103
Beck Institute 91
Beck, J. S. 93, 103, 127, 129
Beck's Cognitive Therapy 85
behaviorism 112
behavioural 'Cs' 6, 8
belief–feeling connection 100
beliefs, irrational 6, 10, 12, 17, 24, 36, 44, 80, 86–7, 98, 108, 123, 150–3
  key questions for 86
  rational 2, 8, 17, 124, 150–2
Bernard, M. E. 24, 28, 99, 103, 144, 145, 152, 153, 157
biopsychiatry 64
Bond, F. W. 99, 103, 128, 129
Borcherdt, B. 55, 56, 59
Bordin, E. S. 3, 13
Bourland, D. 115, 117
Boyd, J. 101, 102, 103, 125, 130

bringing in significant others 70
Brodsky, A. 83, 88
Bufe, C. 83, 88
Burchell, B. 134, 141
Burns, D. D. 80, 88, 126, 129
Buss, D. 113, 117
Butler, G. 122, 129
Cacioppo, J. T. 134, 141
Campbell, D. T. 111, 117
Campbell, I. 99, 103
CARE model 144–8
case conceptualisation 2
    formulation with complex cases
        5–6
challenges, creative 42–4
change 120, 124–5
    cognitive 41–2
    encouraging 127–9
    promoting 12–13
    responsibility for 12
changing the 'As' 62, 65
Childswork, Childsplay 146, 157
Clark, D. M. 128, 129
client, as expert 133
    characteristics 92
    goals, referring back to 136
client's language 136–7
    situation 97
co-therapists 99
cognitive
    'C' 8
    change through rehearsal 41
    distortions 10
Cole, M. 149, 157
Cole, S. R. 149, 157
collaborative relationship 94
combating 'I don't know' 120, 125
commitment 122
compliance, homework 120, 126
consequences 83
    emotional 96–7, 149–50
constructing 'Bs' from emotional and
    behavioral 'C 110
constructive behaviour 8
constructivist or choice theory 17
contract 95

contracts and letters of introduction
    155
cooperation 51
Cormier, L. S. 121, 130
Cormier, W. H. 121, 130
Cosmides, L. 113, 117
counseling, genteel 48, 59
couples 98
Cowan, M. 92, 103
Crawford, T. 110, 117
critical 'As' 2, 6, 8–9
cultural irrational beliefs 98
Cziko, G. 111, 112, 117
Darwinian thinking 111
Davison, G. C. 2, 14, 138, 141
Dawkins, R. 113, 117
Dawson, R. W. 145, 157
deepening affect 68
DeRubeis, R. 35, 45
Descartes, R. 40, 41, 45
developing explanatory schema 37
developmental
    assessment 144, 148–9
    perspective 98–9
diagnosis 16
DiClemente, C. 34, 45
DiGiuseppe, R. 24, 29, 34, 38, 43, 45,
    63, 73, 94, 99, 103, 129, 130,
    141,148, 150, 152, 153, 154, 156,
    157, 158
directiveness 4
disputation of evaluations 99–100
disputes, handling 54–6
    protest, cold war, or strike 54
disputing, gradual 39
    irrational beliefs 32, 42, 144,
        152
Dobson, K. S. 2, 13
doubts, difficulties and obstacles to
    change 12
doubts, reservations and objections to
    REBT concept 2, 11
Dowd, E. T. 121, 130
'downward arrow' technique 70
DRADA 64, 73
Dryden, W. 2, 3, 4, 5, 6, 7, 8, 9, 10,

11, 12, 13, 14, 16, 18, 24, 28, 29, 33, 34, 48, 56, 59, 63, 73, 94, 99, 103, 106, 117, 120, 121, 122, 123, 124, 128, 129, 130, 141, 144, 145, 147, 148, 150, 152, 153, 156, 157, 158

Edelstein, M. 108, 109, 117

Egan, G. 92, 103

elegant and inelegant REBT 102, 114, 153–4

Ellis, A. 3, 6, 13, 14, 16, 18, 21, 24, 27, 18, 29, 34, 44, 45, 49, 59, 63, 72, 73, 78, 83, 86, 87, 98, 89, 101, 102, 103, 106, 110, 113, 114, 116, 117, 120, 122, 123, 130, 140, 141, 144, 145, 148, 150, 152, 153, 156, 157

Emmons, R. 54, 59

emotional and behavioural 'Cs' 2, 5, 8

emotional
  consequences 96–7
  distress 67
  disturbance 67
  responsibility 100

empathy 147

encouraging change 127

encouraging my clients to assertively speak up 135

evaluate the emotional consequences 96

evaluation processes 100

exploring the past 36

failure 111

families 98

family myths 98

family systems perspective 38

fear, of financial harm 54
  of physical harm 54
  of rejection 53

Fechner, G. T. 40, 45

Fingarette, H. 83, 87

focus on one 'ABC' at a time 100

formal/informal issue 139–40

Fox, V. 83, 87

Frank, J. 35, 45

Frankl, V. E. 126, 130

Franklin, R. 101, 103

Fraser, C. 134, 141

frustration tolerance, low 102–3

games 146

Garfield, S. L. 92, 103

genteel counseling 48, 59

Gilbert, D. T. 40, 45

Glover, M. 126, 130

goal-oriented approach 95

goal-setting 154–5

goals 3–4
  and problems 6
  and values 16
  clear 95–6
  client, referring back to 136
  identifying and pursuing 116
  of human interaction 51–2
  SMART 121–2

Goldfried, M. R. 133, 138, 141

Gordon, J. 56, 59

Greaves, D. 99, 128, 130

Greenberger, D. 99, 103, 127, 130

Grieger, R. M. 101, 102, 103, 122, 125, 130

grieving, blocked 68

guilt 53

Haaga, D. A. F. 2, 14

Hahn, Thich Nhat 67, 73

Haley, J. 92, 103

Hanna, F. J. 124, 130

Harper, R. A. 24, 28, 49, 60, 101, 102, 103

Hauck, P. A. 48, 49, 50, 53, 54, 55, 56, 57, 60, 123, 130

Hauserman, N. M. 63, 73

Hawton, K. 99, 103

Hayes, S. C. 67, 73

Hoffman, L. 92, 103

homework 12, 19, 80, 123, 137–8, 156
  compliance 120, 126–7

Horvath, A. T. 34, 45, 78, 81, 87

Human Interaction Program (HIP) 48–50

human interaction, three principles of 50–1

goals of 51–52
human nature and biological effects
113–14
humor, humour 2, 4, 13, 21–4, 62, 44,
72, 140–1
humorous songs 21–3
inelegant solution 153–4
inferential theme 7, 9
influences 90
informal vs. formal relationship 4
informed
    allies 2–3
    consent 3
Internet sessions 28
interpersonal problems 48, 50, 55, 66
intimacy 64
    of sharing 62
intrapersonal problems 48
introductory session 91
irrational beliefs 6, 10, 12, 17, 24, 36,
    44, 80, 86–7, 98, 108, 150
      disputing 32, 42, 123–4, 144,
        152–3
jargon, avoiding 35
jealousy 50
Joyce, M. R. 99, 103, 128, 130, 145,
    152, 153, 157
Just Reasonable Contentment (JRC)
    48, 56
Kabat-Zinn, J. 67, 73
Kelly, G. 19, 29, 37, 45
Klosko, J. S. 64, 73
Korzybski, A. 18, 29
language, client's 136–7
Lavin, P. J. 63, 73
Lazarus, A. 96, 103
Leiber, D. 41, 45
listening to the client's language 136–
7
listening, attentive 17
London, T. 49, 56, 60
love and marriage 48, 50, 52
    psychology of 57–8
low frustration tolerance 102
Luborsky, L. 34, 45
MacLaren, C. 24, 29,150, 152, 156,

157
Madsen, C. H. 52, 60
Madsen, C. K. 52, 60
Mahoney, M. 37, 45
Maultsby, M. C. Jr. 11, 48, 60
McLellarn, R. W. 3, 14, 144, 158
McManus, F. 122, 129
medication 80
Meichenbaum, D. 58, 60
metaphors in psychotherapy 43
metapsychological problems 6
methods, vivid 2, 12
Miller, W. R. 79, 82, 87
Mills, D. 57, 60
mindful acceptance 67
model, of change 40
    of human disturbance 17
Monjes, A. 49, 60
motivation
    for change 34, 81
    re-direction 81
Muran, C. 43, 45
Muran, J. C. 121, 130, 133, 141
musts, three main 109–10
Naimark, H. 99, 104
Neenan, M. 3, 4, 7, 10, 14, 48, 59,
    121, 123, 124, 127, 129, 130
O'Kelly, M. 99, 103, 128, 130
other-pity 53
Owens, K. B. 149, 157
Padesky, C. 99, 103, 127, 130
past, exploring the 36
Peele, S. 83, 87, 88
Pelusi, N. 114, 117
Perkinson, H. J. 111, 117
Perloff, J. M. 80, 88
personality problems: intrapersonal
    and interpersonal 49–50
Persons, J. B. 5, 14, 80, 88
Petty, R. E. 134, 141
philosophy, effective new 154
phone sessions 27
Pinker, S. 113, 117
power 94
Powers, W. T. 112, 117
preferences for certain techniques 71

primary level of 'B' 84
problems and goals 6–8
Problem Separation technique 108
Prochaska, J. 34, 45
Pruitt, D. B. 149, 157
psychology, evolutionary 113
    social 133–4
Rachman, S. 58, 60
rapport 76–7, 92
rational beliefs 2, 8, 17, 124
    full version of 10
Rational Emotive Imagery 112
rational optimism, hope, and faith 81
realistic thinking 8
REBT, hard-hitting approach to 26
    skills 11–12
    special ways of using
        behavioral aspects of 19
    special ways of using emotional
        aspects of 18
    unusual ways of doing 27
    values 154
recorded sessions 27
rehearsal 32
reinforcement 138–9
relationship, collaborative 94–5
    developing 3–5
    therapeutic 120
respect 51, 147
responsibility 94, 120, 125–6
    for change 12
Robb, H. 2, 14, 60
Rogers, C. 34, 45, 147, 157
Rollnick, S. 79, 82, 87
Rorer, L. C. 44, 45
Safran, J. D. 121, 130, 133, 141
Salkovskis, P. 99, 103
schema 32, 84
    explanatory 37–8
    therapy 64
secondary
    emotional problems 101
    emotions 97
    level of 'B' 84
    symptoms 67
self-acceptance 101–2

self-deception 114
self-discipline 49
self-disclosure 65, 147
    use of 135–6
Seligman, M. 35, 45
semantics 115–16
separation or divorce 56
session
    as a television series 140
    introductory 91–2, 107–8
    structure 93–4
    written 27
sharing, intimacy of 64–5
Sherif, C. 40, 45
Sherif, M. 40, 45
skills of REBT 11
Skinner's reinforcement principle 52
social psychology
    incorporating into practice 133–4
socialising
    the client 93
    clients into REBT 79–80
Spinoza 40, 41
Steele, D. R. 108, 109, 117
Strosahl, K. D. 67, 73
structure for the sessions 93–4
style of therapy 20
subconscious 114
SUDS scale 96
Suinn, R. 41, 45
symptom stress 67
systemic
    irrational beliefs 98
    perspective 98
systems theory 98
Tang, T. Z. 35, 45
target problems 2, 7
tasks 4, 12
teaching
    new rational beliefs 41
    the psychology of love and
        marriage 57
    tools 48, 58
Teasdale, J. 58, 60
termination 156
tertiary level of 'B' 85

therapeutic
    alliance 32, 34, 133, 148
    bond 3
    relationship 92, 120–1
    tasks 3
therapist, high-energy 138
therapy
    sequence 94
    style of 20
thinking 'Cs' 2, 9, 10
thought–feeling connection 101
three main musts 109–10
three principles of human interaction 50
three rules of assertion 52
toleration
    with resentment 56
    without resentment 54
Tooby, J. 113, 117
treatment planning 24
trial-and-error philosophy 110–12
Trivers, R. 114, 117
unconditional acceptance 147
unusual ways of doing REBT 27
'UPCP' 5, 6
Velten, E. 78, 81, 82, 83, 86, 87, 88
verbosity 120, 129
Vernon, A. 144, 145, 146, 147, 148, 149, 150, 151, 152, 153, 154, 157
vivid methods 2, 12
von Breton Chart 82, 83
von Breton, J. 78, 82, 88
Walen, S. R. 24, 29, 73, 129, 130, 141, 148, 152, 158
Warren, R. 3, 14, 144, 158
Wessler, R. A. 7, 9, 14
Wessler, R. L. 7, 9, 14, 63, 73, 128, 130
Wilde, J. 144, 145, 157, 158
Wilson, K. G. 67, 73
Wolfe, B. E. 133, 141
Wolfe, J. L. 28, 57, 60, 99, 104
Wolpe, J. 96, 104
Woods, P. 97, 104
working
    alliance 3

    at multiple levels 69
    fast 69
written sessions 27
Yalom, I. 136, 141
Yankura, J. 3, 48, 59, 144, 148, 158
Young, J. E. 64, 73

Are you sitting uncomfortably?
Windy Dryden Live and Uncut

Windy Dryden
1998 ISBN 1 898059 18 7   148x210 pp. 170 £10.50 pb.

12 thought-provoking and challenging lectures delivered by Britain's most widely published counsellor. Readers will probably be familiar with Windy Dryden as author and editor of over 100 books on counselling and psychotherapy. Now read him at his irrepressible best; live and uncensored in these 12 stimulating lectures. Be prepared to be stirred by his outspoken attempts both to provoke and illuminate the world of counselling. Trainers, trainees and practitioners should be ready to respond to his discomforting challenges.

Windy Dryden — Up close and personal

Windy Dryden
2002 ISBN 1 898059 50 0   148x210 pp. 128 £12.00 pb.

Up close and personal does exactly what it says on the cover. It provides an insight into Windy Dryden the man, using articles, humorous pieces, a fascinating glimpse into his personal therapy experiences and an interview with Dave Mearns. *Up close and personal* is an entertaining and illuminating account of Windy Dryden's evolution as an REBT practitioner; to be enjoyed whatever the reader's theoretical persuasion.

Order from our website
www.pccs-books.co.uk

PCCS Books
Llangarron
HR9 6PT
UK
Tel. +44 (0)1989 770 707

The Dynamics of Power in Counselling and Psychotherapy
Ethics, Politics and Practice

Gillian Proctor

2002 ISBN 1 898059 40 3 pp. 154+ii £14.00

The foundation of this book rests on the values and ethics of justice and responsibility, to resist domination and totalising discourses and to deconstruct the discourses behind models of therapy. Given that people who are distressed often choose to go for help in therapy, it is our duty and responsibility, as therapists, to deconstruct our practices and to be clear about the ethics, values and effects of the discourses and practices we use.

'When we enter into therapy we give enormous power to the therapist because we want to see that person as someone who can take our pain away. Such power can be abused. Gillian Proctor's timely, thoughtful book is essential reading for anyone who wants to understand what goes on in that most dangerous of arenas, therapy.'
  Dorothy Rowe

'Gillian Proctor's book makes a significant contribution in bringing to the fore issues of power that have been grossly neglected in psychotherapy up to now.'
  David Smail

'Gillian Proctor has given us a penetrating analysis of the meanings of power and its role in therapy that should become required reading for therapists and a major source book on power in relationships for social scientists.'
  Barbara Temaner Brodley

Gillian Proctor is a clinical psychologist working in Yorkshire, UK. She uses the person-centred approach in all aspects of her work in forensic services (for clients with mental health problems who have committed, or are at risk of committing, serious offences) in the National Health Service. Her particular interests, in relation to clinical practice and mental health systems, are power, ethics and oppression. She is author of several articles concerning power and ethics in therapy and research.

Order from our website
www.pccs-books.co.uk

PCCS Books
Llangarron
HR9 6PT
UK
Tel. +44 (0)1989 770 707